QUOTAS FOR WOMEN
IN POLITICS

Sebastián Molano
2013 — OEA; DC
Euro

QUOTAS FOR WOMEN IN POLITICS

Gender and Candidate Selection Reform Worldwide

Mona Lena Krook

OXFORD

UNIVERSITY PRESS

Oxford University Press, Inc., publishes works that further
Oxford University's objective of excellence
in research, scholarship, and education.

Oxford New York
Auckland Cape Town Dar es Salaam Hong Kong Karachi
Kuala Lumpur Madrid Melbourne Mexico City Nairobi
New Delhi Shanghai Taipei Toronto

With offices in
Argentina Austria Brazil Chile Czech Republic France Greece
Guatemala Hungary Italy Japan Poland Portugal Singapore
South Korea Switzerland Thailand Turkey Ukraine Vietnam

Published by Oxford University Press, Inc.
198 Madison Avenue, New York, New York 10016

www.oup.com

First issued as an Oxford University Press paperback, 2010

Oxford is a registered trademark of Oxford University Press

Library of Congress Cataloging-in-Publication Data
Krook, Mona Lena.
Quotas for women in politics : gender and candidate selection
reform worldwide / Mona Lena Krook.
p. cm.
Includes bibliographical references and index.
ISBN 978-0-19-537567-1; 978-0-19-974027-7 (pbk.)
1. Women in politics—Statistics. 2. Women politicians—Statistics.
3. Women in politics—Cross-cultural studies. 4. Women politicians—
Cross-cultural studies. I. Title.
HQ1236.K76 2009
320.082—dc22   2008032447

Printed in the United States of America
on acid-free paper

For my parents

Acknowledgments

The work in this book has been informed by so many people that it is difficult to know where to start. I have had many mentors. As a graduate student at Columbia University, my two main advisors were Mark Kesselman and Ira Katznelson. Although perhaps they did not realize it, they encouraged me to elaborate this project in opposite directions: Mark advocated exploring the broader implications of my findings and pressed me to incorporate a broader range of cases, while Ira recommended a more fine-grained and nuanced analysis of a more limited range of countries. I have not forgotten their advice. In my dissertation and subsequent work, I have constantly tried to strike a balance between these two goals by elaborating broader comparative frameworks grounded in the details of individual cases. Outside of Columbia University, I am deeply grateful to Drude Dahlerup who was not only my host at Stockholm University in 2001–2002, but who also ultimately inspired me to change direction in my research by inviting me to participate in the compilation of the Global Database of Quotas for Women. The experience of researching gender quota policies around the world opened my eyes to the global nature of this phenomenon, which most scholars to date had treated only as a country- or region-specific trend. As I was finishing up my dissertation, Judith Squires encouraged me to apply for an Economic and Social Research Council Postdoctoral Fellowship, which enabled me to spend a year at the University of Bristol. It was a wonderful research environment, where I shared an office with Johanna Kantola and began a long series of collaborative work with Sarah Childs and Judith Squires. All three were and continue to be some of my closest colleagues and friends, not only providing me with invaluable advice for transforming my doctoral thesis into a book, but also helping me realize what feminist friendship and scholarship is all about. I keep these lessons close to my heart and seek to implement them at every opportunity.

Many of the ideas that appear in this book developed during the course of conversations at conferences, workshops, coffees, dinners, and e-mail exchanges with Lisa Baldez, Karen Beckwith, Christina Bergqvist, Susan Franceschet, Lenita Freidenvall, Anne Maria Holli, Melanie Hughes, Mark Jones, Miki Caul Kittilson, Adrienne LeBas, Joni Lovenduski, Fiona Mackay, Richard Matland, Petra Meier, Rainbow Murray, Katherine Opello, Pamela Paxton, Eeva Raevaara, Shirin Rai, Diane Sainsbury, Leslie Schwindt-Bayer, Ann Towns, and Aili Mari Tripp. I received invaluable comments on early drafts at the European Consortium for Political Research Joint Sessions of Workshops in Edinburgh, Scotland, in April 2003; the American Political Science Association Panel on Gender Quotas in Philadelphia, Pennsylvania, in August 2003; the European Consortium for Political Research General Conference in Marburg, Germany, in September 2003; and the Institute for Social and Economic Research and Policy Graduate Fellows Seminar in New York in April 2004. At two particularly crucial moments, my work also benefited from methods-related feedback from students and faculty at the Society for Comparative Research Graduate Student Retreat in Budapest, Hungary, in May 2002, and the Institute on Qualitative Research Methods in Tempe, Arizona, in January 2003. I am especially grateful to Gary Goertz, Charles Ragin, and Benoît Rihoux, who read some of my subsequent papers and offered advice that I later integrated into this book.

At Washington University in St. Louis, where I have worked since 2005, I have been fortunate to have a number of excellent research assistants. Krista Swip and Brittany Coleman collected information on quota campaigns around the world, and Lydia Anderson-Dana proofread the entire manuscript and helped me with the bibliography. Diana O'Brien has assisted with so many aspects of my research on quotas that it is difficult to remember all the ways that she has contributed to this book. We have not only spent hours discussing gender quotas, but she has devoted many, many long days and nights tracking down the data I used to compile the appendix and update all my case studies. We both benefited from the arrival of Pär Zetterberg from the University of Uppsala as a visiting graduate student in spring 2008; our conversations have led us all to think about quotas in new ways. These various research activities would have been impossible, however, without grants from the Graduate School of Arts and Sciences and the Weidenbaum Center on the Economy, Government, and Public Policy at Washington University in St. Louis. Similarly, my earlier work received generous financial support from the National Science Foundation, the Graduate School of Arts and Sciences at Columbia University, the German Marshall Fund of the United States, the Woodrow Wilson National Fellowship Foundation, and the Economic and Social Research Council. At Oxford University Press, I owe a major thanks to Angela Chnapko, the editor who worked most closely with me and whose enthusiasm for this project provided crucial encouragement and support throughout the process. I would also like to express my appreciation to David McBride, who recommended my project to Angela, as well as Gwen Colvin and Megan Kennedy, who worked on the editing and marketing of this volume, respectively.

Finally, I would like to give a special thanks to the people in my family who have watched this project grow and evolve over the years. On a very practical level, I am particularly indebted to my dear brother Daniel Krook, who despite being two years younger, bought my two computers: one for my years in graduate school, which I used to research and write my doctoral dissertation, and one for my first years as an assistant professor, which I have used to draft and complete this book. To help me connect with scholars around the world, he also designed, on his own initiative, my two academic websites at Columbia University and Washington University in St. Louis. His unconditional support for my research as a feminist scholar goes well beyond the call of duty and has been an important source of strength over the years. In a different way, the enthusiasm for my work on the part of my sister-in-law, Catherine Fugarino Krook, my darling "fake cousins," Lisa and Tina Rinta-Tuuri, and my real cousins, Maria Herlin and Mikaela Mansikkaniemi, has helped on several occasions remind me that scholarly research should always seek to connect to the concerns of women in the real world.

My husband, Ewan Harrison, has been an incredible partner throughout the process of revising the manuscript for publication, taking up way more than his fair share of the household duties and carefully reading—and re-reading—the entire manuscript. He was another outcome of my time at Bristol, so I am multiply grateful to Judith Squires and Johanna Kantola for suggesting that I apply. My in-laws, Frances, John, and Fiona Harrison, cheerfully checked up on my progress, yet another example of how much this project was the product of a broader community of people. This book, however, is dedicated to my parents, Leena and Christer Krook. As immigrants to the United States from Finland, they built up a wonderful life with very few initial resources. In truth, they had very little preparation for how many years I was to spend as an undergraduate and then graduate student at Columbia University. I sincerely appreciate their faith that all of this was going to eventually lead somewhere; at the same time, it did help to have them ask on a regular basis when I was finally going to finish. Their love and support for all my projects, academic and otherwise, is an inspiration and helped keep me on track until the end. For all these reasons, this work is truly for my parents. To them, I owe everything.

Contents

QUOTAS FOR WOMEN
IN POLITICS

Introduction to Gender Quotas

Recent years have witnessed a surge of interest in patterns of political representation. On the one hand, political transformations around the world have stimulated reflection on questions of institutional and constitutional design. In Latin America, Eastern Europe, and Africa, reformers have sought to devise new political arrangements in light of democratic transition, economic crisis, and post-conflict reconstruction. In Western Europe, pressures for devolution have culminated in the creation of new regional bodies which, along with increased European integration, have forced governments to recognize emerging systems of multilevel governance. On the other hand, new scholarship has challenged the dominant conventions of liberal democracy by rethinking the means and ends of the representative process. Rather than viewing politics as a neutral arena in which all citizens play an equal role, these studies argue that liberal political arrangements create systematic distortions in public policies, as well as the potential for equal political engagement. Alternatives they propose include civic republicanism, deliberative democracy, and multiculturalism, all of which promote a notion of equality in a context of difference.

These developments, both empirical and theoretical, have led to various innovations in political participation. The most common reforms, from a global perspective, have been provisions for the increased representation of women. Most of these provisions take the form of quota policies aimed at increasing the selection and election of female candidates to political office. The origins of many of these policies can be traced back to the United Nations' (UN) Fourth World Conference on Women, held in Beijing in September 1995. The resulting Beijing Declaration and Platform for Action, signed unanimously by all 189 member states, called on governments to take measures to ensure women's equal access and full participation in power structures and decision-making, as well as to increase women's capacity to participate in decision-making and leadership (United Nations 1995). Although some quotas appeared before this date, the importance of this event can be seen in patterns of quota adoption around the world.

Between 1930 and 1980, only ten countries established quota provisions, followed by twelve states in the 1980s. Over the course of the 1990s, however, quotas appeared in more than fifty countries, which have been joined by nearly forty more since the year 2000. As a result, quotas now exist in more than one hundred countries around the world, but more than three-quarters of these measures have been passed within the last fifteen years.

In line with these developments, research on gender quotas has become one of the fastest growing subfields of research on women and politics. Most of this work focuses on single countries, or, at most, the diffusion of quotas within a single world region. It thus tends to offer explanations of this phenomenon in relation to dynamics at work within a small number of cases. When juxtaposed, however, these findings often contradict or talk past one another (Krook 2007). This indicates that efforts to generalize based on the experiences of individual countries may be limited in their ability to explain all instances of quota reform. Further, the rapid diffusion of quota provisions implies that these debates may be linked, in the sense that debates in one case may shape how quotas reach the agenda and are formulated in other countries around the world. Alternatively, multiple cases may be swayed by similar international and transnational influences, explaining patterns in the timing and nature of quota proposals. Together, these possibilities suggest that a broader comparative lens may be more appropriate for analyzing gender quotas, both individually and as a group.

Seeking to expand the scope of investigation, this book takes a global perspective to explore the various dynamics at work across the wider universe of quota campaigns and debates. The goal is to use this lens to develop a common framework for understanding the origins and impact of gender quotas, both to produce more cumulative research and to design more effective quota strategies and measures. Comparative work is crucial because an initial glance at quota measures around the world reveals no clear patterns with regard to the source or outcomes of quota policies. Countries with quotas are found in all major regions and have a broad range of institutional, social, economic, and cultural characteristics. Various coalitions of actors may thus pursue quota reforms for any number of different reasons. At the same time, the mere advent of gender quotas has not resulted in uniform increases in the percentage of women in parliament worldwide. Rather, some countries have seen dramatic increases following the adoption of new quota regulations, while others have witnessed more modest changes or even setbacks in the number of women elected to national assemblies. These variations suggest that specific quota provisions, while ostensibly similar, may in fact entail distinct processes of political reform.

The book aims to untangle these dynamics in a theory-building exercise organized around two sets of questions. First, why are quotas adopted? Which actors are involved in quota campaigns, and why do they support or oppose quota measures? Second, what impact do quotas have on existing patterns of representation? Are these provisions sufficient for bringing more women into politics? Or, do their effects depend on other features of the broader political context? The framework developed via this approach identifies a range of actors, strategies, and contexts relevant to quota reform, and as such, offers a template for engaging in single and comparative case studies of quota policies. The utility of these elements is then illustrated through paired comparisons of the origins and impact of quotas in Pakistan and India, Sweden and the United Kingdom (UK), and Argentina and France.

The analysis has several broad implications for the study of politics and efforts to improve women's status around the globe. In particular, the spread of quotas to all world regions signals a major shift in approach from previous patterns of political incorporation, which did not recognize—and, indeed, often explicitly rejected—"women" as a category deserving political representation. Future research on elections and legislatures will thus need to take gender quotas into account, both empirically and theoretically, when investigating political campaigns, candidate selection, and legislative behavior. By the same token the large-scale adoption of gender quotas by national parliaments, as well as individual political parties, raises important challenges for democratic theory and practice, which have often tended to ignore the role of women and gender, despite the fact that women form more than half the population worldwide. More specifically, the diffusion and effects of quotas reveal that women's presence in political assemblies does not simply reflect their broader social and economic status. Rather, measures to increase women's representation may appear even in the absence of previously assumed social and economic prerequisites. In contrast, the adoption and implementation of quotas highlights the recruitment practices of political elites, indicating that political actors and dynamics, not vague forces of development, are the central factor producing and mitigating inequalities in representation.

Gender Quota Policies

The growing literature on gender quotas presents a variety of typologies for classifying different kinds of quota measures. Most scholars recognize three basic types: reserved seats, party quotas, and legislative quotas (Krook 2005; Norris 2004). However, some exclude reserved seats on the grounds that these provisions do not influence candidate nomination processes, but rather make specific guarantees as to who may accede to political office (Dahlerup 2006a). Others divide party quotas into two further types: aspirant quotas, which affect preselection processes by establishing that only women may be considered as nominees, and candidate quotas, which require that parties select a particular proportion of women among their final lists of candidates (Matland 2006). Still others draw distinctions between various kinds of legislative quotas, separating out those quotas instituted through changes to the electoral law from those secured through constitutional reforms (Dahlerup 2007). Despite these various typologies, this book retains a focus on reserved seats, party quotas, and legislative quotas based on the fact that these policies share similar concerns to increase the numbers of women elected to political office, despite their attention to distinct aspects of the selection process. Further, patterns in the timing of their adoption, as well as where particular kinds of quotas appear, suggest that choices to pursue one type of measure over another may stem from country-, region-, and situation-specific "repertoires" of female representation, rather than objective evaluations as to where best to intervene in candidate selection processes.

Reserved Seats

Reserved seats appear primarily in Africa, Asia, and the Middle East (Krook 2004). These measures first emerged in the 1930s, and, indeed, were the main type of quota adopted through the 1970s. Since 2000, however, a new wave of these provisions have been passed in a number of countries that otherwise have had very low levels of female representation. These policies are often established through reforms to the constitution—and occasionally the electoral law—that create separate electoral rolls for women, designate separate districts for female candidates, or distribute seats for women based on each party's proportion of the popular vote. Reserved seats differ from party and legislative quotas in that they mandate a minimum number of female legislators, rather than simply a percentage of women among political candidates. In so doing they revise aspects of the electoral system in ways that guarantee the election of women.

These measures often provide for low levels of female representation, usually between 1 percent and 10 percent of all elected representatives. However, since 2000 a number of countries have instituted much larger provisions of 30 percent.[1] In some instances, reserved seats apply to single-member districts reserved for women, in which only women may run for election (Nanivadekar 2006). In others, they are allocated in multimember districts to the designated number of women who win the most votes (Norris 2006). In yet others, women are selected to these seats by members of the national parliament several weeks after the general elections (Goetz and Hassim 2003). As such these policies confer varying degrees of dependence between the women elected to these seats and the parties and elected officials who make their election possible.

Party Quotas

Party quotas are the most common type of gender quota (see appendix). They were first adopted in the early 1970s by a limited number of socialist and social democratic parties in Western Europe. During the 1980s and 1990s, however, they appeared in green parties, social democratic parties, and even some conservative parties more broadly across Western Europe, as well as in a diverse array of political parties in other regions around the world. In some countries they exist alongside the presence of other types of quotas to promote women's representation (Meier 2004; Araújo and García Quesada 2006). At their most basic, party quotas are measures that are adopted voluntarily by individual parties that commit the party to aim for a certain proportion of women among its candidates to political office. In this sense, they alter party practices by setting out new criteria for candidate selection that require elites to recognize existing biases and consider alternative spheres of political recruitment (Krook 2005; cf. Lovenduski and Norris 1993).

These policies typically mandate that women constitute between 25 percent and 50 percent of parties' electoral slates. However, the particular phrasing of this requirement varies: some policies identify women as the group to be promoted by the quota (Durrieu 1999; Goetz and Hassim 2003; Valiente 2005), while others set out a more gender-neutral formulation, specifying a minimum representation for "each sex" or establishing that "neither sex" can account for more than a particular proportion of a party's candidates (Freidenvall, Dahlerup, and Skjeie 2006; Guadagnini 2005). Parties implement these measures in a number of ways. In countries with proportional representation (PR) electoral systems, party quotas govern the composition of party lists. While some parties apply the quota to the list as a whole, others direct it to the number of seats on the list that they anticipate winning in the next elections. In countries with majoritarian systems, party quotas are often directed at a collection of single-member districts. This may entail nominating a proportion of women across all the districts where the party is running candidates (Opello 2006). Alternatively, the policy may apply to a designated set of seats that the party expects to win; for example, seats where one of the party's incumbents is stepping down, or seats that the party expects to capture in the next round of elections (Campbell, Childs, and Lovenduski 2006; Russell 2005).

Legislative Quotas

Legislative quotas tend to be found in developing countries, especially Latin America, and post-conflict societies, primarily in Africa, the Middle East, and Southeastern Europe (Krook 2004). These patterns are explained in part by the fact that legislative quotas are the newest kind of quota policy, appearing first only in the 1990s, at a time when issues of women's representation reached the agenda of many international organizations and transnational non-governmental organizations (NGOs). Enacted through reforms to electoral laws and sometimes constitutions, legislative quotas are similar to party quotas in that they address party selection processes, but differ in that they are passed by national parliaments to require that all parties nominate a certain proportion of female candidates. As such, they are mandatory provisions that apply to all political groupings, rather than only those that choose to adopt quotas. In the course of setting these requirements, these policies take important steps to legitimize positive action and recognize "gender" as a political identity by altering the basic meanings of equality and representation that inform candidate selection processes.

Similar to party quotas, legislative quotas call for women to form between 25 percent and 50 percent of all candidates. However, they involve broader processes of reform focused on changing the language contained in constitutions and electoral laws, rather than the content of individual party statutes. As such, their passage usually requires some degree of cross-partisan agreement; indeed, most legislative quotas are approved nearly unanimously by legislators representing parties from across the political spectrum. The language contained in these measures is typically gender-neutral, speaking of women and men together or making reference to the "underrepresented sex." All the same, these provisions vary in terms of how strictly their goals are articulated: some speak vaguely about "facilitating access" (Giraud and Jenson 2001), while others offer more concrete prescriptions regarding the selection and placement of female candidates (Jones 2004; Meier 2005). Like party quotas, legislative quotas are implemented in different ways depending on the electoral system, applying alternatively to party lists (Meier 2004) or to a broader group of single-member districts (Murray 2004). However, given their status as law, a distinctive feature of legislative quotas is that they usually contain sanctions for noncompliance and are subject to some degree of oversight from external bodies (Baldez 2004; Jones 1998).

Gender Quota Adoption

Gender quotas thus take a number of different forms in countries around the world. To explain their adoption, studies of cases around the world offer four main accounts. The first is that women mobilize for quotas, usually when women's groups come to realize that quotas are an effective—and perhaps the only—means for increasing women's political representation. These women may include women's organizations inside political parties, women's movements in civil society, women's groups in other countries, and even individual women close to powerful men (Bruhn 2003; Kittilson 2006). In all of these instances, women pursue quotas for both normative and pragmatic reasons. They believe that there should be more women in politics in order to achieve justice, promote women's interests, and make use of women's resources for the good of society (Phillips 1995). However, in the absence of any natural trend toward change, they acknowledge that this is likely to be achieved only through specific, targeted actions to promote female candidates (cf. Krook 2006a).

A second common explanation is that political elites adopt quotas for strategic reasons, generally related to competition with other parties. Various case studies suggest, for example, that party elites often adopt quotas when one of their rivals adopts them (Caul 2001;

Meier 2004). This concern may be heightened if the party is seeking to overcome a long period in opposition or a dramatic decrease in popularity. In other contexts, elites view quotas as a way to demonstrate a degree of commitment to women without actually intending to alter existing patterns of inequality (Htun and Jones 2002; Mossuz-Lavau 1998). Alternatively, they treat quotas as a convenient means to promote other ends, like maintaining control over rivals within or outside the party (Chowdhury 2002). If these motives are correct, the adoption of quotas may be less about empowering women in politics and more about how quotas fit in—perhaps serendipitously—with various other struggles among political elites.

A third view is that quotas are adopted when they mesh with existing or emerging notions of equality and representation. Evidence indicates that gender quotas are compatible in distinct ways with a number of normative frameworks. Some scholars view quota adoption as consistent with ideas about equality and fair access. They point out that left-wing parties are generally more open to measures such as quotas because these match with their more general goals of social equality (Hassim 2002; Opello 2006). Others interpret quotas as a method to recognize difference and the need for proportional representation. According to this view, quotas for women can be seen as a logical extension of guarantees given to other groups based on linguistic, religious, racial, and other cleavages (Inhetveen 1999; Meier 2000). A final observation is that quotas tend to emerge during periods of democratic innovation. In these countries, quotas may be seen as a way to establish the legitimacy of the new political system during democratic transition or the creation of new democratic institutions (Bauer and Britton 2006). Taken together, these arguments analyze quotas in relation to their "fit" with features of the political context; they do not reflect principled concerns to empower women or pragmatic strategies to win or maintain power.

A fourth explanation is that quotas are supported by international norms and spread through transnational sharing. During the last ten years, a variety of international organizations—including the UN, the Socialist International, the Council of Europe, the European Union, the Commonwealth, the African Union, the Southern African Development Community, and the Organization of American States—have issued declarations recommending that all member-states aim for 30 percent women in all political bodies.[2] These norms shape national quota debates in at least four ways (Krook 2006b). International imposition occurs in cases where international actors are directly involved in quota adoption, either by directly applying quotas when devising electoral regulations or by compelling national leaders to do so themselves. Transnational emulation takes place in cases where local women's movements and transnational NGOs share information on quota strategies across national borders. International tipping appears in cases where international events provide new sources of leverage in national debates, shifting the balance in favor of local and transnational actors pressing for quota adoption. International blockage, finally, happens in cases where international actors seek to prevent the adoption of gender quotas, despite mobilization by local women's groups and transnational NGOs in favor of these policies.

Gender Quota Implementation

Quota measures are diverse, and, thus, differences in their impact are to be expected. Yet, pinpointing why some quotas are more effective than others is a complicated task: in addition to features of specific quota policies, which affect their likelihood of being implemented, quotas are introduced when variations already exist in the percentage of women in national parliaments. Cross-national variations are thus the combined result of quotas, where they are present, and other factors that were likely at work before quotas were established. As a result, quotas do not simply lead to gains proportional to the quota policy, but also interact, both positively and negatively, with various features of the broader political context.

Three broad explanations have been offered to untangle these effects. The first links variations in quota implementation to details of quota measures themselves. Some studies connect quota impact to the type of measure involved. Although most agree that reserved seats generally produce small changes in the numbers of women elected, some claim that party quotas are more effective than other types of quotas because they are voluntary measures, adopted from concerns about electoral advantage. Others insist that legislative quotas have more force because they bind all parties, not simply those that choose to adopt quotas, and are enforced by state bureaucracies and the courts, rather than party leaders (Jones 1998; Norris 2006). More recent work delves deeper into variations within and across types to understand why specific quotas are more or less effective in achieving changes in women's representation. It argues that the success or failure of quotas stems from their wording (Htun 2002), requirements (Chama 2001; Meier 2004), sanctions (Murray 2004; Schmidt and Saunders 2004), and perceived legitimacy (Yoon 2001), all of which may have intended and unintended effects.

A second account relates quota impact to the "fit" between quota measures and other political institutions. Most research in this vein focuses on characteristics of the electoral system, examining how electoral rules influence quota effects. It observes that these policies have the greatest impact in PR electoral systems with closed lists and high district magnitudes (Caul 1999; Htun and Jones 2002), although it also identifies idiosyncratic features of particular electoral systems that negatively affect quota implementation (Htun 2002). Other studies consider characteristics of the party system, as well as the features of parties themselves, to discern dynamics that may aid or subvert quota implementation. They argue that quotas are more likely to have an impact in party systems where several parties coexist and larger parties respond to policy innovations initiated by smaller parties, as well as in parties with left-wing ideologies where the party leadership is better able to enforce party or national regulations (Caul 1999; Davidson-Schmich 2006). Still others note higher rates of implementation across all parties in countries where the political culture emphasizes sexual difference and group representation, and lower rates of compliance in countries where it stresses sexual equality and individual representation (Inhetveen 1999; Meier 2000).

A third explanation outlines the actors who support and oppose quotas and their respective roles vis-à-vis quota implementation. Much of this literature targets party elites as the group most directly responsible for variations in the success or failure of quotas, since the effective application of quotas largely hinges around elites' willingness to recruit female candidates. Most of these accounts expose the ways in which elites seek to mitigate quota impact through passive refusal to enforce quotas to more active measures to subvert their intended effects (Araújo 2003; Costa Benavides 2003). Many also mention other actors who may play a direct or indirect role in enforcing quota provisions, including women's organizations inside and outside political parties (Durrieu 1999; Sainsbury 1993), national and international courts (Chama 2001; Jones 2004), and ordinary citizens (Baldez 2004; Kolinsky 1991), all of whom may monitor party compliance with quota measures in ways that lead elites to ignore or honor—and possibly even exceed—quota requirements.

Analyzing Gender Quotas

Existing research thus presents four answers as to who supports quotas and why these policies are adopted, related to the mobilization of women's groups, the calculations of political elites, the links between quotas and prevailing political norms, and the convictions of international organizations and transnational networks. It also offers three reasons for variations in quota effects, stemming from the features of particular quota measures, their "fit" with institutional frameworks, and their support among actors in positions to guarantee or undermine quota effects. Despite the substantial evidence behind these accounts, a more comprehensive review reveals that while these arguments are supported by many case studies, they are often contradicted in important ways by others (Krook 2007). Because these explanations emerge largely from the analysis of single cases, these patterns raise two possibilities: (1) some accounts may characterize only some countries, and (2) some may tell only part of a story that engages several of these narratives.

Dynamics such as these are difficult to study using traditional approaches in political science, which tend to gravitate toward one of two poles: large-n statistical analyses or small-n case studies. The former use quantitative methods to analyze many cases, establish relations between variables, and infer causality from statistical significance. The latter apply qualitative techniques to focus on a few cases, situate variables in the context of the whole, and detect causality through process-tracing (Brady and Collier 2004; Mahoney and Goertz 2006). Despite these differences, conventional ways of employing these methods share two core assumptions: causal homogeneity, the notion that factors work the same way in all cases, and causal competition, the belief that variables exert independent effects on outcomes (Ragin 1987). Although several central contributions in qualitative political science depart from this approach (Moore 1966; Katznelson 1997), most qualitative scholars of comparative politics draw heavily on John Stuart Mills's (1874) methods of agreement and difference in developing tenets of research design. The basic intuition behind the method of difference, the one most widely used in political science (cf. King, Keohane, and Verba 1994), is that cases be matched on all attributes but one and then outcomes examined to see whether that difference led to a distinct outcome; if so, the element can be credited as the cause of that outcome.

Recent innovations in comparative methods criticize these conventional perspectives. Although these scholars are especially interested in developing techniques for analyzing medium-n populations (Ragin 1987; Ragin 2000), they are primarily joined by a desire to explore the potential for causal heterogeneity, the possibility that variables may not work the same way in all instances, and causal combination, the idea that the effects of particular factors may depend on the presence or absence of other conditions (Mahoney and Rueschemeyer 2003; Ragin 2000). As such, the goal of this work is often to formalize comparisons in a manner that incorporates information from a larger sample but still retains the integrity of individual cases, thus achieving a middle ground between covering laws and idiographic descriptions. Adopting these assumptions, however, has crucial implications for political analysis. Recognizing causal heterogeneity opens up the potential for equifinality, the idea that there may be multiple paths to the same outcome, while acknowledging causal combination requires that analysts map and evaluate various possible configurations of causal conditions. These perspectives are less well-known, but there are good reasons to believe that they will provide greater leverage than traditional approaches in explaining the origins and effects of quotas around the globe. As already noted, existing research offers various accounts as to why quotas are adopted, involving multiple actors and motivations coming together in complex and even contradictory ways, as well as diverse intuitions as to why some quotas are more successful than others, producing breakthroughs in distinct countries despite being designed along a variety of different lines. The analysis in this book thus takes advantage of these novel methodological tools to theorize paths to quota reform and analyze configurations of causal conditions, both systematically and comparatively, in careful dialogue with evidence from around the world.

Overview of the Book

Studies of gender quotas have quickly become a major new area of research on women and politics. Given the relative newness of this phenomenon, most work to date has sought to document patterns in the adoption and implementation of quotas in countries around the world. The aim of this book is to build on these studies in order to move this literature forward, as well as facilitate the emergence of new quota campaigns and the design of more effective quota policies. To this end, it takes a global perspective to synthesize these explanations and elaborate a more general framework for analyzing the origins and impact of quota policies. The tools derived from this theory-building exercise are then used to investigate the origins and effects of reserved seats in Pakistan and India, party quotas in Sweden and the UK, and legislative quotas in Argentina and France.

Chapter 2 addresses quota adoption by, first, reviewing the four existing explanations and, second, considering the evidence for and against each account. It suggests that each argument may characterize only some cases, at the same time that some may tell only part of a larger story that engages several of these narratives. To devise a more general framework, the chapter disaggregates these explanations into their component parts to identify three sets of actors and seven possible motivations for quota reform.

Chapter 3 examines quota implementation using a similar method. After elaborating and evaluating the three accounts often presented in the literature, it stresses the need to relate these reforms to existing dynamics of candidate selection and makes a case for reconciling the three narratives to explore how structures, practices, and norms might work together to produce the effects of quota policies. It sketches an alternative model of candidate selection based on three types of gendered institutions and argues that each category of gender quota attempts to reform a different kind of political institution.

Chapters 4, 5, and 6 then undertake paired comparisons of six cases of quota reform. The cases were selected according to two criteria. First, in all of the chosen cases, multiple attempts at quota reform have taken place. This enables closer examination of iterated sequences of reform and their relation to changing patterns of political representation over time. Second, within each pair, one country has witnessed dramatic shifts following the implementation of quota policies, while the other has seen little change or even stagnation in the numbers of women elected. The goal of each comparison is to assess the role of quotas by exploring the actors, motivations, and contexts that are relevant to the origins, adoption, and implementation of each measure, drawing on various primary and secondary sources. Crucially, this analysis focuses on shifts in configurations of conditions, meaning that it is not necessary to match the cases on all attributes minus one; rather, differences across the cases are incorporated into the comparison by virtue of the configurations themselves.

Chapter 4 examines campaigns for reserved seats in Pakistan and India. Despite a common colonial history, opposite approaches were taken with regard to reserved seats for women following independence. In Pakistan, regimes of all types reserved seats for women from the early 1950s until the late 1980s, with a new round of reforms being introduced in 2002. In India, reservations for women were not on the agenda until the late 1980s, when they were established in various states. This led to proposals in the early 1990s to set aside seats for women in local government through constitutional reform. Although these provisions were quickly passed, efforts to extend these provisions to the national parliament have failed, despite being introduced in every legislative session since the mid-1990s. As a result of these distinct developments, women occupy 23 percent of the seats in parliament in Pakistan, but only 9 percent of these seats in India (Inter-Parliamentary Union 2008a).

Chapter 5 engages in a similar examination of campaigns for party quotas in Sweden and the UK. Before quotas were adopted, both countries had relatively similar levels of female representation. By 2008, however, women constituted 47 percent of members of parliament (MPs) in Sweden but only 20 percent of MPs in the UK (Inter-Parliamentary Union 2008a). In Sweden, advocates initially pressed parties to adopt softer recommendations and targets in the 1970s and 1980s. In the course of the 1990s, they gradually radicalized their demands and eventually gained commitments from most parties to alternate between women and men on their candidate lists. In the UK, the Labour Party adopted a quota in the early 1990s, which an industrial tribunal later declared illegal on the grounds that it violated the terms of the country's Sex Discrimination Act. After various attempts to work within a context of substantial legal ambiguity, MPs eventually reformed this act to allow—but not require—parties to pursue positive action in candidate selection, leading to important variations among parties in terms of their recruitment of women.

Chapter 6 explores campaigns for legislative quotas in Argentina and France. In Argentina, a quota law was adopted in the early 1990s that required all parties to nominate 30 percent women. Although this provision amended only the electoral code and did not specify how the quota would be implemented and monitored, by the late 2000s the policy had resulted in the election of 40 percent women (Inter-Parliamentary Union 2008a). In France, by contrast, legislators altered both the constitution and the electoral law to mandate that parties nominate equal numbers of women and men, with specific regulations as to how quotas would be applied in various kinds of elections and sanctions would be imposed on parties that did not meet these requirements. Despite these apparently radical reforms, the representation of women increased only incrementally to 12 percent and then 19 percent (Inter-Parliamentary Union 2008a), still only barely approximating the world average of 18 percent (Inter-Parliamentary Union 2008b).

Chapter 7 presents an overview of the theoretical and empirical findings of the book. After reviewing the framework, as well as the insights generated by the paired comparisons, the chapter takes this discussion one step further by juxtaposing trends across the case studies as a whole. It concludes with six main observations regarding quota campaigns. In terms of actors, a global lens indicates that (1) the key actors in quota debates vary widely across countries, pursuing quota reform for both feminist and nonfeminist reasons, and (2) the actors that are most often overlooked are international organizations and transnational networks. When it comes to strategies, (3) normative issues are a central concern in quota debates, but (4) strategic motivations often play a significant role in getting quotas on the political agenda. In terms of context, (5) the impact of quotas depends on how they interact with elements of the political environment, whose various effects must be disentangled by tracing changes in the configurations of these conditions over time. Crucially, however, given the central importance of causal combination and the possibility of multiple paths to the same outcome, (6) there are limits to prediction and prescription when it comes to quota adoption and implementation. Yet, these insights are not intended as the final word on quotas: in the spirit of theory-building, they are offered rather as a means for taking the first steps toward developing more cumulative research on strategies to increase women's political representation worldwide.

The Adoption of Gender Quotas

Gender quotas take a wide range of forms in countries around the world. The mere presence of these measures, however, does not explain why they have been adopted. Indeed, the countries where they exist seem to have little else in common, given their diverse political, social, economic, and cultural characteristics. The present literature offers a number of important insights into this question, as most research thus far has focused on explaining quota adoption by identifying the core actors in quota campaigns and their reasons for pursuing or opposing quota reform. Yet, the vast majority of these studies emphasize domestic explanations, despite the fact that quotas appeared on political agendas in many countries around the same time (Krook 2006b). In contrast, the approach developed in this chapter seeks to draw connections among campaigns and promote more explicit comparisons among cases to elaborate a common framework for analyzing quota adoption, open to the possibility of multiple models of quota reform. The result is a more inclusive model of quota adoption that considers various actors and motivations while also enabling scholars to situate their findings more readily in relation to studies of other countries.

The chapter starts by organizing explanations as to why quotas have been adopted, drawing on the broad body of research that has been carried out on individual cases. Although these studies address developments in a remarkable number of contexts, they can be condensed into a limited number of narratives: women mobilize for quotas to increase women's representation, political elites recognize strategic advantages for pursuing quotas, quotas are consistent with existing or emerging notions of equality and representation, and quotas are supported by international norms and spread through transnational sharing. Evaluating the evidence, it becomes clear that no single account describes all cases. Rather than search for another universal explanation, the analysis draws instead on patterns of quota adoption around the world to make a case for treating quotas as a global phenomenon, and thus, for exploring the possibility of causal diversity among quota campaigns. It suggests that these four accounts together contain elements that operate within the wider universe of quota debates, but not necessarily within every single campaign. As such, some accounts may characterize only some cases, at the same time that some may tell only part of a larger story that engages several of these narratives.

To manage this complexity, and thus use it to understand individual cases, the chapter disaggregates these explanations to identify three categories of potential actors in quota campaigns: civil society actors, like women's movements and women's sections inside political parties; state actors, like national leaders and courts; and international and transnational actors, like international organizations and transnational nongovernmental organizations (NGOs). By the same method, it outlines seven possible motivations for reform: principled stands, electoral considerations, empty gestures, promotion of other political ends, extension of representational guarantees, international pressure, and transnational learning. To illustrate how these various elements may come together in particular campaigns, the chapter concludes with a discussion of typical alliances in quota debates, which suggests that most quota policies may result from multiple groups of actors who support reform for various and perhaps even conflicting reasons. Although attuned to causal diversity, the resulting framework thus presents common concepts—if not common findings— with regard to the origins and spread of gender quota policies.

Mapping the Field: Current Perspectives on Quota Adoption

The emerging literature on gender quotas offers several distinct perspectives on quota adoption. Despite being framed in general terms, most of these studies focus on the experiences of individual cases in order to comprehend why quotas—which appear to challenge many important aspects of the political status quo—not only reach the political agenda, but are also passed in a variety of contexts around the world. This research identifies four basic patterns as to who supports quotas and why these policies are adopted, related to the mobilization of women's groups, the calculations of political elites, the connections between quotas and reigning political norms, and the convictions of international organizations and transnational activists. Taken together, these narratives present conflicting views on the actors involved in quota campaigns, as well as their reasons for pressing for quota adoption. Further, each rests on evidence from some cases that is contradicted by details from others, suggesting that none of these accounts on their own explain all cases of quota reform.

Women's Movements

Most research on quota adoption views women as the source of quota proposals. These scholars argue that efforts to nominate more women never occur without the prior mobilization of women, even when male elites are ultimately responsible for the decision to establish quotas. While often motivated by principled concerns to empower women, these campaigns also have a pragmatic dimension, as they tend to emerge when women's groups perceive quotas as not an ideal but perhaps the only effective means for increasing female representation. However, the specific groups vary across cases and may include grassroots women's movements that work both nationally and internationally to promote women's political participation (Baldez 2004; Beckwith 2003; Lubertino Beltrán 1992; Pires 2002); cross-partisan networks among women that make connections with each other through national and international women's gatherings, as well as via transnational women's networks, to exchange information on successful strategies for increasing women's representation (Bruhn 2003; Chama 2001; Howard-Merriam 1990; Hassim 2002); women's organizations inside political parties that propose specific quota policies or draw on gains made by women in other parties to press for changes within their own organizations (Connell 1998; Skjeie 1992); individual women inside parties who lobby male leaders to promote female candidates (Abou-Zeid 2006; Araújo 2003; Kittilson 2006; Schmidt 2003); and women involved with the national women's machinery who support gender quotas as a means for accomplishing broader goals of women-friendly policy change (Costa Benavides 2003; García Quesada 2003; Jones 1996).

Evidence from many cases indicates that efforts to nominate more female candidates rarely occur in the absence of women's mobilization. However, stressing the support of women's groups has a tendency to gloss over the many women who oppose quota policies. As a smaller group of studies has shown, women as a group are in fact frequently divided as to the desirability of gender quotas. Indeed, some of the strongest opposition comes from feminists, both inside and outside the political parties, who argue that quotas do not further the cause of female empowerment (Amar 1999; Huang 2002; Kishwar 1998b). This resistance takes on a variety of different forms, ranging from limited mobilization by grassroots women's groups to more active denunciations by prominent female politicians (Badinter 1996; García Quesada 2003). Other individual scholars point out, further, that even in cases where a large number of women do support quotas, their proposals rarely gain consideration until at least one well-placed elite man embraces them and pressures his own party, or his own colleagues in parliament, to approve quotas for women (Schmidt 2003). These insights may be more broadly valid: before such leaders come out in favor of quotas, such measures are often ridiculed as a demand made by a minority of radicals who are out of touch with more moderate women. While women's groups are important, therefore, their role is more complex—and mixed—than much of the literature suggests.

Political Elites

Other scholars emphasize political elites and the strategic advantages they perceive for adopting quotas, focusing on the role of these elites—who are usually overwhelmingly male—in blocking or opening up opportunities for women to run for political office. Most accounts point to the importance of party competition, noting that elites tend to embrace quota reform only after one of their electoral rivals establishes them (Caul 2001; Davidson-Schmich 2006; Matland and Studlar 1996; Meier 2004). These effects are especially strong when parties seek to overcome a long period in opposition or a dramatic decrease in popularity by closing a gap in support among female voters (Kolinsky 1991; Perrigo 1996; Stevenson 2000). They also appear in cases where elites promote female candidates to win an electoral campaign or sustain an existing regime (Howard-Merriam 1990; Millard and Ortiz 1998; Schmidt 2003), engage in empty gestures to express apparent commitment to women's rights without necessarily altering existing patterns of representation (Htun and Jones 2002; Mossuz-Lavau 1998; Rai 1999), apply quotas in an effort to consolidate control over party representatives and political rivals (Chowdhury 2002; Goetz and Hassim 2003), and defend quotas to demonstrate autonomy from other branches of government (Baldez 2004).

Although a great deal of evidence supports these arguments, most accounts overlook instances where quotas meet with strong opposition from party leaders and male politicians (Haug 1995; Huang 2002). Instead of outspoken and pragmatic convergence on quota policies, some elites abstain from taking public positions on quotas (Sgier 2003), adopt quotas but do not publicize this policy widely (Bruhn 2003), or engage in acrimonious debate within and across their own parties as to the desirability of quotas (Scott 1998; Squires 1996). In addition, a limited number of studies cast doubt on the general applicability of these purported incentives. They find that competition among parties may in fact work against the selection of female candidates, as parties that are uncertain about electoral outcomes often fall back on more traditional male politicians (Murray 2008; Randall 1982; Stevenson 2000). Conversely, the lack of party competition may sometimes facilitate women's recruitment, as in cases where single party regimes use inclusion as a means to gain social legitimacy (Goetz and Hassim 2003; Nechemias 1994). In yet other instances, elites appear to act more from normative rather than strategic concerns to improve women's access to political office by engaging in repeated attempts to institute or extend quota policies (Araújo 2003; Meier 2004; Mossuz-Lavau 1998; Stevenson 2000). Finally, some evidence suggests that elites do not always espouse quotas in efforts to consolidate control, but rather as a response to internal party struggles initiated among the rank-and-file (Bruhn 2003; Kittilson 2006).

Norms of Equality and Representation

Still other work views quota adoption as an extension of existing or emerging notions of equality and representation. All the same, scholars interpret consistency in distinct ways, depending on how they relate quota provisions to reigning political norms. Some equate quota adoption with ideas about equality and fair access by observing that quotas in left-wing parties match their more general goals of social equality and grassroots decision-making (Hassim 2002; Kolinsky 1991; Opello 2006). Others view quotas for women in terms of other representational guarantees meant to recognize sexual difference and the need for proportional representation (Inhetveen 1999; Meier 2000; Sgier 2003). Yet a third group associates quota adoption with democratic innovation by observing that demands for quotas emerge during periods of democratic transition or the creation of new democratic institutions as a means for guaranteeing the representation of traditionally underprivileged groups or establishing the national and international legitimacy of the new regime (Bauer and Britton 2006; Brown et al 2002; Camacho Granados et al 1997; Reyes 2002).

These accounts are certainly correct in observing connections between quotas and broader political ideals. Emphasizing the "fit"

between policies and contexts, however, neglects cases where proposals for gender quotas encounter fierce opposition among a wide
range of domestic groups. Findings from several studies undermine
these generalizing claims. For example, in countries where quotas are
framed as a means for promoting equality and fair access, detractors
have argued against them on the grounds that quotas for women discriminate against men and thus are unconstitutional or illegal (Guadagnini 2005; Haug 1995; Lovenduski 1997; Mossuz-Lavau 1998).
Where quotas aim to recognize difference and proportional representation, quotas for women may interact in various ways with claims for
the representation of other groups: some governments recognize certain groups to the exclusion of others (Goetz and Hassim 2003; Jenkins
1999; Sgier 2003), while others simply avoid adopting quotas for any
group at all (Diop 2002; Scott 1998). In countries where quotas are
linked to democratic innovation, finally, reformers sometimes reject
special provisions for women—especially in cases where the former
regime applied quotas as a means for gaining social legitimacy—on
the grounds that such measures are fundamentally anti-democratic
and thus contrary to the spirit of the transition (Antić and Gortnar
2004; Waylen 1994; Yoon 2001).

International Organizations and Transnational Networks

A final vein of research that often coexists with the first three
accounts refers to the role of international norms and transnational
information sharing in shaping national quota debates. This work
generally locates the origins of these policies in international meetings and conferences that generate recommendations for member–
states to improve women's access to political decision-making. For
many countries, the two most important documents in this regard
are the Convention on the Elimination of All Forms of Discrimination Against Women, passed in 1979, and the Beijing Platform for
Action, approved in 1995, both elaborated within the framework of
the United Nations (UN). However, other international organizations
have issued similar resolutions in recent years embracing quotas for
women, including the Inter-Parliamentary Union, the Socialist International, the Council of Europe, the European Union, the Organization for Security and Co-operation in Europe, the Commonwealth, the
African Union, the Southern African Development Community, and
the Organization of American States. At the same time, numerous

transnational actors have emerged and served as catalysts to the rapid spread of quota policies around the world, particularly in the years following the UN's Fourth World Conference in Beijing in 1995 (Htun and Jones 2002; Leijenaar 1997). These actors include NGOs, groups formed under the auspices of international institutions, and formal and informal networks of scholars, activists, and politicians, who share information across national borders that enables domestic campaigns to learn new tactics for reform and import strategies from other countries into their own (Krook 2006b).

In a striking number of cases, gender quotas are adopted in the wake of recommendations issued by international organizations. Yet, this literature rarely traces the explicit causal connections between international and transnational trends and domestic quota campaigns. Instead, most scholars mention these effects only in passing and limit their observations to a restricted number of well-known international and transnational events. A range of disparate studies suggests, however, that national campaigns interact in a number of ways with international and transnational trends. In some post-conflict societies, for example, international actors play a direct role in pressing for the adoption of quotas for women (Bauer 2002; Corrin 2001; Ballington and Dahlerup 2006). In other cases, campaigns develop locally, prior to international conferences establishing the legitimacy of quotas as a measure to increase women's representation (Kassé 2003; Lubertino Beltrán 1992; Wisler 1999). As such, international events act as catalysts to domestic campaigns already in progress, rather than as initial inspirations for these campaigns (Araújo and García Quesada 2006; Yáñez 2003). Finally, in some contexts, international actors turn out to be pivotal to the rejection, rather than the promotion, of quotas, despite the mobilization of local women's groups and transnational NGOs in support of these measures (Ciezadlo 2003; Pires 2002).

Toward a New Framework: Actors and Motivations in Quota Campaigns

Current research on gender quotas thus offers four basic accounts as to why quotas are adopted and which actors are involved. Each of these claims, however, is subject to challenge based on evidence from a smaller number of cases, where quotas are opposed by feminists as demeaning to women, rejected by elites due to concerns about electoral competition, blocked by guarantees for other groups, and obstructed by international actors as a violation of electoral best practices. In addition, these four arguments appear to contradict one another, as they draw attention to distinct actors and motivations for quota reform. Because these arguments emerge from the study of single cases, these patterns raise two possibilities: some accounts may characterize only some cases, at the same time that some may tell only part of a story that engages several of these narratives. As such, each story may capture a dynamic at work within the wider universe of quota campaigns, rather than a mechanism that describes all cases of quota adoption. Alternatively, each may constitute only one element within a larger sequence of events: women's mobilization may precede and influence elite decision making, while international and transnational norms may affect democratic innovation at the local and national levels. If this is true, the search for a single explanation may be misguided.

This case for a new approach hinges on establishing that quotas are a global phenomenon, such that it would be plausible to assume some degree of diversity across quota debates, given other points of difference among countries, like their history, geography, language, and position within the world economy. If quotas are a global phenomenon, it then makes sense to use existing accounts to generate a list of actors and motivations to consider when analyzing individual instances of reform. This approach offers important advantages for understanding and comparing quota campaigns, as it (1) requires scholars to explore factors they might otherwise overlook, and (2) enables researchers to identify similarities and differences between their studies and the findings of other cases. Conflicting assessments are thus used as a resource—rather than as a stumbling block—for devising a common set of tools for engaging in single and comparative case studies of quota adoption. While recognizing that all factors will not be relevant in the same way in all countries, this lens obliges all researchers to view quota adoption simultaneously in the context of national and international developments.

Quotas as a Global Phenomenon

A survey of gender quota policies around the world reveals a number of interesting trends related to the timing, location, and context of quota reforms, all of which provide evidence for the argument that quotas are a global phenomenon—and, perhaps more intriguingly, that many quota campaigns appear to be linked across national borders. Most of the literature on quotas gives little theoretical attention to the issue of when these measures were adopted, apart from noting the year when these policies were initially approved. Yet, even a brief look at the emergence of quotas indicates that this question merits further consideration: more than three-quarters of all quota policies have been passed within the last fifteen years. These developments are more striking still when viewed over time. Between 1930 and 1980, ten countries established gender quotas, followed by twelve other states in the 1980s. In the 1990s, however, quotas appeared in more than fifty countries, which have been joined by nearly forty more since 2000 (Krook 2006b, 312–313). These waves intersect with differences in the timing and prevalence of distinct kinds of quota measures. Reserved seats were the earliest policies devised to guarantee women's representation and were the main quota type adopted between 1930 and 1970. However, they have become increasingly popular since 2000. Party quotas emerged in the early 1970s, but grew more widespread over the course of the 1980s and 1990s. Legislative quotas appeared for the first time in the 1990s and have gained momentum through the 2000s. Given this structure of diffusion, it is difficult to explain these patterns as the result of parallel processes which have independently produced the same policy outcomes across many countries within the same span of time.

In addition to these differences in timing, the types of quotas adopted also follow certain geographic patterns and make similar provisions across the regions in which they appear (see appendix). Reserved seats exist in countries in Africa, Asia, and the Middle East. In most instances, they set aside a small number of places for women, with the exception of some more recent provisions for national and local government that approximate 20 percent to 30 percent of all seats. Party quotas, in contrast, were initially adopted almost exclusively by left-wing parties in Western Europe. However, they have now spread to parties across the political spectrum and in all regions of the world, although they continue to be the most prevalent measure employed in Europe. These policies typically make provisions for women to form between 25 percent and 50 percent of all party candidates. Legislative quotas, finally, were first passed in Argentina but are now found in countries in Latin America, Africa, and various parts of Europe. They also mandate that women constitute between 25 percent and 50 percent of all candidates.

These patterns suggest that there may in fact be region-specific "repertoires" of female representation. In research on social movements, the concept of repertoires refer to "a limited set of routines that are learned, shared, and acted out through a relatively deliberate process of choice," which constitute "the established ways in which pairs of actors make and receive claims bearing on each other's interests" (Tilly 1995, 42, 43). Because they constitute a set of measures that actors employ to make their actions understood, prevailing repertoires are likely to guide decision-making with regard to the particular types of measures that are adopted to guarantee the representation of identity groups (Krook and O'Brien 2007). This intuition is corroborated by evidence from quota debates around the world, which points to the importance of learning processes generated by the work of international and regional organizations (Krook 2004), contacts among civil society groups across national borders (Lubertino Beltrán 1992; Short 1996), and even straightforward emulation of the policies adopted in neighboring countries (Guadagnini 2005; Valiente 2005; cf. Ellerby 2008; Krook 2006b).

A closer look at these patterns, in turn, points to shared elements of the political contexts in which quotas are introduced. On the one hand, many of the countries that might be engaged in learning processes tend to be linked to outside actors in relatively structured ways. Women's groups in countries with similar languages, for example, have been documented as exchanging information on quota policies—and effective strategies for gaining their passage—across national borders (Htun and Jones 2002; Lubertino Beltrán 1992). Analogous transnational effects have also been observed among women's groups in parties with similar political ideologies (Russell 2005; Wisler 1999). More diffuse evidence for cross-national sharing is the prevalence of 30 percent quota policies around the world, a proportion which matches the recommendation made in most international documents concerning women's representation (Childs and Krook 2006).

On the other hand, most cases of quota adoption, while varied in many other ways, are nonetheless similar in that they tend to emerge during moments of crisis or change. National legislatures generally approve quotas when countries are undergoing constitutional reform (Baines and Rubio-Marin 2005), democratic transition (Araújo and García Quesada 2006), post-conflict reconstruction (Hughes 2007), or regime change (Goetz and Hassim 2003). Along comparable lines, parties typically adopt quotas when elites are seeking to overcome a long period in opposition (Perrigo 1996), counteract a dramatic decrease in popularity (Baldez 2004), sustain an existing regime (Howard-Merriam 1990), or simply respond to the adoption of quotas by one their rivals (Caul 2001). These trends suggest that quotas are not only a global phenomenon, but are also connected to, or share important commonalities with, other quota campaigns around the world. Importantly, however, these links—especially dynamics of learning—may lead particular actors and motivations for quota reform to differ in important ways across national and party contexts.

Elements of Quota Campaigns

Disaggregating the four stories of quota adoption points to three broad groups of actors involved in quota campaigns, as well as at least seven possible motivations for quota reform. Actors may mobilize for or against quotas, while motivations may be principled or pragmatic. As a result, together they may produce varied results with regard to the design and intended impact of quota policies. Actors may be located in civil society, the state, or the international and transnational spheres. Those in civil society may include grassroots women's movements, women's movement organizations, women's sections inside political parties, cross-partisan networks of female politicians, and individual women active inside and outside parties. Most of these actors support quotas (Bruhn 2003; Dahlerup 2006b; Kittilson 2006; Lovenduski 2005), but some organize against them (Amar 1999; Howard-Merriam 1990; Kishwar 1998b). They are frequently the actors who initiate quota campaigns, which they direct toward state actors, sometimes with ideas or help from international and transnational actors.

State actors may encompass national women's policy agencies, national leaders, governing coalitions, members of parliament, party leaders, and judges in national and local courts. They are often the most powerful voices in quota debates in light of their broad visibility and their capacity to institute or reject quotas (Lovenduski 2005; Lubertino Beltrán 1992). They may propose quotas, but are most often the targets of campaigns waged by civil society and international and transnational actors. International and transnational actors, finally, may comprise international organizations of global and regional scope; transnational NGOs; and various kinds of transnational networks, usually composed of activists, politicians, or scholars. In a handful of earlier cases,[1] they also included colonial governments that played a central role in instituting quota reforms. Almost all of these actors support quotas, but some have been effective obstacles to quota adoption (Ciezadlo 2003; Pires 2002). For the most part, they provide inspiration and resources for civil society actors in their quest to convince state actors of the virtues of gender quotas.

Motivations for quota reform may include principled stands, electoral considerations, empty gestures, promotion of other political ends, extension of representational guarantees, international pressure, and transnational learning. Most of these contain normative and pragmatic elements, and in many cases, several distinct motives may operate simultaneously to promote or foil quota reform. Principled stands are engaged when women's groups pursue quotas out of the belief that women should be better represented (Dahlerup 2006b; Lovenduski 2005; Opello 2006), elites undertake repeated quota reform out of concerns to improve women's political access (Meier 2004; Mossuz-Lavau 1998), party and state actors adopt quotas to redefine citizenship in more inclusionary ways (Inhetveen 1999; Meier 2000), and international and transnational organizations recommend quotas as a means to foster gender-balanced decision-making (Krook 2006b). Normative arguments may also offer strong ammunition against quotas, however, in instances where opponents insist that they discriminate against men, restrict voters' choices, and contravene articles of the law that enshrine equality between women and men (Guadagnini 2005; Russell 2000; Varikas 1995).

Electoral considerations come into play when elites decide to introduce quotas after one of their rivals adopts them (Davidson-Schmich 2006; Kaiser 2001; Matland and Studlar 1996). A key element is often mobilization by women's sections inside political parties, which may draw on gains made by women in other parties to press for quotas in their own parties (Lovenduski and Norris 1993). They usually succeed when advocates frame quotas as an effective tool for winning women's votes, which can be an especially effective argument in cases where parties seek to overcome a long period in opposition or a dramatic decrease in popularity (Perrigo 1999; Stevenson 2000). Electoral incentives may all the same prove to be a double-edged sword, as opponents also argue against quotas for women on the grounds of electoral competition, claiming that women are less effective candidates than men and thus that increasing the proportion of women threatens to decrease the party's electoral fortunes (Bruhn 2003; Murray 2004). Empty gestures are related to electoral considerations and occur in instances where elites view quotas as a relatively easy way to demonstrate commitment to women's rights without necessarily altering existing patterns of representation (Htun and Jones 2002). In these cases, leaders enthusiastically embrace gender quotas because they believe that these policies will not personally affect them, will never be implemented, or will be deemed unconstitutional before they can ever be applied (Araújo 2003; Durrieu 1999; Mossuz-Lavau

1998). In this sense, empty gestures embody both a strategy and a counterstrategy for quota adoption and implementation.

Promotion of other ends may take a number of different forms in quota campaigns. It may enter into elite calculations when they realize that pursuing quotas may also help them achieve other political goals. From this perspective, quota adoption enables elites to hand-pick "malleable" women who will not question or challenge the status quo (Costa Benavides 2003; Goetz and Hassim 2003), institutionalize procedures for candidate selection that enforce central party decisions (Baldez 2004; Bruhn 2003), build alliances with potential coalition partners (Chowdhury 2002; Shaheed, Zia, and Warraich 1998), manifest independence from other centers of government (Baldez 2004), and—more broadly—establish the national and international legitimacy of a particular regime (Nechemias 1994; Howard-Merriam 1990; Reyes 2002). The promotion of other ends may also undermine quota adoption, however, if opponents argue that other projects are more pressing than women's political representation (Waylen 1994).

The extension of representational guarantees, in turn, operates when the adoption of gender quotas is linked to existing approaches for recognizing difference. In some countries, advocates argue that quotas for women simply build on various guarantees already given to other groups based on language, religion, race, ethnicity, youth, or occupation. These measures are typically intended to safeguard the participation of vulnerable groups or simply to ensure some degree of proportional representation (Bih-er, Clark, and Clark 1990; Bird 2003; Meier 2000). Yet, in some cases, the measures that already exist may also be used to argue effectively against quotas on the grounds that "sex" is not a category of political representation on par with other recognized group identities (Jenkins 1999; Sgier 2003).

International pressure may influence quota adoption when leaders incorporate a range of different social groups in political assemblies in attempts to establish the international legitimacy of a new regime (Nechemias 1994; Howard-Merriam 1990), conform to emerging international norms following the direct intervention of international and transnational organizations (Dahlerup and Nordlund 2004; Krook 2006b), or—in several historical instances of quota reform—maintain colonial-era policies following independence or secession (Afzal 1999; Everett 1979). In rare cases, pressure from international actors may force country-level actors to abandon quotas as a strategy to increase women's representation, based on the argument that quotas do not constitute international "best practice" for conducting elections (Pires 2002).

Finally, transnational learning occurs when women's groups share information on successful strategies for increasing women's representation with each other across national borders (Lubertino Beltrán 1992; Tripp 2004), or transnational organizations and networks transmit information to domestic groups to suggest new tactics for reform (Russell 2005). These processes rarely reveal direct application of lessons learned, but frequently involve efforts to "translate" quotas to suit specific domestic contexts (Krook 2006b). Opponents hardly ever use this strategy, apart from efforts to delegitimize quotas through association with ex-Communist regimes (Matland and Montgomery 2003).

Combinations in Quota Campaigns

Reaggregating these elements, it becomes clear in many cases that feminist and nonfeminist actors are frequently involved on both sides of these debates, influencing at least to some extent the degree to which quotas can be considered feminist reforms. Most strikingly, the adoption of gender quotas does not always stem from principled concerns to empower women in politics. Rather, most policies are the result of a combination of normative and pragmatic motivations, pursued by varied but multiple groups of actors who may support reform for various and often conflicting reasons. Understanding individual quota campaigns thus requires careful attention to the alliances— both intended and unintended—that come together to promote quota reform. Many scholars implicitly trace these alliances, recounting how actors work together in various ways within and across civil society, the state, and the international and transnational spheres. However, their research rarely "speaks" to the findings of other cases, given the lack of a shared vocabulary for organizing their conclusions.

Although the potential combinations are endless, it is possible— based on the broad range of case studies reviewed here—to discern a number of common coalitions that come together during quota campaigns. One brings together women in civil society and women in the state, who both take principled stands on the need for increased female representation. Examples include campaigns that mobilize women's movement organizations and/or women inside political parties, who work with members of women's policy agencies to support quota reform (Durrieu 1999; Franceschet 2005; Kittilson 2006; Lovenduski 2005). A second joins women in civil society and men in the state. Although civil society groups generally assume principled stands, elites typically espouse quotas for pragmatic reasons: they respond to electoral considerations, make empty gestures, promote other political ends, or extend representational guarantees. In some cases, women inside the parties gain concessions from party leaders when the former convince the latter that doing so will attract more female voters (Lovenduski and Norris 1993; Perrigo 1999; Wängnerud 2001). In others, women's movement organizations press for quotas, and elites take up this demand in order to appear open to demands from civil society or to consolidate control over their political rivals (Baldez 2004; Htun and Jones 2002). In these instances, quotas do originate with women's movements, but serve other—sometimes pernicious and even anti-democratic—goals.

A third alliance occurs between women in civil society and various kinds of transnational actors, including transnational NGOs and transnational networks. Both groups are generally inspired by principled concerns, but transnational actors are also interested in transnational sharing. Indeed, most transnational networks exist to serve as conduits of information on various policy models and tactics for change (cf. True and Mintrom 2001), as well as to act as allies in persuading governments to adopt new policy innovations (Keck and Sikkink 1998). In quota campaigns, this dynamic is present in countries where women's movement organizations learn new tactics for reform through their involvement in various kinds of regional networks (Htun and Jones 2002; Tripp 2004; cf. Adams and Kang 2007). It also exists in cases where women inside the parties discover that quotas have been used effectively in similar parties abroad over the course of international meetings of their party federations (Lubertino Beltrán 1992; Russell 2005).

A fourth coalition links women in civil society with global and regional international organizations. Although both sets of actors are publicly committed to gender quotas for principled reasons, international organizations—by virtue of the fact that they bring together but also stand above national governments—also exert international pressure in order to gain compliance with emerging international norms. Examples include campaigns where international organizations give new force to the normative arguments presented by women's movement organizations by framing quotas as a central feature of a modern state, and even as the best route to economic modernization and development (Krook 2006b; Towns 2004). This partnership is particularly effective when states are sensitive to international scrutiny, where elites come to view quotas as a means to cultivate international legitimacy, foster perceptions of domestic legitimacy, or avoid being viewed as pariahs in the international community (Ellerby 2008; Howard-Merriam 1990; Reyes 2002).

A fifth possible partnership appears between women in civil society across two or more countries. These groups—usually women's movement organizations or women's sections inside political parties—espouse similar normative beliefs regarding the need to increase the numbers of women in elected office. However, their interest in exchanging information on concrete strategies for adopting and implementing quota policies means that they are also motivated by a need for transnational sharing. These groups often organize sessions during meetings of regional and global organizations (Araújo and García Quesada 2006; Tripp, Konaté, and Lowe-Morna 2006), but they also frequently initiate their own contacts by planning conferences, arranging personal visits, and circulating memos (Lubertino Beltrán 1992). In some cases, their contacts with one another are facilitated through financial and logistical assistance from national and transnational research centers.

Comparing Campaigns: Quotas, Actors, and Motivations for Reform

Although "ideas can come from anywhere" (Kingdon 1984, 75), tracking the origins of public policies is crucial for understanding how and why they come to be adopted, and in many instances, the particular forms they ultimately take. To date, much of the literature on quotas has focused on explaining their adoption within the context of a single case. While crucial for mapping developments around the world, this type of approach has important limitations, as it says little about whether these arguments might hold in other countries. Even more seriously, it may—and often does—lead scholars to overlook actors and motivations that are central to quota adoption, but which are perhaps less obvious given the lack of a comparative lens. In addition, attention to single cases—to the exclusion of broader trends—cannot by definition account for the rapid diffusion of quota policies to nearly all corners of the globe during the last fifteen years. Conducting more accurate case studies thus requires a more comprehensive framework for analyzing the actors and strategies involved in particular quota campaigns. The approach elaborated here is rooted in the details of individual studies, but draws on conflicting assessments across the literature to map a template of elements to consider when analyzing developments in a single case. The aim is to facilitate more informed comparisons on the role of various actors and motivations in quota debates, rather than provide a single model of quota adoption. Indeed, the goal is to privilege the possibility of causal diversity across quota campaigns, recognizing that these may be linked in various ways as part of a broader global wave leading to distinct trajectories of quota reform. Establishing the reasons for quota adoption, however, does not say anything about how effective these policies actually are. These questions are addressed in the next chapter, which seeks to explain why some quotas come closer than others in achieving higher levels of female representation.

The Implementation of Gender Quotas

Gender quotas have now been adopted by political parties and national legislatures in more than one hundred countries around the globe. The mere advent of these measures, however, has not resulted in a uniform rise in the numbers of women elected to national parliaments. Rather, some countries have experienced dramatic increases following the adoption of quota regulations, while others have witnessed more modest changes or even setbacks in women's representation. To date, reasons for these variations are not well-understood. This stems in part from the fact that quotas are a relatively new phenomenon. As such, most research carried out thus far focuses on detailing the features of these reforms and exploring motives for their adoption as a "first cut" at understanding where quotas come from. However, it also emerges from the lack of comparative research on this question: although case studies are important, without some contrasts it is difficult to know the extent to which the insights generated can be used to explain patterns in other cases. A number of recent studies have sought to bridge this gap by including quotas as one variable among many that might account for cross-national variations in women's representation (Matland 2006; Schwindt-Bayer 2007; Tremblay 2006; Tripp and Kang 2008; Yoon 2004), in an effort to discover how much "work" quotas do in comparison to the electoral system, indicators of women's social and economic status, and cultural attitudes toward women in politics. The approach elaborated in this chapter departs from this work on methodological grounds, arguing that it is necessary to undertake the analysis in two steps by first modeling dynamics of candidate selection, and then exploring the degree to which quota reforms reinforce or disrupt these dynamics. Organizing the investigation in this way not only affords greater analytical precision, but also provides a means to account for distinct routes to the same outcome, as well as instances where similar policies produce differing results.

This chapter begins by reviewing reasons for variations in quota implementation, as revealed in a wide range of case studies. Although this work is diverse, it tends toward one of three broad explanations: the impact of quotas is linked to details of the measures themselves, the institutional framework in which they are introduced, and the balance of actors for and against quotas. Weighing the evidence, this chapter makes a case for reconciling these accounts to consider how structures, practices, and norms work together to produce the effects of quota policies. To this end, it develops an alternative model of candidate selection based on configurations of three categories of gendered institutions: systemic institutions, the formal features of political systems; practical institutions, the formal and informal practices that shape political behavior; and normative institutions, the formal and informal principles that guide and justify the means and goals of political life. It then proposes that distinct quota types reform different kinds of political institutions: reserved seats alter systemic institutions, party quotas change practical institutions, and legislative quotas reframe normative institutions. Individual policies, however, may vary in their degree of reform, at the same time that these changes may interact with shifts and stability in the other two kinds of institutions. The result is a framework that analyzes quota implementation in relation to the extent to which quota policies affect existing institutional configurations in ways that facilitate or undermine transformation in women's political representation. This framework is illustrated in greater depth in the next three chapters through three sets of paired comparisons, which reveal—with reference to structures, practices, and norms—why some quotas are more successful than others in altering women's access to political office.

Mapping the Field: Current Perspectives on Quota Implementation

Recent studies offer a variety of insights into the dynamics of quota implementation in an effort to understand why some policies are more effective than others in achieving their stated goals. Despite their attention to individual cases, this work converges on three accounts related to the details of quota measures, their "fit" with existing institutional frameworks, and their support among actors in positions to guarantee or undermine quota success. Although this research rarely reflects on how particular conclusions might "speak" to the findings of another case, these "stories" nonetheless produce a list of details, institutions, and actors that appear favorable to the implementation and impact of quota policies. However, all three narratives are challenged by evidence from other cases, suggesting that none of these factors—at least when viewed in isolation from others—has a single set of generalizable effects.

Details of Quota Policies

A large group of studies analyzes implementation with regard to the details of quota policies. Initial surveys focused on the type of quota: most agreed that reserved seats tended to produce only small changes in women's representation (Chowdhury 2002; but see Norris 2006), but debated whether party quotas or legislative quotas were ultimately more effective (Leijenaar 1997; Jones 1998; cf. Krook 2006b). More recent work delves deeper into variations within and across these three categories. It argues that the impact of particular measures stems from their wording, that is, whether the language used in the policy introduces or reduces ambiguity regarding the process of implementation (Chama 2001; Schmidt and Saunders 2004); their requirements, that is, whether the policy specifies where female candidates should be placed and to which elections the policy applies (Jones 2004; Murray 2004); their sanctions, that is, whether the policy establishes organs for reviewing and enforcing quota requirements and procedures for punishing or rectifying noncompliance (Baldez 2004; Guldvik 2003); and their perceived legitimacy, that is, whether the policy is viewed as legal or constitutional from the point of view of national and international law (Mossuz-Lavau 1998; Russell 2000).

The details of individual provisions clearly shape implementation, as they set out the means and goals of specific quota policies. However, measures that appear similar sometimes have distinct effects on women's representation—at the same time that provisions that seem dissimilar may achieve comparable results. Notably, all three types of quotas have practically the same range in terms of their impact: reserved seats produce between 6.4 percent and 48.8 percent of women in parliament, party quotas between 4.1 percent and 47.3 percent, and legislative quotas between 9 percent and 40 percent (Inter-Parliamentary Union 2008a). A closer look at the dynamics of particular cases, further, reveals a number of unanticipated consequences related to the wording, requirements, sanctions, and legitimacy of quota measures. In some instances, for example, strong wording inadvertently establishes a ceiling for women's access, because elites interpret positions not designated for women as seats thereby reserved for men (Huang 2002; Nanivadekar 2006). In others, policy requirements, however strict, are less important to outcomes than related pieces of legislation passed at later moments in time (Chama 2001; Meier 2004). Sanctions have similarly mixed effects: their presence does not always suffice for gaining elite compliance, especially if they are not applied consistently by oversight bodies (Jones 1996; Schmidt and Saunders 2004), while their absence does not necessarily preclude compliance, if parties perceive other normative or strategic incentives for implementing quota provisions (Leijenaar 1997; Opello 2006). Finally, in some cases, measures viewed as illegitimate have resulted in dramatic increases in women's representation (Yoon 2001), while others seen as legitimate have lost their effectiveness over time, leading to stagnation in the numbers of women elected (Dahlerup 2001).

Institutional Frameworks and Quota Policies

A second common thread in research on this topic relates quota impact to the "fit" between quota measures and existing institutional frameworks. Most studies focus on characteristics of the electoral system, examining how electoral rules facilitate or hinder the potentially positive effects of quotas on women's representation. They observe that quotas tend to have the greatest impact in proportional representation (PR) electoral systems with closed lists and high district magnitudes (Caul 1999; Htun and Jones 2002; Matland 2006). Some also identify more idiosyncratic features of particular electoral systems that negatively affect quota implementation, including possibilities for parties to run more than one list in each district (Costa Benavides 2003), the presence of distinct electoral systems for different types of elections (Jones 1998), and opportunities for parties to nominate more candidates than the number of seats available (Htun 2002). Other scholars point to features of party systems, as well as parties themselves, to draw attention to the partisan dynamics that might aid or subvert quota impact. They find that quotas usually have stronger effects in party systems where several parties coexist and larger parties respond to innovations initiated by smaller parties (Kittilson 2006), as well as in parties with left-wing ideologies that have leaders who are able to enforce party or national regulations (Caul 1999; Davidson-Schmich 2006). A third group points to higher rates of implementation across all parties in states where political cultures emphasize sexual difference and group representation (Meier 2004), and lower rates in countries where political cultures stress sexual equality and individual representation (Inhetveen 1999).

These accounts are persuasive in connecting quota effectiveness to the presence of certain electoral, partisan, and normative characteristics. Other studies suggest, nonetheless, that quotas may succeed in a variety of institutional contexts. Most strikingly, in some cases quotas do have a strong impact on the proportion of women elected, despite the use of first-past-the-post (FPTP) and mixed electoral systems (Russell et al 2002; Tripp, Konaté, and Lowe-Morna 2006). Similarly, open lists and low district magnitudes sometimes magnify rather than dilute the influence of quotas through the dynamics of preferential voting, the distance between legislated and "effective" quotas, and the relative magnitude of the largest political party (Araújo 2003; Schmidt and Saunders 2004).[1] As for party systems, the presence of several parties is not necessary for quotas to have an impact: some of the most effective policies are those applied by single-party regimes as a form of political patronage or as a means for establishing social legitimacy (Goetz and Hassim 2003; Nechemias 1994). Further, some right-wing parties have greater rates of quota implementation than those on the left (Murray 2004), similar to decentralized parties in comparison to more centralized ones (Kolinsky 1991). Lastly, norms emphasizing sexual equality and individual representation can be powerful tools for increasing women's representation (Dahlerup 2001). Further, because quota campaigns frequently transform discourses, variations in the implementation of these measures can be related to new and emerging norms, as much as they are constrained by more traditional ideas about gender and politics (Sgier 2004; Squires 1996).

Actor Support and Quota Policies

A third set of explanations centers on the actors who support and oppose quotas and their respective roles with regard to quota implementation. Much of this literature focuses on party elites, exposing—in most cases—the ways in which elites seek to mitigate quota impact through passive refusal to enforce quotas to more active efforts to subvert their intended effects (Araújo 2003; Holli, Luhtakallio, and Raevaara 2006; Murray 2004), including large-scale electoral fraud and widespread intimidation of female candidates (Delgadillo 2000; Human Rights Watch 2004). Many studies also make reference to other actors who may play direct or indirect roles in enforcing quota provisions. These include women's organizations inside and outside the parties, who pressure elites to comply with quota provisions, distribute information on quota regulations both to elites and voters, and train female candidates to negotiate better positions on their respective party lists (Durrieu 1999; Lokar 2003; Sainsbury 1993); national and international courts, which provide an arena to challenge noncompliance and require parties to redo lists that do not comply with the law (Chama 2001; Jones 2004);[2] and finally ordinary citizens, who engage in public scrutiny of parties' selection practices through reports and reprimands that lead elites to honor and even exceed quota commitments (Baldez 2004; Kolinsky 1991).

Evidence from many cases indicates that party elites often oppose quotas and take steps to reduce their impact, in contrast to other state and social movement actors, who support quotas and pressure elites to ensure their implementation. All the same, several studies discover that these same groups may in fact play several distinct roles *vis-à-vis* quota regulations. For example, some elites implement quotas despite varying degrees of public opposition: they introduce quotas gradually over the course of several elections in order to reduce resistance among incumbents, voters, and local party organizations (Dahlerup 1988; Steininger 2000), or perhaps more conveniently, embrace these measures as a pretext for eliminating male rivals in favor of less-experienced female candidates (Bird 2003). At the same time, some women's groups do not support quotas and instead actively seek to undermine these provisions, although in some cases this is because they aim to gain the passage of more radical measures, such as alternative policies providing for higher levels of female representation (Chowdhury 2002; Huang 2002). Similarly, some judges dismiss allegations of noncompliance, issue erroneous decisions regarding the applicability of quota laws, and reduce their judicial activism over time, leading to decreases in quota effectiveness (Chama 2001; Schmidt 2003). Many citizens, finally, are not even aware of the existence of quota provisions, much less variations in their impact, thus diminishing the possibility for public oversight of the implementation process (Htun and Jones 2002; Zetterberg 2008).

Toward a New Framework: Quotas and Institutions of Candidate Selection

The existing literature thus offers no single definitive factor that explains all variations in quota implementation. Much of this work, however, points to the need to consider the combined role of details, institutions, and actors, in terms of the ways in which conditions come together to shape how quotas influence women's representation. In other words, there may be multiple paths to the same outcome, at the same time that the effects of various factors may be contingent upon the presence or absence of other conditions (cf. Ragin 2000). In order to incorporate this intuition into an analysis of quota impact, it is first necessary to revisit explanations for cross-national variations in women's representation. This is because, although it is rarely noted, quotas are introduced when differences already exist among countries with regard to women's access to national parliaments. Understanding the effects of quotas thus requires separating out analytically: (1) the factors that influence women's representation before quotas are adopted, and (2) the ways and degrees to which quotas alter these dynamics. Upon closer inspection, most research on cross-national variations speaks implicitly to the importance of combinations of causal factors, even as it purports to discuss the distinct and relative effects of individual conditions. This revised perspective suggests that a more fruitful approach to the study of quota impact should begin with these causal configurations, with an eye to how quotas may shift their various parts over the course of quota reforms.

Institutions of Candidate Selection

The factors that scholars analyze to explain variations in women's representation can be organized into three broad categories: formal features of political systems, formal and informal practices of political elites, and formal and informal principles of equality and representation. It is useful to think of these factors as three kinds of political institutions, where the term "institution" is understood in its broadest sense as the structures, practices, and norms that guide political action as if they were formal rules (Hall and Taylor 1996; Thelen and Steinmo 1992). Most research on gender and politics explores these three elements in relation to women's representation, but usually employs "institution" to refer only to formal structures (Krook and Freidenvall 2007). The approach developed here, however, draws on the insights of new institutionalism, which defines institutions in terms of "formal constraints—such as the rules that human beings devise—and informal constraints—such as conventions and codes of behavior" (North 1990, 4). The focus of inquiry is thus the continuum between formal and informal institutions, "mov[ing] from the study of such intangible phenomena as ideas, meanings, signifiers, beliefs, identities, attitudes, worldviews, discourses, and values to such tangible entities as states, constitutions, bureaucracies, churches, schools, armies, parties, and groups" (Ethington and McDonagh 1995, 470).

Although institutional scholars often allude to many different kinds of institutions, in empirical analyses many restrict their focus to a single institution in order to understand its particular origins and effects. This strategy misses an opportunity to explore how various kinds of institutions fit together as part of a "complicated ecology of interconnected rules" (March and Olsen 1989, 170). These webs may be characterized by various dynamics. On the one hand, they may form part of a self-enforcing, mutually reinforcing set of "institutional elements that motivate, coordinate, and enable individuals to follow particular regularities of behavior" (Greif and Laitin 2004, 635). On the other hand, they may involve ongoing clashes between different institutions, as "the institutions of a polity are not created or recreated all at once, in accordance with a single ordering principle; they are created instead at different times, in the light of different experiences, and often for quite contrary purposes" (Orren and Skowronek 2004, 112). While these two perspectives often remain implicit in institutionalist analysis, they suggest that various institutions may "surround, support, elaborate, and contradict" (March and Olsen 1989, 22) the effects of other institutions. Conceptualizing structures, practices, and norms as "institutions" thus has the advantage that it compels scholars to consider the role of all three at all points in the analysis, in order to discern how they interact to shape political outcomes. Taking this idea seriously, however, requires a shift to "configurational thinking" (Ragin 2000, 71), which recognizes that the effects of one institution may depend on the shape of other institutions operating within the same political context.

To emphasize their shared institutional nature, the analysis in this chapter conceptualizes structures, practices, and norms as three categories of political institutions: systemic, practical, and normative. *Systemic institutions* refer to the formal features of political systems, namely the laws and organizations officially structuring the conduct of political life. Their effects are among the most studied in the field of gender and politics. Amid these variables, scholars have focused on the electoral system as one of the most important, if not *the* most important factor, explaining cross-national variations in women's representation. They note that PR electoral systems, especially when combined with closed party lists and higher district magnitudes, tend to have much higher numbers of women in parliament than

FPTP electoral systems, which involve direct election of candidates in single-member districts (Caul 1999; Kunovich and Paxton 2005). However, a closer look at causal explanations reveals that PR systems promote women to the extent that their structural features combine with concerns to actually select more women—that is, practices and norms that support and even compel the recruitment of female candidates. More specifically, scholars speculate that PR systems offer more opportunities to women, because the presence of party lists and multimember districts means that parties are able, and may even feel pressed, to nominate at least a few women to "balance" their lists (Caul 1999; Matland 1995). By the same token, FPTP systems do not necessarily preclude the election of more women. Although balancing nominations is impossible, given the presence of single-member districts, parties that resolve to elect more women may devise new practices of candidate selection to accomplish this goal, like all-women shortlists, guaranteeing that whichever candidate is chosen in a particular district will be female. Implementing such a controversial policy, however, often requires linking it to other party practices or justifying it through appeals to broader notions of equality.

The formal and informal practices of elites can, in turn, be classified as *practical* institutions. In the case of political recruitment, these encompass the procedures and criteria that parties employ to select their candidates. Qualifications required by law include age, citizenship, country of birth, party membership, and in some cases, collection of a certain number of signatures or the payment of a fee to register the candidacy. Informal criteria are more numerous and may comprise education, party service, legislative experience, speaking abilities, financial resources, political connections, kinship, name recognition, membership group networks, and organizational skills (Rahat and Hazan 2001). These requirements are influenced by the location of candidate selection, groups in the party that are entitled to suggest or to veto candidates, methods of ballot composition, and rules about secret or open ballots during candidate selection. These processes invariably produce distortions between the features of candidates and the characteristics of voters, as legislatures worldwide contain a larger share of affluent, male, middle-aged, and white-collar members than exist proportionally in the electorate (Norris 1997b). Scholars disagree as to whether supply or demand side factors play a greater role in fostering inequalities in political recruitment. However, in many of their accounts they explain party selection practices in terms of party characteristics and underlying popular beliefs about the political qualifications of women—that is, structures and norms that influence how party selectors and voters perceive female candidates. Numerous studies find, for example, that the criteria that a party requires of candidates are largely a function of its organization and its ideology, with centralized left-wing parties being more likely to recruit women (Matland and Studlar 1996; Norris and Lovenduski 1995). All the same, decentralized parties provide opportunities for women to become more active in local party organizations that can, in turn, offer a crucial stepping stone for attaining higher political office (Caul 1999), shifting party practices and norms.

Formal and informal principles, finally, can be viewed as normative institutions that set forth the values informing the means and goals of political life. Here, they refer to hegemonic interpretations of "equality" and "representation" shaping patterns of candidate selection, including beliefs about the legitimacy of elite intervention to promote equal representation. They may be enshrined formally in constitutions, legal codes, electoral laws, and party statutes, as well as informally in public speeches, political ideologies, and voter opinions. Norms of equality may support "equality of opportunities," focused on inputs, or "equality of results," focused on outputs. Principles of representation, in turn, may emphasize a "politics of ideas," a belief that ideas are important and thus the personal traits of representatives are irrelevant, and a "politics of presence," an assertion that the personal features of representatives are crucial because they influence the substance of public policies (Phillips 1995; cf. Krook, Lovenduski, and Squires 2006). Signaling the importance of an equality of results, most scholars find that countries with more egalitarian political cultures, as well as parties on the left, are more likely to promote women (Inglehart and Norris 2003; Kittilson 2006). Indicating the need for a politics of presence, research on electoral systems suggests that parties in PR systems feel pressed to nominate at least a few women in order to balance their lists of candidates, in line with broader goals of fostering the participation of many different groups (Matland 1995). In these explanations, the role of norms is thus largely embedded within discussions of structures and party practices. All the same, a more comprehensive review reveals that concepts of equality and representation may take a number of different forms as they interact with party ideologies regarding sex and gender. While some conservatives oppose quotas because they support equal opportunities, others defend such measures on the grounds that men and women are different. Conversely, some progressives resist quotas because they fear that these essentialize gender differences, while others defend such policies because they favor equality of results (Inhetveen 1999; Skjeie 1992). Similar trends are evident with notions of representation, with many parties shifting their views regarding which groups "deserve" representation depending on the sectors they view or seek to capture as primary constituencies (Krook and O'Brien 2007; Sgier 2003).

Quotas as Institutional Reforms

Studies that emphasize individual institutions, therefore, almost invariably include references to the other two categories of institutions when seeking to explain their causal effects. This insight is crucial for theorizing quota impact, as these policies affect not only single institutions, but also entire institutional configurations. At the same time, the three categories of quota measures seek to reform these configurations in distinct ways: reserved seats revise systemic institutions, party quotas rework practical institutions, and legislative quotas redefine normative institutions. Reserved seats mainly entail systemic reform because they alter the formal mechanisms of election to set aside a certain number of seats for women. They are usually enacted through constitutional changes that establish separate electoral rolls for women, designate particular districts for female candidates, or allocate women's seats to political parties based on their proportion of the popular vote. Initial provisions for reserved seats in Pakistan in the 1950s, for example, created a separate ballot that would allow only women to vote for the women who would fill the reserved seats (Afzal 1999). In comparison, quotas in Uganda require that women run in specially designated electoral districts, overlapping the "regular" constituencies, in a vote that takes place as many as two weeks after the general elections (Goetz and Hassim 2003; Tripp 2000). The most common arrangement, however, is one in which women's seats are distributed to parties based on their degree of voter support. In some countries, like Pakistan, this policy enables several parties to fill the reserved seats in proportion to their share of the popular vote (Krook 2005). The policy is different in other countries, like Bangladesh, where the party that wins the most votes earns the right to designate all the seats. This enables parties to pack seats with their own supporters or to utilize the seats as a tool for gaining coalition partners (Chowdhury 2002).

Party quotas, in contrast, primarily involve practical reform because they alter the criteria for candidate selection in ways that require elites to devise new practices of political recruitment. They are typically introduced through changes to party statutes that commit the party to field a certain percentage of women. In most cases, this requirement compels elites to find new ways of locating prospective female candidates and persuading them to run for office, thus overcoming some of the important biases that result in fewer women standing forward and being chosen as party candidates (cf. Krook 2006a; Lawless and Fox 2005). This dynamic plays itself out in similar ways across many political parties. The Social Democratic Party in Germany, to take one instance, introduced a 25 percent quota in 1988, which it raised to 33 percent in 1994 and 40 percent in 1998. In order to implement these quotas, party elites were obliged to relax traditional expectations regarding candidate nomination, which had earlier required prospective candidates to spend years working inside the party as political apprentices. Having adopted the quota, elites were compelled to recognize that this "qualification" tended to exclude women, who had less time than men to devote to party work, even though they were competent at many other levels to run for political office. The policy thus forced the party to uncover other ways of finding candidates, like tapping activists in the party's youth organization, organizing training sessions for possible female candidates, and encouraging talented women to consider running (Kolinsky 1991; McKay 2005).

Legislative quotas, finally, predominantly engage in normative reform because they revise definitions of equality and representation to call on all parties to nominate a greater proportion of female candidates. They entail amending constitutions or electoral laws to legitimize positive action, foster more equal results, and recognize "sex" as a category of representation. In France, for example, a 50 percent quota was introduced following constitutional reform in 1999 and changes to the electoral law in 2000. Parties must now nominate 50 percent male and 50 percent female candidates to almost all political offices, suffering various sorts of financial and political penalties if they do not comply (Murray 2004). By way of contrast, the quota law approved in Argentina in 1991 involved reforms to the electoral code that stated that parties must present 30 percent female candidates in positions where they are likely to be elected. Combined with other decisions and legislation, this law requires that parties not only nominate, but also elect, 30 percent women (Chama 2001; Jones 1996). The requirements of a similar law passed in Bosnia in 2000 were made more precise in 2001 to specify the positions on party lists where female candidates had to be placed: at least one woman among the first two candidates, two among the first five, and three among the first eight (Lokar 2003; Rukavina et al 2002). Both individually and as a group, therefore, these policies seek to shift the effects of reigning notions of equality and representation from supporting the exclusion to promoting the inclusion of women as political actors.

Quotas and Institutional Configurational Change

Gender quotas thus vary in terms of the kinds of reforms they initiate in candidate selection processes. To add a further layer of complexity, specific quota policies also achieve varying degrees of institutional reform, interact in numerous ways with existing institutional arrangements, and intersect—at the moment of reform or at a later point in time—with the reform and nonreform of other institutions. All of these dynamics, whether intended or unintended, play a central role in shaping the impact of quota policies. As such, they offer crucial clues as to why attempts to reform the same type of institution may lead to radically different outcomes, at the same time that efforts to change distinct institutions may produce relatively similar results across cases. The explicit focus on single institutions in existing institutionalist research offers only limited leverage for modeling these dynamics. Nonetheless, it does provide tools for analyzing institutional transformation through two broad theories of institutional stability and change.

The first draws a sharp analytical distinction between moments of change and mechanisms of reproduction. In this approach, new institutions emerge rarely and often only in the context of crisis or great uncertainty. These "critical junctures," which cannot be predicted from prior events or initial conditions, serve as major turning points in which the—often contingent—decisions of actors establish new directions of change (Collier and Collier 1991; Mahoney 2000). A dynamic of "path dependence" then precludes the emergence of other options over time through such mechanisms as increasing returns, sunk costs, durable commitments, personal and social conservatism, and learning curves (North 1990; Pierson 2000). These reinforce movement along a given trajectory, even when other choices appear better or more efficient (Aminzade 1992; Tilly 2001). This perspective thus resembles a "punctuated equilibrium" model in which long periods characterized by path dependence alternate with brief and dramatic turns of event (cf. Krasner 1984).

While widely applied, this approach has been increasingly challenged in recent years by scholars in various institutional traditions who criticize the sharp separation between institutional creation and institutional reproduction. In its place, a pair of rational choice theorists develop the notion of endogenous "institutional refinement," whereby "institutions organically evolve (or are intentionally designed) through changing, introducing, or manipulating institutional elements while supplementing existing elements (or responding to their failure to generate desire behavior)" (Greif and Laitin 2004, 640). Along similar lines, some historical scholars note that "when institutions have been in place for a long time *most* changes will be incremental" (Pierson 2004, 153). Consequently, they theorize that institutions more typically survive through dynamics of institutional conversion, in which existing institutions are directed to new purposes, and institutional layering, in which some elements of existing institutions are renegotiated but other elements remain (Thelen 2003). These intuitions are echoed by several sociological institutionalists, who observe that "ideas about appropriate behavior ordinarily change gradually through the development of experience and the elaboration of worldviews" (March and Olsen 1989, 171). They are also the focus of various discursive institutionalists, who call attention to how elements of one discourse are translated into another through "discursive alliances or bricolage" (Campbell and Pedersen 2001, 12). Taken together, these views are closer to a "bounded innovation" model in which periods of institutional reproduction overlap with moments of institutional creation in partial and often unanticipated ways (cf. Weir 1992).

Both of these perspectives call attention to the "sticky" nature of institutions, observing that once in place, structures, practices, and norms are generally difficult to alter. Nonetheless, actors sometimes do attempt to reform institutions, although their efforts rarely achieve exactly what they set out to do, stemming from a tendency to overlook—at least in initial stages—how these reforms will interact with broader institutional configurations. Understanding why quotas have varied effects on women's representation thus requires a more careful look at how particular policies interact with elements of the wider context. Prevailing methods in political science point to two possible research strategies for gauging these effects.

A quantitative solution would involve gathering information on a large number of countries with and without quota policies in order to determine what sort of impact on average quotas exert on patterns of representation (cf. Matland 2006; Tremblay 2006; Yoon 2004). The main drawback of this approach, as noted above, is that quotas do not exert independent effects on political outcomes. Rather, their impact depends closely on existing—as well as changing— configurations of other conditions, which themselves may shift as a result of quota adoption. A qualitative solution, in contrast, would trace events as they evolve in countries that adopt quotas, paying close attention to the factors that facilitate or undermine quota success (cf. Bradbury et al 2000; Davidson-Schmich 2006; Meier 2003; Murray 2004). Although this approach offers greater potential for unraveling causal configurations, it is limited in that it examines developments in a small number of cases, largely avoiding comparisons with other instances of quota reform.

A third alternative, and the one advocated here, is to devise a middle-range approach that enables both cross- and within-case comparisons. To implement this strategy, the remaining chapters of this book focus on countries that have witnessed multiple attempts at quota reform, analyzing what Jeffrey Haydu (1998) describes as "sequences of reiterated problem-solving." This perspective reconciles the two models of institutional change outlined above: it "constructs narratives of historical switch points that are followed by more or less durable social regimes" but also "links these historical junctures into coherent sequences [by exploring] how earlier historical turning points shape later ones" (Haydu 1998, 349–350). The intuition is that actors almost always devise new strategies in relation to what has come before, even when they seek to initiate dramatic reform. Examining the course of these trial-and-error processes thus offers a novel means for constructing and comparing how configurations of institutions change or remain stable over time.

Although this lens can only be applied to the few cases where actors pursue multiple attempts at reform, attention to these campaigns can provide crucial insights for understanding the larger universe of cases. First, as has been shown with regard to the existing literature on quotas, comparing single reforms tends to uncover a host of contradictions regarding the causal function of individual institutions. This leads to less, but also potentially misleading, theoretical leverage on the importance of specific institutions. In contrast, analyzing instances of multiple reforms helps clarify the dynamics at work across all campaigns by making use of the extra data provided by cases of iterated reforms to discern the part played by individual institutions within broader institutional configurations as one or both of these evolve over time. Second, focusing on single attempts at reform enables researchers to observe connections between inputs and outcomes, but leaves little theoretical space for exploring actors' reactions or intentions in the face of expected or unexpected results. In comparison, closer scrutiny of iterated reforms affords a clearer view of actors' own interpretations as to why certain strategies fail or succeed, and thus the intended and unintended consequences of individual reforms.

The literature on institutions, as alluded to above, offers two views—albeit largely implicit—on relations between different kinds of institutions, which may be mutually reinforcing (Greif and Laitin 2004) or conflicting (Orren and Skowronek 2004), by historical accident or intentional design. When linked to the concept of iterated reforms, these perspectives suggest two ideal-typical models of institutional configurational change that reflect how, and the extent to which, attempts to reform one institution intersect with the reform and nonreform of other institutions. The contrast between them can be described as harmonizing versus disjointed sequences of reform. In most cases, actors do not appear, at least initially, to be aware of how structures, practices, and norms work together to shape patterns of political representation. As such, in nearly all instances of quota reform,[3] advocates typically begin by focusing on one type of institution: systemic institutions in the case of reserved seats, practical institutions in the case of party quotas, and normative institutions in the case of legislative quotas. Supporters then discover after one or more rounds of implementation that the policy has little or no effect on women's representation: the number of women elected remains relatively stable because elites treat reserved seats as a ceiling on women's recruitment, flout party quota requirements, or misinterpret legislative quota provisions. Thus, systemic reform is not matched by practical and normative reform, practical reform is thwarted by lack of systemic and normative reform, or normative reform is undone by the absence of systemic and practical reform.

The nature of the sequence that then follows depends closely on the strategies that actors, both advocates and opponents, pursue in the wake of these events. In *harmonizing sequences,* actions are taken that lead the three categories of institutions to fit together increasingly over time. In the run-up to subsequent elections, for example, supporters may pursue reforms that aim to improve quota impact by acknowledging how they interact with features of other institutions.

Their line of attack may include matching the policy to various aspects of the electoral system,[4] reducing any lingering ambiguity regarding the details and scope of the quota and sanctions for noncompliance, or establishing or confirming the legitimacy of the policy in relation to national or international law. In this way, during the course of the campaign advocates grow to recognize, implicitly or explicitly, that structures, practices, and norms interact. They thus work cumulatively to adjust institutions of candidate selection in mutually reinforcing ways. Because these campaigns complement institutional reform with institutional configurational reform, they generally experience dramatic success in the implementation and impact of gender quota provisions.

Disjointed sequences, in contrast, result when actors pursue strategies that cause the three types of institutions to clash with one another, producing conflicts and tensions that undermine efforts to promote change. In many of these cases, efforts to adopt and implement quotas inspire a backlash that leads opponents to challenge and successfully overturn quota policies. These setbacks not only prevent further institutional reform, but also strongly de-legitimize quotas themselves as a strategy for increasing women's representation. In some instances, supporters respond by identifying one pivotal institution of candidate selection—sometimes, but not always, the same institution as before—whose reform they believe is vital to quota adoption and implementation. However, the effort to reject one institutional form in favor of another often requires them to justify radical change within a largely hostile environment to generate an entirely new path to reform. Waging an uphill battle, they may focus only on revising elements of the electoral system, enforcing an overhaul of party selection procedures, or achieving a constitutional amendment to allow positive action. In the course of privileging one kind of institution, they may ignore and even downplay the importance of the others, fostering competition—rather than mutual support—across their causal effects. By separating institutional reform from institutional configurational reform, these campaigns usually produce mixed results in terms of quota adoption and limited success with regard to quota implementation and impact. However, in some instances these sequences may become harmonizing, if campaigners eventually come to realize the importance of broader institutional configurations. By the same token, harmonizing and disjointed sequences may coexist across parties or levels of government, depending on the form and reach of particular quota debates. As such, sequences of reform may play out in a variety of ways across countries, with diverse effects on women's political representation.

Comparing Cases of Reform: Quotas and Shifts in Institutional Configurations

Quotas are introduced when cross-national variations already exist in terms of the numbers of women elected to political office. Further, specific policies enact differing degrees of reform to reigning candidate selection processes. Analyzing variations in the effects of gender quotas thus requires an approach sensitive to the substantial causal complexity at work in these diverse cases. First, no single factor explains all variations; instead, multiple conditions combine to influence how quotas affect women's access to political office. Second, quota reforms do not take place in a vacuum: they proceed in a temporal relation to previous institutions within the same category, as well as the causal context of broader institutional configurations. These various features go far in explaining why "institutional change rarely satisfies the prior intentions of those who initiate it [as] change cannot be controlled precisely" (March and Olsen 1989, 65), as "changes in the environment of any complex system produce a series of actions and reactions that need to be calibrated before the ultimate consequences are understood" (March and Olsen 1989, 57). Evaluating the form and impact of institutional reform thus requires a three-stage research strategy that (1) maps existing institutional configurations, (2) evaluates the nature and degree of attempted institutional change, and (3) explores the ways in which these reforms interact with stability and change in other political institutions. Applied to the case of quotas, this approach not only enables better knowledge of quota campaigns, but given more careful attention to institutional configurations, should also facilitate the design of more effective quota policies.

The next three chapters apply this framework to analyze and compare instances of iterated quota reform, with the goal of illuminating through cross- and within-case comparisons why some quotas are more effective than others in achieving their stated aims. To select countries for closer analysis, quota campaigns around the world were reviewed to discover which cases had experienced sequences of iterated reform. At least fourteen countries met this criterion: Argentina,

Austria, Bangladesh, Belgium, Costa Rica, France, Germany, Mexico, Pakistan, Spain, Sweden, Tanzania, Uganda, and the United Kingdom (UK). Six of these cases were then chosen for further investigation based on quota types and sequences of reform: Argentina, France, India, Pakistan, Sweden, and the UK (see table 3.1). The form and content of these campaigns are diverse, beginning as early as the 1920s and as late as the 1980s, spanning periods from as little as fifteen to as many as seventy years, involving both slow and quick rates of change, and resulting in below average to nearly equal levels of female representation in parliament. The group also offers a relatively accurate reflection of the range of countries that have witnessed quota campaigns, given their wide array of political, social, economic, and cultural characteristics. They include democratic and nondemocratic regimes; varying histories of political stability and instability; FPTP and PR electoral systems; no-party, two-party, and multiparty systems; and low, medium, and high levels of socioeconomic development. While traditional qualitative methods would preclude these comparisons on the grounds that these cases cannot be matched on all characteristics but one, these differences can be accommodated within an analysis focused on configurations of causal conditions, because attention is focused on how these factors combine, rather than on the causal effects of any single condition.

A preliminary mapping of the impact of the policies in these six countries provides initial corroboration of the intuition that harmonizing reforms are more effective than disjointed reforms in increasing women's representation (see table 3.2). However, to explore this point more carefully, and thus evaluate the arguments in this chapter in greater depth, the next three chapters undertake paired comparisons of countries with similar kinds of quota policies. Within these pairs, one country has seen dramatic shifts following the implementation of a gender quotas, while the other has witnessed little change or even stagnation in the numbers of women elected. To assess the nature and effects of institutional reform, as well as the degree of

Table 3.1. Case Selection by Type and Sequence of Reform

Type of Reform	Harmonizing Sequence	Disjointed Sequence
Systemic Reform	Pakistan	India
Practical Reform	Sweden	United Kingdom
Normative Reform	Argentina	France

Table 3.2. Sequences of Reform and Women's Political Representation

Type of Sequence	Women in Parliament, 2008 (%)	Change, 1950–2008 (% points)
Harmonizing Sequences		
Pakistan	22.5 (2008)	18.7[a]
Sweden	47.3 (2006)	42.3
Argentina	40.0 (2007)	40.0
Disjointed Sequences		
India	9.1 (2004)	5.1
United Kingdom	19.5 (2005)	16.2
France	18.2 (2007)	14.4

Source: Inter-Parliamentary Union (1995); Inter-Parliamentary Union (2008a).

[a]Data for Pakistan since 1962.

institutional configurational change, each set of campaigns is examined with reference to the actors, motivations, and contexts that are relevant in the origins, adoption, and implementation of each quota measure. To ensure their accuracy, the case studies incorporate evidence from a variety of primary and secondary sources, including interviews, parliamentary debates, newspaper editorials, personal testimonials, online election reports, media articles, and scholarly analyses. The chapters draw on these diverse materials to explore links between earlier events and later strategies and how these may shed light on the presence—and actors' awareness—of broader institutional constellations. The case studies are thus embedded in an explicitly comparative framework that combines attention to temporality and causal configurations, in this way going beyond attention to the cause and effect of particular quota policies in individual cases around the world.

FOUR

Reserved Seats in Pakistan and India

For many years a number of countries around the world have reserved seats for women in politics by reforming constitutions, and sometimes electoral laws, to establish separate electoral rolls for women, designate separate districts for female candidates, or allocate women's seats to parties based on their proportion of the popular vote. These provisions thus alter systemic institutions by revising mechanisms of election to mandate a minimum number of female representatives. As such, they differ from party and legislative quotas in that they guarantee women's presence, although the proportion of women they stipulate is generally much lower than these other types, often less than 10 percent but sometimes as much as 30 percent. Reserved seats also have a longer history than these other measures, appearing as early as the 1930s, and tend to be concentrated geographically in Africa, Asia, and the Middle East. As more countries have adopted quotas over the last several years, reservations have become an increasingly popular solution for including women, especially in countries with very low levels of female parliamentary representation.[1]

To understand why reserved seats have been adopted in various countries, when these policies entail setting aside positions for women that men are not eligible to contest, this chapter analyzes the cases of Pakistan and India, where a shared colonial past witnessed attempts in the 1930s by the British to reserve seats for women in politics, in line with reservations for a range of other groups based on race, religion, education, and occupation. After independence, however, the two countries took opposite approaches to the issue of reserved seats, with Pakistan introducing measures for women in the early 1950s and India rejecting such proposals until the late 1980s. Today, both have adopted a one-third quota for women in local government, but only Pakistan has reserved seats for women in the national parliament. As a result, women occupy 23 percent of the seats in parliament in Pakistan, but only 9 percent of these seats in India (Inter-Parliamentary Union 2008a). As these measures most often entail full implementation,[2] the question emerges: Why have leaders in Pakistan, both democrats and dictators, repeatedly insti-tuted reserved seats for women, while leaders in India have consis-tently rebuffed proposals for reserved seats at the national level?

Employing the framework elaborated in the two previous chapters, the analysis explores the actors, strategies, and institutions that have played a role in decisions to adopt—and not adopt—gender quotas by comparing efforts to establish reserved seats in Pakistan between 1988 and 2002 with debates over the Women's Reservation Bill in India between 1988 and 2008. As both countries have witnessed numerous attempts at quota reform, each case study is situated within the context of its historical antecedents, which include shared experiences under the Government of India Act of 1935, but distinct approaches following independence. While leaders in Pakistan con-tinually reserved seats for women in national and state assemblies until 1988, governments in India repeatedly resisted such demands until the early 1990s, when national legislators finally approved a 30 percent reservation for women, but for local government only. In analyzing the origins, adoption, and implementation of the present quota provisions, the chapter reveals that reform processes in Pakistan are harmonizing while those in India have been disjointed. In Paki-stan, a military regime restored reserved seats and enacted a series of other systemic reforms that in the run up to new popular elections spilled over into partial practical and normative reform, enabling women to win more reserved and nonreserved seats than ever before. In India, in contrast, supporters sought to extend the successes of systemic reform at the local level by pursuing systemic reform at the national level, ignoring the possibilities for practical and normative reform even as existing practices and norms undermined their efforts for systemic change. These distinct trajectories not only explain vari-ations in women's representation across these two countries, but also call attention to the multiple dimensions of reform—and the some-times crucial importance of unintended consequences—in campaigns to bring more women into political office.

Reserved Seats for Women in Pakistan

Campaigns for reserved seats in Pakistan reach back nearly seventy years, with the first decisions to institute quotas appearing in 1935 and the most recent reforms taking place in 2002. During this time, the actors involved in these campaigns have included civil society actors like women's movement organizations, religious authorities, and women in the parties; state actors like colonial officers, parliamentary representatives, presidents, prime ministers, military leaders, cabinet ministers, state committees, women's policy agencies, parties, and the courts; and international and transnational actors like the British government, the United Nations (UN), the United Nations Development Program (UNDP), and transnational nongovernmental organizations (NGOs). Involved in different ways at various points in these campaigns, these actors have advocated and rejected reserved seats in the service of normative objectives as well as pragmatic goals. The role of systemic provisions in maintaining a minimum level of female representation became clear in 1990, when the expiration of the reserved seats policy resulted in a dramatic drop in the number of women elected to the lower house of parliament. Twelve years later, reserved seats were restored and increased through systemic reform that, combined with new restrictions on political candidacy, spilled over to practical and normative reform, resulting in the election of more women to reserved and nonreserved seats than ever before.

Antecedents to Reserved Seats

Reserved seats, most recently adopted as part of a package for national elections in 2002, have a long and relatively continuous history in Pakistan. They were first introduced in 1935, when the country was part of India and ruled by the British Empire, through the Government of India Act, which enfranchised women and allocated seats for them in the Council of State and the Federal Assembly. Although women had already gained the right to vote in provincial elections with strong property qualifications, this act marked the first attempt to include women in elected assemblies. Six seats were reserved for women in the Council of State, one each to be selected by the provincial legislatures of Madras, Bengal, Bombay, the United Provinces, Punjab, and Bihar. Nine seats were reserved for women in the Federal Assembly—two from Madras, two from Bombay, one from Bengal, one from the United Provinces, one from Punjab, and one from the Central Provinces—and were to be chosen by an electoral college consisting of the female members of each respective provincial legislature. These numbers remained extremely small, however, amounting to less than 4 percent of both chambers and excluding five and four provinces in the Council of State and Federal Assembly, respectively (Afzal 1999).

Various women were subsequently elected to provincial and national assemblies, but most politically active Muslim women turned their attention instead to the movement for Pakistan and formed the All India Muslim Women's Sub-Committee in 1938 to support the idea of a separate homeland for Muslims. Playing a central role in the revival of the Muslim League, they mobilized voters during the 1930s and 1940s to gain the support of the Muslim population. When Pakistan gained independence in 1947, the new regime quickly adopted a provisional constitution and organized elections for a Constituent Assembly, charged with the task of writing a permanent constitution. Mohammad Ali Jinnah, the founder of Pakistan and leader of the Muslim League, reserved two of these seats for women, emphasizing the need for women to participate in politics as an essential condition for women's progress, even though the number of seats set aside for women represented less than 3 percent of all members of the Constituent Assembly (Ikramullah 1976; Mumtaz 1998). Provincial elections were then held under the terms of the Government of India Act, with some amendments and alterations. The Third Amendment reserved seats in all four provincial assemblies—nine seats in East Pakistan (309 total), five seats in Punjab (197 total), three seats in Sind (111 total), and two seats in North West Frontier Province (NWFP) (85 total)—for women who would be elected by female voters through separate constituencies (Afzal 1999, 18–19).

Despite these concessions, women stepped up their demands for reserved seats over the next several years, although they had not made reserved seats a central issue before independence and, indeed, had initially believed that the state had more pressing priorities than enhancing women's legal status (Afzal 1999; Ali 2000). In 1948, however, thousands of women marched to the assembly chambers in Lahore to press for women's right to inherit property and an increase in the number of seats reserved for women, leading to the creation of the All Pakistan Women's Association (APWA) in 1949 with the goal of promoting the welfare of women in Pakistan (Zafar 1991). The following year, the Basic Principles Committee (BPC), responsible for drafting the fundamental principles of the constitution, considered a range of proposals from individuals and organizations on the issue of women's representation. Because Pakistan sought to define itself as an Islamic republic, religious groups sent numerous recommendations aimed at restricting women's political activity.

One group of religious scholars, for example, stated that women should be barred from the position of head of state. Another religious leader expressed the belief that women should have the right to vote, but the election of women to legislative bodies was against the spirit of Islam. He suggested instead creating a separate women's assembly, elected entirely by women, to handle all issues related to women and the general welfare of the country, but serving only a consultative role in relation to the members of the national assembly. The Board of *Ta'limaat-i Islamia*, whose task was to advise the Constituent Assembly on principles of Islam, echoed many of these sentiments in its report to the BPC, in which it argued that the free mixing of men and women was the greatest cause of social disorder. Although it preferred that women be barred from legislative participation, it conceded that modern times might require some women in politics. In that case, women should become assembly members only if they were over the age of fifty and observed purdah, physical segregation or covering with a veil or burqa, during the performance of their legislative duties. The report stated categorically, however, that women should not be allowed to become the head of state under any circumstances. The BPC ignored these various suggestions and instead recommended in 1952 that every citizen over the age of twenty-one have the right to vote and run for political office, with no special seats for women (Afzal 1999).

The APWA responded to these proposals by demanding that 10 percent of all seats be reserved for women in national and provincial assemblies for a period of at least ten years. In 1953, the two female members of the Constituent Assembly presented this request to the Franchise Committee, which reduced the recommendation to 3 percent. One year later, the 10 percent reservation reappeared in the draft Charter of Women's Rights, which included demands for equal status and opportunity, equal pay for equal work, and guarantee of rights for women under Muslim law. Critics argued that many of these rights had not even been granted in the West, while supporters pointed out that women constituted 50 percent of the voting population and thus could not be ignored (Haroon 1995; Mumtaz and Shaheed 1987). The Constituent Assembly eventually approved the charter, but again reduced the proportion of reserved seats to 3 percent. After numerous delays, it then officially adopted the report of the BPC, which in the end reserved two seats for women in the 52-member House of Units and 14 seats for women in the 314-member House of People. The two seats in the upper house would be designated by the provincial legislature in East Pakistan and the electoral college in West Pakistan, respectively, while the fourteen seats in the lower house—seven seats in East Pakistan; three seats in Punjab; one seat in Sind and Khairpur;

one seat in the NWFP, the Frontier States, and the Tribal Areas; one seat in Baluchistan, the Baluchistan States Union, and Bahawalpur; and one seat in Karachi—would be chosen by female voters on the basis of territorial constituencies drawn by the National Assembly (Afzal 1999, 24–25). In line with women's demands, the provisions would last ten years, in the hope that reserved seats would enable women to gain the necessary experience to contest general seats in the future (Shaheed, Zia, and Warraich 1998).

However, before the final version of the constitution materialized, the governor general dissolved the assembly and ordered new elections in 1955. Despite the efforts of female politicians, no seats were reserved for women and no parties gave any tickets to female candidates (Afzal 1999). All the same, the new all-male Constituent Assembly only slightly modified the existing provisions for women's representation by setting aside ten seats for women in the 310-member National Assembly, the new unicameral institution that replaced the earlier bicameral arrangement. Divided equally between East and West Pakistan, these seats would be elected by female voters on the basis of territorial constituencies for a period of ten years. The result was that women gained a double right to vote, for the general seats and the seats reserved for women. Although this Constitution came into force in 1956, the Constituent Assembly assumed the role of interim National Assembly for nearly two years, as ongoing conflicts over the details of voting—combined with other political disagreements—repeatedly delayed the holding of new elections.

In response to these disputes, President Iskander Mirza abrogated the constitution and imposed martial law in October 1958. General Muhammad Ayub Khan, commander-in-chief of the army, was appointed chief martial law administrator and replaced Mirza as president a short while later. Ayub Khan argued that parliamentary democracy was unlikely to work in Pakistan, because low literacy rates prevented most people from being sufficiently informed to cast a meaningful vote (Sayeed 1963–1964). To resolve this problem, he devised a five-tiered system in which 80,000 locally-elected Basic Democrats would comprise an electoral college that would vote for all higher tiers of government, including the presidency. This system did not reserve seats for women, but following a vote of confidence from the newly elected Basic Democrats in 1960, Ayub Khan appointed an eleven-member Constitution Commission, which recommended that seats be reserved for women and that women also have the right to contest the general seats. The Constitution of 1962 thus reserved six seats for women in the

156-member National Assembly and five seats for women in each of the two 155-member Provincial Assemblies in East and West Pakistan. These provisions decreased the number of seats reserved for women in both the national and provincial assemblies and discontinued the system of female suffrage on the basis of territorial constituencies, delegating this responsibility to the male members of the national and provincial assemblies (Shaheed, Zia, and Warraich 1998; Zafar 1996).

Nonetheless, the issue of reserved seats for women remained alive and resurfaced again in 1964 during deliberations in the National Assembly over the Electoral College Bill and the National and Provincial Assemblies (Elections) Bill. Roquayya Anwar, a female member from East Pakistan, proposed during the early stages of debate that half of all seats in the electoral college—composed of the 80,000 Basic Democrats—be reserved for women to reflect their share of the population. When this idea found little support, she presented two amendments to the Electoral College Bill: one to reserve 10,000 seats for women as Basic Democrats and the other to provide for separate polling stations and registration offices for women in every electoral unit. With little input from the other female members, the National Assembly approved a plan to establish separate polling places for women, but it flatly rejected the proposal for reserved seats. Despite this setback, Anwar continued to lobby for an increase in the number of seats reserved for women. During debates over the National and Provincial Assemblies (Elections) Bill, she introduced another amendment to guarantee that at least 25 percent of all seats be reserved for women.[3] Supporters argued that reserved seats provided the only means to protect women's rights because men deliberately excluded women from all spheres of public life. Opponents, including some women, maintained that women already enjoyed basic rights and that reserved seats only prevented them from gaining increased political understanding and awareness. While some went so far as to suggest that reserved seats be abolished, the Assembly simply rejected the proposed amendment and retained the status quo (Afzal 1999; Mumtaz 1998).

The issue of women's political participation returned to public debate the following year, when opposition parties nominated Mohtarma Fatima Jinnah, the sister of Mohammad Ali Jinnah, to run against General Ayub Khan in the 1965 presidential elections. Her campaign was supported by the Combined Opposition Parties, which included a number of religious–political leaders who had argued earlier against giving women the right to vote and, indeed, had been especially adamant that a woman could never become the head of an Islamic state (Mujahid 1965; Shahab 1993). Forced to justify their reversal, several explained that a woman could serve in this capacity in extraordinary circumstances, although normally only men could fill this function (Sayeed 1966). In response, Ayub Khan got another set of religious officials to issue a series of *fatwas* against appointing or electing a woman as the head of an Islamic state (Ali 2000; Mujahid 1965). In an unusual twist, the APWA then stood behind Ayub Khan and actively campaigned against Fatima Jinnah (Afzal 1999). Despite these vivid debates, Ayub Khan eventually won re-election with more than 60 percent of the vote, made possible—at least in part—by the structure of the Basic Democrat system (Sayeed 1966, 80).

As a result, the question of whether or not a woman could serve as the head of state quickly dissipated after the elections. However, the issue of reserved seats remained firmly on the agenda. In 1966, Begum Dolly Azad, a female member of the National Assembly, proposed to increase the number of seats reserved for women in the national and provincial assemblies. The government did not respond immediately, but in December 1967, the law minister announced that the number of seats reserved for women would increase from six to eight in the National Assembly and from five to eight in each Provincial Assembly, to accommodate an expansion in the number of seats in all assemblies to 218. These provisions, which formed part of the Constitution (Eighth Amendment) Bill, introduced a new method of election—provinces were now to be divided into four zones for the purpose of electing each female member of the National Assembly—and eliminated any time restriction for reservation. However, they sparked controversy because they came at the initiative of individual government ministers, rather than the governing Pakistan Muslim League. At the same time, these reforms triggered an entirely new debate on reservation for women in union and district councils. Women argued for greater representation in local government on the grounds that they formed 50 percent of the population, but several prominent men claimed that women were already represented in local politics—pointing to two women who had been elected—and that women themselves were responsible for any disparity between actual and desired numbers of elected women. Although reserved seats were not ultimately extended to local government, legislators approved the small increase in the number of reserved seats in the national and provincial assemblies, which simply constituted an attempt to retain a similar proportion of women as were present in the earlier assemblies (Mumtaz 1998).

Before these reforms were applied, however, a country-wide movement to remove Ayub Khan resulted in a return to martial law in 1969. General Agha Muhammad Yahya Khan, the commander-in-chief of the army, assumed power and, after conferring with various political forces, issued a Legal Framework Order (LFO) in March 1970 to replace the Constitution. The LFO increased the number of seats reserved for women in the National Assembly to thirteen, distributed among the provinces on the basis of the 1961 census: seven seats in East Pakistan (162 total), three seats in Punjab (82 total), one seat in Sind (27 total), one seat in Baluchistan (4 total), one seat in NWFP (18 total), and no seats in the Centrally Administered Tribal Area (7 total). It also reserved seats for women in the provincial assemblies: ten seats in East Pakistan (300 total), six seats in Punjab (180 total), two seats in Sind (60 total), one seat in Baluchistan (20 total), and two seats in NWFP (40 total) (Afzal 1999, 31). Similar to the early constitution, it specified that women would be elected to the reserved seats by members of the national and provincial assemblies. These elections were scheduled for the day before the first official session of the National Assembly, but a deadlock in political negotiations following the elections resulted in a military crackdown in East Pakistan. As such, the Election Commission simply authorized the returning officer to fill the reserved seats with the thirteen women who had filed nomination papers (Afzal 1999, 32). One year later, the country split, and West Pakistan took the name Pakistan and East Pakistan became Bangladesh.[4]

The members of the National Assembly elected from West Pakistan assumed responsibility for drafting the new constitution for Pakistan. The legislators nominated a 25-member Constitution Committee to prepare a report on recommended institutional reforms for debate in the Assembly at the beginning of 1973. The committee had received authorization from the National Assembly to allocate ten seats for women—at 5%, this reflected a slight improvement over earlier provisions—for a period of ten years, but more than twenty women's organizations lobbied for an increase in the number of seats reserved for women, as well as for direct elections to these seats. In its final report, the committee suggested the creation of a bicameral legislature, with no seats reserved for women in the Senate and ten seats reserved for women in the 200-member National Assembly, in addition to ten seats reserved for women in the various provincial assemblies. A large number of male assembly members expressed their support for these measures, although one argued that the number of women's seats should be increased, a second questioned whether women should be allowed to contest the general seats when seats were reserved for women, and two claimed that women should not participate in politics at all on religious grounds (Mumtaz 1998). Several female members responded by noting that the Senate would play a central role in policy-making, since its approval would be required for every bill, and argued that without reserved seats parties would not nominate women to the Senate, thus excluding women's views from the broader legislative process. For this reason, they presented amendments proposing that one or two seats in each province be reserved for women in the Senate. Nonetheless, the National Assembly rejected these proposals and upheld the Committee's recommendations regarding the number and distribution of reserved seats.

Seeking another way to improve women's influence in policy-making, female legislator Begum Nasim Jehan subsequently introduced an amendment to replace indirect elections by male legislators with direct elections by female voters as a means of fostering accountability between elected and ordinary women. She reasoned that if seats were reserved for women at all, these seats should serve to represent women's views and interests in political debates. However, the prevailing method of election made this impossible, because whenever female legislators took positions on issues of concern to women, their male colleagues reminded them that they had been elected by men, and not by women. As such, indirect elections simply enabled male elites to increase their parties' share of assembly members, without any corresponding obligation to represent "women" as a group (Mumtaz 1998; Pakistan Commission on the Status of Women 1989).

Not surprisingly, these arguments provoked strong hostility among male assembly members, who claimed that limiting the electorate for these seats to female voters would create a gulf between men and women, as well as aggravate existing inequalities between women in the urban and rural areas. According to them, a system of female suffrage would leave rural women unrepresented, since women in the cities were more politically active, whereas the existing system would at least guarantee that peasant and laborer women entered the Assembly. In the end, no other legislators—women or men—spoke up in favor of the proposal, leading Jehan to withdraw the bill in protest.[5] Later, she became the most vocal opponent of a third amendment seeking to establish that only male Muslims could serve as head of state. Members eventually rejected this bill, but primarily on the grounds that it was not necessary, as the small number of women in the National Assembly suggested that a woman was unlikely to stand for the office of president any time soon (Afzal 1999; Mumtaz 1998). All the same, they limited reserved seats in the national and provincial assemblies to a decade out of the belief that ten years would be sufficient for women to gain a foothold in politics (Baqai 1976).

In spite of these struggles, the Constitution of 1973 represented a significant advance in the recognition of women's rights in Pakistan. Distinct from earlier constitutions, it made women and men equal before the law and outlawed any discrimination on the basis of sex. It also mandated that at least one woman be included on the Islamic Ideological Council, an advisory board charged with balancing the principles of Islam with the needs of the modern world (Afzal 1999). As a result of these changes, women began to organize increasingly over the next several years, building on their participation in the anti-Ayub agitation and the establishment of women's wings inside the political parties (Mumtaz 1998). The country then signed the Mexico Declaration at the UN's World Conference on Women in 1975, which led the government to set up a thirteen-member Women's Rights Committee in 1976 to determine the status of women in Pakistan to make recommendations for improvement (Haroon 1995; Zafar 1991). The next year, elections brought ten women into the National Assembly on the reserved seats and, for the first time, one woman on a general seat. This woman never took office, however, because her coalition, the opposition Pakistan National Alliance, boycotted the National Assembly on charges that the government had rigged the voting.

These disputes culminated in yet another period of martial law, this time under the leadership of General Zia-ul-Haq, who brought an abrupt end to women's advances in Pakistan by allying with fundamentalist religious forces to "Islamize" the legal code, primarily through "Islamic" laws focused on reducing women's rights and freedoms. After repeatedly cancelling new elections, Zia eventually introduced a new legislative form in 1980 known as the *Majlis-e-Shoora*, or Council of Advisors, which he presented as a new form of "Islamic democracy," although its members were all appointed by Zia himself and exercised no effective legislative powers. Despite the anti-woman image of his government, he hand-picked twenty women as members of the 284-member *Majlis*, a slight improvement on the proportion of women in earlier legislative assemblies (Khan 1985; Shaheed, Zia, and Warraich 1998).

In 1983, Zia set up the Ansari Commission to submit proposals regarding a future system of government. The commission recommended that the office of head of state be closed for women and all female candidates to the National Assembly be over the age of fifty and provide the written permission of their husbands in order to contest assembly seats. Although it claimed that these regulations derived from Islam, many speculated that they were in fact directed at Benazir Bhutto, a prominent figure in the opposition who was female, thirty years old, and unmarried (Korson and Maskiell 1985). All the same, the commission did advocate reserving at least 5 percent of the assembly seats for women on the basis of separate electorates for women and men. The *Majlis* took up these issues several months later, with at least one female member arguing for an increase in the number of seats reserved for women and several men presenting motions to exclude women from the office of head of state (Mumtaz 1998).

Zia responded to these recommendations in Martial Law Ordinance 1984, which set out the terms of the 1985 elections, by doubling the number of seats reserved for women in the National Assembly and maintaining the number of seats reserved for women in the provincial assemblies by the Constitution. The ordinance thus set aside twenty seats for women in the 200-member National Assembly, but did not reserve any seats for women in the Senate.[6] In addition, it banned political parties and automatically disqualified all current party leaders from standing for election. Thirteen women ran for general seats, although only one won election, while sixty-four ran for the twenty reserved seats chosen indirectly by the members of the National Assembly (Pakistan Commission on the Status of Women 1989, 119). Shortly thereafter, the Assembly began deliberations over the Eighth Constitutional Amendment Bill, which sought to indemnify the ordinances and laws promulgated by the military regime to ensure that they could not be challenged in the future in any court of law (Zia 1991). Although not its primary focus, the bill included a proposal that would extend provisions for reserved seats for one more set of elections. Female members were divided on this issue: the woman who won the general seat felt that reserved seats implied that women were not capable of winning election on their own, while women in the reserved seats argued that removing these would lead to a dramatic decline in the number of elected women. To empower non-elected women, the Women's Action Forum lobbied for a double vote that would allow women to cast votes for general and reserved seats. Despite these various suggestions, the National Assembly decided simply to retain the current provision for reserved seats for one more election cycle (Haroon 1995; Mumtaz 1998).

The next several years witnessed contradictory tendencies regarding women's status. On the one hand, the Frontier Assembly voted to put all women into purdah, or seclusion. On the other hand, the state-sponsored Commission on the Status of Women (CSW) recommended that at least 20 percent of seats in national and provincial assemblies be reserved for women,[7] while Benazir Bhutto returned from self-imposed exile to demand new democratic elections. When Zia died in a plane crash in August 1988, new elections were organized that restored democratic rule and brought Bhutto to power as the first female prime minister of Pakistan. Four women were elected on general seats, including Benazir Bhutto and her mother Nusrat Bhutto, in addition to the twenty women selected to the reserved seats, elevating women's representation in Pakistan for the first time to more than 10 percent (Mumtaz 1998). With these elections, the policy of reserving seats for women formally lapsed after having been applied continuously by a range of different regimes since 1935.

The Origins of Reserved Seats

The election of Benazir Bhutto, combined with the expiration of reserved seats provisions, triggered a new series of debates on women's political participation in Pakistan. Despite the return to democracy, several groups raised the question of whether or not a woman could serve as the head of government of a Muslim state. Although political opponents sought unsuccessfully to place the issue at the center of the election campaign in order to undermine the Pakistan People's Party (PPP), it gained new life once Bhutto assumed power and political religious groups revived the matter as a means to destabilize her government.[8] In February 1989, more than five hundred *Ulama*, men with religious education responsible for interpreting the true content of Islam, came together from all over Pakistan for the United Ulama Convention, which passed a resolution calling on citizens to reject Bhutto's premiership as "anti-Islamic." In making their case, they made reference to a *Hadith*, or a saying of the Prophet, proclaiming that "those who entrust their affairs to a woman will never know prosperity."[9] They interpreted this as an injunction against female leadership on the grounds that it would culminate in the destruction of the state.[10]

Interestingly, some of the most vociferous advocates of this stance were the very same people who had supported Fatima Jinnah against Ayub Kahn in the 1962 presidential elections (Shahab 1993). Only

Shias took a different view, arguing that Islam did not prohibit women from ruling states, and for that reason they advised the *Ulama* not to undertake any decisions that might upset the existing political equilibrium (Zakaria 1990). Following the convention's verdict, the Supreme Shariah Council took up the issue and decided by a majority of four against two, with one abstention, that Bhutto could continue as prime minister of Pakistan, because the case against her relied on a weak *Hadith* whose reporters included a man who had been flogged for committing a crime against Islam (Shahab 1993).[11] The council noted, further, that the prime minister was not the head of state but the head of a political party and, as such, the same restrictions did not apply. These arguments were enough to convince most *Ulama* to cease their campaign against Bhutto, at least on religious grounds (Weiss 1990).

Following these debates, attention turned again to the question of reserved seats. In line with her campaign promises to empower women, Bhutto elevated the Women's Division to a Ministry of Women's Development and, as a first order of business, asked it to develop an affirmative action proposal to ensure that women occupied at least 5 percent to 10 percent of all decision-making positions within each ministry (Weiss 1994). Concerned that women would not be able to win election in other political bodies, women's organizations pressed her to make a similar commitment to reinstate and expand the number of seats reserved for women to 20 percent in the national and provincial assemblies. They also suggested that 10 percent of the seats in the Senate be set aside for women and that all reserved seats be determined on the basis of separate female constituencies (Pakistan Commission on the Status of Women 1989; Zafar 1996). The government responded by sending Rehana Sarwar, the Federal Minister for Women's Affairs, to confer with the various parties to gain a consensus on extending the provisions for reserved seats, as a two-thirds majority would be required to enact a constitutional amendment. A bill was then introduced in the upper house in November 1989, but before the vote could take place, the Bhutto government was dismissed and new elections were scheduled for October 1990 (Shaheed, Zia, and Warraich 1998). In the absence of reserved seats, only thirteen women stood as candidates and only two women, Benazir Bhutto and Nusrat Bhutto, won election to the 217-member National Assembly (Zafar 1996, 57).

Nawaz Sharif replaced Bhutto as prime minister and immediately reversed all progress on women's rights by dissolving the Marriage Act and Family Protection Bill and passing the Shariah Law Bill, which gave religious courts power to overrule the existing laws to reduce any protections previously granted to women (Goodwin 1994). In this environment, the new government made no attempts to promote women in politics, despite efforts by women's groups to secure a new bill on reserved seats (Shaheed, Zia, and Warraich 1998). Three years later, Sharif himself was dismissed as prime minister and new elections were organized for October 1993. Seeking to bolster women's rights, women's groups met with the leaders of the various parties to pressure them to include a special chapter on women's issues, including reserved seats, in their election manifestos (Ali 2000). As a result, both major parties—the Pakistan Muslim League N (PML-N), Nawaz's party, and the PPP, Bhutto's party—pledged to revive the constitutional provision by reserving seats for women in the national and provincial assemblies. Nonetheless, the parties nominated only sixteen women as candidates and only four women, including the two Bhuttos, were elected (Zafar 1996, 58).

Bhutto was returned to power as prime minister, and soon after the elections, the Women's Action Forum and the state CSW initiated discussions with the new government and opposition parties to devise more specific plans for restoring reserved seats (Zafar 1996). As a consequence, one of the first bills drafted by the PPP government proposed to amend the constitution to reserve twenty-five seats for women in the National Assembly, nine seats for women in the Senate, and 5 percent of all seats in the various provincial assemblies, with no time restrictions. The PML-N responded with two proposals of its own. The first pledged to increase the number of seats reserved for women in the National Assembly to forty, to be filled directly by female voters or through a system of proportional representation based on the number of votes received by each party, while the second required all parties apply a 10 percent quota for female candidates (*Report of the Commission of Inquiry for Women* 1997). However, in the course of the parliamentary session, the PML-N reversed itself and announced that it would not support a separate constitutional amendment on the issue of reserved seats for women, but would instead seek to include it as part of a broader package of constitutional reform. Some suspected that this move was an effort to undermine the bill due to disagreements within the party on the method for selecting women to these seats, a strategy that eventually led to the defeat of both bills (Gulrez and Warraich 1998; Shaheed, Zia, and Warraich 1998).

Women's groups kept the issue alive, even though some members were skeptical that reserved seats would translate into improvements in women's status, because most agreed that women were unlikely to gain access to legislatures without positive action. They pointed to reserved seats policies in countries like Bangladesh, India, Nepal, and Tanzania, and noted that even developed countries were increasingly adopting measures to promote women's access to political decision-making (Mumtaz 1998). The government responded by setting up a National Consultative Committee to confer with members of the National Assembly on the question of reserved seats. By July 1995, the committee had obtained 148 signatures in favor of reform. In addition, a workshop organized by women's organizations succeeded in getting representatives of the three largest parties in Pakistan—the PPP, the PML-N, and the Awami National Party (ANP)—to agree to sign a joint declaration calling for restoration of reserved seats and extension of these provisions to the Senate. In light of this consensus, the government introduced a bill to reinstate reserved seats. Despite its apparent support across the parties, the measure was soundly defeated, supposedly because concerns that reserved seats might increase the strength of political rivals led the PML-N to change its mind and vote against the amendment (*Report of the Commission of Inquiry for Women* 1997; Sarwar 1997).

When the government ratified the UN's Convention on the Elimination of All Forms of Discrimination Against Women the following year, the CSW took a slightly different approach and drew on international norms to formulate new demands for reserved seats. Noting that the UN recommended at least one-third women at all tiers of representation, it proposed that all political bodies be expanded to incorporate a larger proportion of women, elected directly by female voters (*Report of the Commission of Inquiry for Women* 1997). The parties, however, made no additional commitments until they produced their manifestos for the 1997 elections. The PPP and the PML-N pledged to restore reserved seats, but gave no detailed proposals regarding the number of seats or means of elections, while the right-wing *Jamiat-e-Islami* called on women to take part in public life, but outlined no specific plans for increasing women's representation. The newly formed Pakistan *Tehreek-I-Insaaf* (PTI), in contrast, promised to amend the electoral law to ensure that only parties which allocated at least 10 percent of their general seats tickets to women would be allowed to compete in elections (Gulrez and Warraich 1998, 73–74). Despite their rhetoric, the parties nominated only thirty-four female candidates, claiming either that women did not volunteer to run or that they could not risk awarding tickets to women due to increased chances of defeat, and only six women were elected (Gulrez and Warraich 1998, 71–72). In an ominous new development, political and religious leaders in several provinces took actions to restrict women's right to vote, either by mutually agreeing not to let their female supporters come out and vote or by issuing special announcements over mosque loudspeakers that voting by women was un-Islamic, with the result that in some areas not a single female vote was cast (*Report of the Commission of Inquiry for Women* 1997).

In this environment, the PML-N won a majority of seats in the National Assembly and Sharif was returned to power as prime minister. As the new parliamentary session got underway, women's groups—including the Aurat Foundation, the Women's Action Forum, the Human Rights Commission of Pakistan, Bedari, the Sustainable Development Policy Institute, and the Progressive Women's Association—organized demonstrations calling on members to reinstate reserved seats for women in the national and provincial assemblies and to institute reserved seats for women in the Senate. Although they agreed with the CSW on the need for one-third reservation, they argued that the National Assembly should at least begin by doubling the number of seats previously reserved for women (Baruah 1997; Sarwar 1997). In power with a massive majority, the prime minister pursued policy changes that reversed many of the reforms enacted during the martial law period, including the Eighth Amendment that had increased the power of the president over the parliament. When the opposition sought to introduce a constitutional amendment to restore women's seats, the ruling party rejected the initiative, claiming that it would put forward a broader constitutional reform package that would include reserved seats for women. The PPP complained that this move was simply an act of retribution, noting that several PML-N legislators had made frivolous objections to the proposal by comparing reserved seats for women with reserved seats for children (Sarwar 1997; Siddiqui 1997). The federal minister for law and justice, Khalid Anwar, maintained that reserved seats were not controversial and therefore the matter would be easily sorted out in an upcoming constitutional amendment package. By mid-1998, however, no package had materialized and women continued to occupy less than 3 percent of all political bodies in Pakistan (Gulrez and Warraich 1998).

The Adoption of Reserved Seats

In October 1999, General Pervez Musharraf, then chief of army staff, deposed Sharif in a bloodless coup and took over as chief executive and then as president of Pakistan. The Supreme Court validated his rule but gave his government three years to restore democracy. To meet these goals, he appointed a National Reconstruction Bureau (NRB) to formulate plans for new political arrangements, including a new constitution. As its first order of business, the NRB developed a plan to devolve administrative power through a new three-tier structure of local government. Although Article 32 of the existing constitution provided for elections to local government, as well as the special representation of women, peasants, and workers on local councils, only six elections had ever been organized and no seats had ever been reserved for women.[12] Announced in August 2000, the devolution plan set aside one-third of all seats for women—as well as one-fifth of all seats for workers and peasants—at the union, municipality, and district levels, with reserved seats filled through direct elections at the union council level and through indirect elections at the municipality and district levels. Women's groups viewed the provision as a positive change, but religious groups objected to these reforms on religious and cultural grounds, arguing that women should stay within the four walls of the home. These measures fulfilled the National Plan of Action, developed within the framework of the Gender Programme for Pakistan coordinated by the UNDP, which prescribed reserving 33 percent of all seats for women in local and national elective bodies through direct and joint elections (Bari 2001; Reyes 2002).

As these elections got underway, the government organized a referendum to determine whether Musharraf should remain in power for another five years, regardless of the national election results in late 2002. After this referendum was approved, the cabinet presented an election package in January 2002 that reserved 60 seats for women in the 342-member National Assembly, 17 seats in the 100-member Senate, and 22 percent of all seats in the various provincial assemblies. Some citizens protested that women should be subject to election on the same terms as men (*Radio Nederlands Wereldomroep*, 18 January 2002), but the PPP and PML-N opposed the measures on the grounds that reserved seats would simply enable the army to send its own supporters to parliament (*News India-Times*, 8 March 2002). While some individual women worried that reservations would leave women in a weak position, most women's groups—including the

CSW, women's movement organizations, and women inside the four major parties—mobilized to increase the provisions in both houses of parliament from 17 percent to 30 percent (National Commission on the Status of Women 2002; *DAWN: Internet Edition*, 19 February 2002). Although the government responded that the new election package already constituted a significant advance over earlier policies, women's groups pointed out that it overlooked repeated calls for 30 percent reservations, as reflected in the *Report of the Commission of Inquiry for Women* (1997), the National Plan for Action in 1998, and the national consultation conducted by the Ministry of Women and Development in 2001. Further, the government policy ignored women's demands for direct elections. For them, assigning reserved seats according to the proportion of the vote received by each party transformed women into second-class members of political assemblies, reinforced their dependence on the male leadership of the party, and thus undermined their ability to pursue policy reforms favorable to women (Reyes 2002; Tinker 2004).

In light of these reactions, Musharraf issued a series of constitutional amendments several months later to clarify the procedures for the general elections in order to ensure a relatively smooth return to democracy. These amendments, collectively known as the Legal Framework Order (LFO), were extremely controversial in that they bypassed parliament to strengthen the power of the presidency, formalize the role of the army in governance, and diminish the authority of elected representatives (Human Rights Watch 2003). In addition, they imposed a ban on public rallies, limited the activities of parties, and curbed the rights of individuals to stand for public office by restricting candidacy in the National Assembly and the Senate to those who had attained a university degree, at the same time disqualifying those who had been convicted of a crime, defaulted on loans and utility bills, or absconded from court proceedings. These regulations aimed to mute outward opposition to the regime and drastically reduced the pool of potential candidates, conveniently eliminating any competition from former prime ministers Bhutto and Sharif and other politicians convicted under the National Accountability Ordinance following the military coup (Human Rights Watch 2002; Human Rights Watch 2003; Talbot 2003). The LFO, however, also granted seats to technocrats in the lower house of parliament and abolished the system of separate electorates for religious minorities, a system that minority leaders had long opposed on the grounds that it effectively marginalized these groups from mainstream politics. The amendments further outlined the procedures for filling seats reserved for women, technocrats, and minorities and specified that parties would have to win at least 5 percent of the seats in the national and provincial assemblies in order to nominate representatives (Reyes 2002; Rizvi 2002).

The Implementation of Reserved Seats

The current policy on reserved seats for women extended an earlier tradition of setting aside a limited number of seats in parliament for women, but compared with these provisions, it increased the proportion of seats allocated to women, expanded the scope of this practice to other political bodies, and accompanied a dramatic jump in the number of women elected to nonreserved seats. The proportion of seats reserved for women in 1954, 1956, 1962, 1967, 1970, and 1973—between 3 percent and 4 percent—was no higher than in the Government of India Act 1935. While Zia doubled this proportion to 9 percent in 1984, Musharraf doubled it again to 17 percent in 2002. Similarly, earlier measures applied to the national and provincial assemblies, while the new reform addressed these but also included Senate and local elections, enabling women to contest and win elections at all levels of government for the very first time. Most significantly, however, previous policies resulted in the election of women almost exclusively to the reserved seats, even though women were eligible to contest the general seats, because few women were willing to step forward as candidates and few parties were willing to nominate them (Afzal 1999) (see tables 4.1 and 4.2). Those women

Table 4.1. Women's Legislative Representation in Pakistan

National Assembly		Senate	
Year	Women (%)	Year	Women (%)
1973	4.1	1973	2.2
1977	4.6	1975	2.2
1985	8.9	1977	4.8
1988	10.1	1985	0.0
1990	0.9	1991	1.1
1993	1.8	1994	1.1
1997	2.3	1997	1.1
2002	21.3	2003	18.0
2008	22.5	2006	17.0

Sources: Inter-Parliamentary Union (1995, 199); Inter-Parliamentary Union (1998); Inter-Parliamentary Union (2008a).

Table 4.2. Women's Election to Reserved and General Seats in Pakistan, 1962–2008

Year	Reserved Seats	General Seats	Total Number	Total (%)
1962	6	0	6	3.8
1965	6	0	6	3.8
1970	13	0	13	4.2
1973	6[a]	0	6	4.1
1977	10	1[b]	10	4.6
1985	20	1	21	8.9
1988	20	4	24	10.1
1990	0	2	2	0.9
1993	0	4	4	1.8
1997	0	5	5	2.3
2002	60	13	73	21.3
2008	60	16	76	22.5

Sources: Inter-Parliamentary Union (1995, 199); Inter-Parliamentary Union (2008a); Pakistan Commission on the Status of Women (1989, 116); Shaheed, Zia, and Warraich (1998, 22).

[a]Thirteen seats were reserved for women in the National Assembly, but due to the break up of Pakistan, the seven seats reserved in East Pakistan were eliminated when the province declared independence and became Bangladesh.
[b]The first woman elected to a general seat did not enter the National Assembly because her party boycotted the Assembly following the elections.

who did attain office typically served as surrogates for their fathers, husbands, or sons, whose illness, death, exile, or imprisonment prevented them from continuing their own political careers (Shaheed 1991). As a result, the lapse of women's seats after the 1988 elections did not result in higher numbers of women being elected to the general seats, even though the Aurat Foundation organized a campaign before elections in 1993 to call attention to the need for more women in politics (Wilder 1995). Following local and national elections in 2002, more women were elected to reserved and nonreserved seats from more diverse backgrounds than ever before.

Local elections were implemented in five phases between December 2000 and August 2002 for union, municipality, and district councils, as well as for the positions of mayor and vice-mayor. Because of the large number of seats reserved for women, workers, and peasants, more than half of all candidates—or members of their families—had never contested elections before (Bari 2001, xiii; Reyes 2002). In the first round, 2,621 women competed for 1,867 reserved seats, although in 20 percent of districts social and religious leaders prevented women from becoming candidates and in 40 percent of districts female candidates were elected unopposed (Rizvi 2001). All women elected in this round won reserved seats—either seats reserved for women or seats reserved for workers and peasants—and tended to be under the age of forty-five, illiterate, landless, housewives, and with little or no prior political experience (Bari 2001; Reyes 2002). Recognizing a need for training, government agencies and various national and international NGOs began to hold workshops for newly elected female councilors. The mainstream parties criticized women's groups for supporting the reserved seats—and by extension, the military regime—but the latter responded that they felt compelled to participate so that no government in the future could say that women were not willing to contest elections (Bokhari 2001).

More serious obstacles came in the form of social and religious groups, which engaged in various acts of intimidation to dissuade women from coming forward as candidates. In some districts, election officers rejected women's nomination papers and advised them to concentrate on their domestic duties instead of running for political office (Bari 2001). In other districts, especially NWFP, religious leaders sought to prevent women from contesting the reserved seats by threatening their families with social boycotts, which meant losing access to the water supply and the grazing grounds for cattle; persuading judges to invalidate their candidacies in instances where women did stand for election; and passing local laws permitting the houses of female voters—not even just candidates—to be demolished (Human Rights Watch 2002; Human Rights Watch 2004; McCarthy 2001). In extreme cases, women received death threats, were subject to rumors that they had been unfaithful to their husbands, were beaten and paraded naked through the streets of their villages, and even killed by their husbands after refusing to withdraw (Human Rights Watch 2004). Although the Aurat Foundation estimated that between 85 percent and 90 percent of women's seats were contested during the first two phases of the elections, activities in NWFP meant that more than six hundred reserved seats were not filled in this region (Bokhari 2001; Reyes 2002, 2).

Elections to the National and Provincial Assemblies followed in October 2002.[13] Although some observers estimated that women were not able to exercise their right to vote in almost 30 percent of the country (Ahmed 2002), more women ran for political office than ever before, with 281 women contesting the sixty seats reserved for women in the National Assembly and 878 women running for the 188 seats reserved for women in all assemblies (*Pakistan Review*, 2001). In addition, thirteen women won unreserved seats in the National Assemblies, while eleven women won unreserved seats in the provincial assemblies. These patterns varied across provinces, however, with women winning nine general seats in Punjab, three general seats in Sindh, one general seat in Balochistan, and no general seats in NWFP in elections to the National Assembly (Rizvi 2002). Although the new electoral rules provided for the presence of sixty women in the new assembly, the provisions of the LFO shaped its composition in a number of unanticipated ways that ultimately benefited women.

Most notably, the requirement that candidates be university graduates caused some male politicians to step down in favor of their better-educated sisters and wives, although it also disqualified some lesser-educated women who had been working inside the parties and seeking nominations for years (Talbot 2003). The ban on candidates who had engaged in criminal activities had a similar effect, fostering the election of women related to political leaders who could no longer run themselves (Rizvi 2002). Pointing to these patterns, a male parliamentarian called on reserved seats to be abolished, because women had no role in parliament and, he remained convinced, would never win election if seats were not reserved for them (Shehzad 2003). Over time, some female MPs began making related criticisms, pointing out that many women in the National Assembly did not have the political experience to press for changes in women's status (*The Muslim News*, 21 January 2004). Despite the dominating presence of *Muttahida Majlis-e-Amal*, an alliance of six Islamist parties, several women elected to the reserved seats nonetheless campaigned relentlessly for changes in women's status, including legislation to ban the custom of trading women in exchange for crimes committed by family members and to classify as a crime the act of throwing acid at someone's face (Human Rights Watch 2003; Rizvi 2002).

Using these gains to lobby for a "critical mass" of female legislators, the CSW continued to organize workshops to devise ways of improving women's political involvement as voters and as policymakers to achieve and fully realize the goal of one-third female representation (National Commission on the Status of Women 2002). Activists stepped up these demands in the ten-year evaluation of the country's implementation of the UN's Beijing Platform for Action, which called for the reserved seats to be filled on the basis of direct elections by joint electorates of women and men (Shaheed and Zaidi 2005). Female representatives, in turn, began to mobilize for rises in the number of reserved seats. In early 2005, the Women Councilors' Network called for an increase from 33 percent to 50 percent in the proportion of seats reserved for women in local elections (*The Nation*, 15 January 2005).

In mid-2006, parliamentarian Kashmala Tariq suggested that lawmakers consider amending the Political Parties Act and People's Representation Act to expand the percentage of reserved seats to 30 percent. This proposal was embraced by the Speaker of the National Assembly, Chaudry Amir Hussain, following a workshop organized by the Commonwealth Parliamentary Association and the Gender Section of the Commonwealth Secretariat, in collaboration with the Pakistan Parliament (*Balochistan Times*, 19 July 2006; *Business Recorder*, 21 July 2006). By November, a watchdog network was launched to try to persuade parties to allocate quotas to women (*Daily Times*, 22 November 2006), although skeptics remained who claimed that 76 percent of women in parliament and 82 percent of local government were relatives of other politicians (*Daily Times*, 9 November 2006). In October 2007, Bhutto returned from exile, and one month later, it was announced that new elections would be held in January 2008. After Bhutto's assassination in December 2007, elections were postponed until mid-February 2008. Despite widespread intimidation of female voters, as well as the closing of several women-only polling stations (*International Herald Tribune*, 19 February 2008), female candidates filled all sixty reserved seats for women and won sixteen general seats, increasing the proportion of women in parliament to 23 percent (Inter-Parliamentary Union 2008a). In addition, Fahmida Mirza was elected as the speaker of the National Assembly, becoming the first woman ever to hold this position in a Muslim country.

Reserved Seats and Women's Political Representation in Pakistan

Efforts to institute reserved seats in Pakistan thus have survived several cycles of military intervention and democratic restoration, with debates over these measures continuing through the only period characterized by lack of reserved seats. Existing research on women and politics rarely addresses the case of Pakistan, but would anticipate relatively low levels of representation given the country's unstable democratic history, low social and economic development, and strong identity as an Islamic republic. The narrative of events presented in this chapter, however, uncovers enduring attention to and acceptance of reserved seats for women, even in the face of religious challenges to women's political participation and growing restrictions in women's social and economic rights. A broader temporal lens, therefore, sheds crucial light on the impact of systemic reform: women's representation remained stable during the earlier period of reserved seats, dropped significantly during the years without reserved seats, and increased dramatically when reserved seats were restored and women were elected in large numbers to the reserved and nonreserved seats. The first period thus reveals the effect of systemic reform in the absence of practical and normative reform, the second period the absence of all types of reform, and the third period the dynamics of harmonizing reform, as systemic reform spills over and combines with practical and normative reform to produce substantial increases in the number of women elected to parliament (see table 4.3).

Table 4.3. Quota Reforms and Institutional Configurations in Pakistan

Systemic Institutions	Practical Institutions	Normative Institutions
Period 1 (1935–1988):		
Reserved seats for women FPTP electoral system	"Sex" as irrelevant criteria in direct elections Placement in unwinnable districts	Equality before the law Representation as partial politics of presence
Period 2 (1988–2002):		
No reserved seats for women FPTP electoral system	"Sex" as irrelevant criteria in direct elections Placement in unwinnable districts	Equality before the law Representation as politics of ideas
Period 3 (2002–present):		
Reserved seats for women FPTP electoral system	"Sex" as relevant and irrelevant criteria Placement in winnable and unwinnable districts	Equality before the law Representation as politics of presence

Seats have been reserved for women in Pakistan since the time when the country was still part of India and ruled by the British Empire. After independence, democratic and nondemocratic regimes established similar provisions in 1954, 1956, 1962, 1967, 1970, 1973, 1980, and 1984. These policies were solely responsible for women's representation in parliament until 1977, when a woman first won a general seat, and accounted for the election of the overwhelming majority of women in parliament through 1988. As such, systemic institutions largely sustained women's representation from the 1950s to the 1980s, at the same time that practical and normative institutions that did not view "sex" as a central criteria for candidate selection or recognize "women" as a category deserving equal representation largely prevented women from contesting and winning nonreserved seats. As the final reserved seats policy expired following elections in 1988, therefore, women's representation dropped from more than 10 percent to less than 1 percent, although all major parties pledged to restore and even extend the number of seats reserved for women. No democratic government succeeded in fulfilling this promise, however, and with rules, practices, and norms working against the selection of female candidates, the proportion of women in parliament remained below 3 percent.

Although democratic governments failed to restore reserved seats, these measures remained on the agenda and were eventually revived following a military coup in 1999. The new government did not simply introduce the same provisions as before, but instead doubled the proportion of seats reserved for women in the national and provincial assemblies and extended reservations to local and Senate elections for the very first time. Yet, in clarifying the procedures for parliamentary elections, a series of controversial constitutional amendments were issued that restricted candidacy to those who met particular qualifications. The first set of policies deliberately reformed systemic institutions by setting up separate elections for the reserved seats. However, the second set inadvertently shifted practical and normative institutions in ways that benefited women, because the new requirements disqualified many former and aspiring male politicians and thus forced elites to reconsider their pool of potential candidates.

The new election regulations took effect at the local level between December 2000 and August 2002 and came into force at the national and provincial levels in October 2002. At the local level, these policies inspired many women, workers, and peasants to run for office for the very first time, but also sparked various acts of intimidation carried out primarily by religious leaders against prospective female candidates and their families. Yet, despite these attempts to thwart systemic reform with normative arguments, nearly all local seats reserved for women were contested and filled by the end of 2002. Several months later, national elections guaranteed the election of at least sixty women to the National Assembly. However, the disqualification of many prominent political leaders, most of whom were men, inspired many to nominate female relatives who were better-educated or did not possess criminal records. In this way, attempts to reform the mechanisms of election spilled over into a certain degree of practical and normative reform, which acknowledged "sex" as a criteria for candidate selection and accepted women—perhaps begrudgingly— as a vehicle for political representation. As a result, more women were elected directly than ever before, bringing the combined proportion of women in the National Assembly to 22 percent in 2002 and 23 percent in 2008.

The Women's Reservation Bill in India

Campaigns for reserved seats in India cover a period of about fifteen years, with the first calls to establish quotas at the local level emerging in the late 1980s and the most recent discussions on quotas at the national level taking place in 2007. As in Pakistan, however, efforts to reserve seats for women in India appeared initially in the 1930s, when the country still formed part of the British Empire. Across these various periods of time, the actors involved in quota campaigns have included civil society actors like women's movement organizations and women in the political parties; state actors like state committees, local governments, women's policy agencies, parties, prime ministers, cabinet ministers, parliamentary representatives, parliamentary committees, and party leaders; and international and transnational actors like the British government, the UN, the Inter-Parliamentary Union (IPU), and international conference delegates. Engaged at different stages of these campaigns, these actors have supported or opposed reserved seats for reasons including principled stands, promotion of other political ends, electoral considerations, and empty gestures. Although a law reserving one-third of all seats for women in local government was approved relatively quickly, a bill that would extend similar reservations to state assemblies and the national parliament has not yet reached a vote, due outwardly to normative arguments insisting on sub-quotas for lower castes and religious minorities, but inwardly to the unstated practical concerns of male members of parliament (MPs), one-third of whom would lose their positions with passage of the bill.

Antecedents to the Women's Reservation Bill

Reserved seats for women have a long but disjointed history in India. They appeared first in 1935 as part of the Government of India Act, disappeared in 1950 as per the provisions of the new Constitution, and resurfaced again in 1988 as part of the government's National Perspective Plan on Women. As the various provincial legislatures gave women the right to vote during the 1920s, women's groups began to press for the right to stand for election and at this time first raised the possibility of reserving seats for women in various political bodies. This suggestion provoked a vivid debate between the nationalist movement and various women's organizations when the British government set up the Simon Commission in November 1927 to decide whether and when self-government should be established in India. Although all major political groupings agreed with the need to extend women's right to vote and increase the number of women in elected positions, the British committee members and one section of the women's movement supported special franchise qualifications and the reservation of seats for women, while the nationalist movement and another section of the women's movement strongly opposed any mechanisms that would not provide for universal suffrage and would recognize divisions among the population (Everett 1979). The former claimed that women would not be able to win election without the help of reserved seats, while the latter argued that women should stand for election on the same terms as men because legislators should rise above their personal identities to consider the country's best interests. For this reason, nationalists viewed reserved seats for all groups—including Anglo-Indians, Christians, Muslims, Sikhs, and "depressed classes"— as a strategy for creating divisions within the movement.

Protesting the fact that the Simon Commission was composed entirely of British members, the Congress Party and the Muslim League rejected its activities and eventually brought about its demise. The British responded by authorizing the local parties to draft a new constitution for India on which Hindus and Muslims could both agree. Coming together in an All-Parties Conference in January 1928, however, these parties could not overcome their differences, especially with regard to the rights of minorities. After meeting several more times, the Conference eventually appointed a committee to work out the details of the constitution. The resulting Nehru Report, issued in August 1928, reserved seats for Muslims but introduced a system of joint electorates in which Hindus and Muslims would vote for the Muslim seats. The report sparked a great deal of civil disobedience, as various groups supported reserved seats for women and minorities, supported reserved seats for women but not for minorities, and opposed reserved seats for both women and minorities. The British sought to suppress these protests, and thereby undermine the Congress Party, by retaining separate electorates and reserved seats for minorities and urging provincial governments to nominate women if no women were elected directly. In response, the women's group associated with the Congress Party drafted a memorandum in 1931 in which it reiterated its opposition to reserved seats for women and all other social groups (Jenkins 1999). The other faction of the women's movement, however, continued to maintain that women were unlikely to gain election without reserved seats and proposed that at least 5 percent of the seats in the first three legislatures be reserved for women on the basis of indirect election by the generally elected members of these legislatures (Everett 1979).

To find a resolution to these debates, the British prime minister appointed the Indian Franchise Committee to tour the country and form an opinion on the questions of suffrage and political representation. Subsequently known as the Lothian Committee, this group heard arguments for and against franchise qualifications and reserved seats for women. At the end of 1932, it recommended that women's right to vote be expanded and that 2.5 percent of the seats in all political bodies be set aside for women. To guarantee that these women were not drawn disproportionately from one community, the committee proposed electing women on the basis of communal electorates so that, for example, Muslims would elect Muslim women and Sikhs would elect Sikh women. This idea overlapped with the committee's broader recommendation that all minority groups be assigned reserved seats on the basis of separate electorates, an idea which sparked another round of civil disobedience among all communities, including those supposedly favored by these provisions (Everett 1979; Mahan 1999). Wary of political instability, especially stemming from the opposition of more conservative elements of Indian society, subsequent British government reports imposed greater restrictions on women's suffrage and right to political representation.

By 1934, however, the Joint Committee on Indian Constitutional Reform had revised some of these restrictions—perhaps under the influence of British advocates for the rights of Indian women (Jenkins 1999)—to reduce suffrage requirements and reinstate reserved seats. As a result, the Government of India Act of 1935 reserved six seats for women in the Council of State, nine seats for women in the Federal Assembly, and forty-one seats for women in the various provincial legislatures (Afzal 1999). The Act also reserved seats for fourteen other groups based on profession, race, religion, social backwardness, and other minority status, such that the 145 special seats actually outnumbered the 105 open seats based on territorial representation (Clokie 1936; Tinker and Walker 1956). Although earlier acts had set aside seats for Muslims, Sikhs, Christians, and "depressed classes," the dramatic increase in the number of reserved seats and recognized categories of representation led many nationalists to conclude that reservations and separate electorates were simply tactics to perpetuate British control by dividing the population into numerous special interests. For this reason, the Indian National Congress objected to special rights for any of these groups, and its women's section issued a statement denying special privileges for women for the sake of the common good. Some minority groups, for their part, protested the requirement to include some women within their allocation of reserved seats, concerned that this effectively diluted their own quota (Jenkins 1999).

Congress condemned the Government of India Act on a number of grounds, but decided to contest the first elections to be held under the terms of the act in 1937. Final details regarding the franchise and shape and size of electoral constituencies were delegated by the British government to the Delimitation Committee, which recommended that special constituencies composed of male and female voters be established for the women's seats to ensure that the women elected to these seats were more concerned with social welfare than with party politics. Women's groups criticized these separate constituencies in favor of reserved seats for women in large multimember constituencies, which they felt would enable them to learn to compete under the same conditions as men. However, as parties began to prepare for the elections, these women soon discovered that parties were largely unwilling to nominate women for the general seats and were in fact disinclined to nominate any more women than necessary for the reserved seats (Everett 1979; Jenkins 1999).

Concerned that women would not win any general seats, the nonpartisan All-India Women's Conference (AIWC) met with the leaders of the various parties to request that they nominate at least a few women to the general constituencies (Agnew 1979). As a result, fifty-six women won election across all the provincial assemblies: forty-one in the reserved seats, ten in the general seats, and five in the nomi-nated seats (Everett 1979, 138). Although most of these women were affiliated with the Congress Party, the system of minority reservations ensured that both Hindu and Muslim women were elected (Agnew 1979). Despite these relative successes, women's organizations came to play a reduced role in subsequent elections even as women's electoral turnout increased. Nonetheless, the issue of reservations remained on the agenda, and two years later the Women's Subcom-mittee within the National Planning Committee firmly rejected the option of quotas for women as a policy for women's empowerment (Lama-Rewal 2001).

In the following years, relations between Hindus and Muslims deteriorated and both groups began to press for independence from British rule. At the end of World War II, the triumph of the Labour Party in the first post-war elections led the new prime minister to announce that Britain would grant independence to India. As nego-tiations got underway, growing conflicts between the Congress Party and the Muslim League led British officials to abandon plans to transfer power to a single country and to sanction the creation of two countries, India and Pakistan, in August 1947. In the months before official independence, however, the Congress Party began organizing elections to a new Constituent Assembly that first met in December 1946. Although members of this assembly were chosen indirectly by members of the provincial legislatures, the leadership of the party— along with the AIWC—succeeded in convincing each province to send at least one female representative (Agnew 1979).

The first draft of the constitution contained provisions reserving seats for religious groups on the basis of joint electorates, as well as seats for members of various professions on the basis of appointment, but debate within the assembly following independence eventually persuaded the Muslims, Sikhs, and Indian Christians to drop their demands for special treatment (Rasul 2001; Tinker and Walker 1956). In contrast, the draft enshrined equality between women and men as a fundamental right and thus did not include any special provisions for women, on the grounds that these were simply unnecessary. Despite their desire to abolish all reservations, however, delegates ultimately decided to retain those provisions in place for Scheduled Castes (SCs) and Scheduled Tribes (STs), the two groups that had traditionally been the most marginalized members of Indian society, distributed according to their proportion of the population in the various states and elected on the basis of joint electorates. The resulting Constitution of 1950 also made reference to a third category—later known as the Other Backward Castes (OBCs)—who did not merit reserved seats but who had the right to other types of assistance from the state.

Proposals to reserve seats for women, while not included in the constitution, resurfaced in 1957 in the context of discussions regarding a new system of local government, when the committee in charge of making recommendations advised that all local councils include at least two women. The final version of the law passed in 1959 did not make any specific requirements regarding women, but did empower local leaders to nominate some to the council if no women were elected directly. During the next two decades, most local councils adopted this practice and co-opted one or two women if no women were elected, but policies varied across the states and often became a tool of patronage for local leaders.[14] This practice eventually became a crucial, and often the only, vehicle for women's participation in local government: among the 320 women in local councils in the state of Maharastra in 1978, for example, only six had been elected directly (d'Lima 1993, 22). By the 1980s, however, several states abandoned these policies in favor of seats reserved specifically for women. Karnataka introduced 25 percent reservation for women in local councils in 1983, Andhra Pradesh extended 9 to 25 percent reservation for women in various levels of local government in 1986, and Maharastra announced 30 percent reservation in local bodies in 1990 (Balasubrahmanyan 1998; Manikyamba 1989).

The Origins of the Women's Reservation Bill

Despite the existence of some policies at the local level, the faith—both among women's groups and within the Congress Party—that women would be elected to parliament without the need for special intervention meant that no initiatives were taken in this area in the years following independence. However, in the run-up to the UN's Year of the Woman in 1975, the government set up a Committee on the Status of Women to examine the social, economic, and political standing of women in India. Although the Committee did not initially include a question on reserved seats in its questionnaire as it toured the country and interviewed more than five hundred women in each state, the women's groups with whom it met repeatedly raised reserved seats as the only viable solution for improving women's access to political office at the local, state, and national levels (Keating 2002; Rai and Sharma 2000).

The committee included these arguments in its final report, but ultimately took the view that reserved seats were retrogressive measures that contradicted the principle of equality in the constitution. Some members went so far as to criticize the existing system of reservations for SCs and STs as a colonial strategy that institutionalized the backwardness of these groups (Jenkins 1999). Recording two notes of dissent, the report more specifically rejected reservations on three grounds: separate constituencies for women threatened to narrow the political outlook of female voters and representatives, women's interests were not distinct from men's interests, and women were not a minority group. The committee conceded, however, that reservations might be necessary at the local level to ensure the interests of rural and poor women (Raman 2002). For this reason, it recommended that women's councils, elected directly by local women, be formed in every village and given the responsibility of managing and administering women's and children's welfare and development programs as part of the broader system of local government. At the same time, it encouraged political parties to increase the proportion of women among their candidates, using party-based quotas if necessary (Swarup et al 1994).

These recommendations were passed on to the state governments, but most responded negatively and therefore took no concrete actions to facilitate women's access to political office. Several states, however, returned to the issue of women's representation during debates over local government reform during the 1980s (Sinha 2000). These initiatives were rarely preceded by a widespread mobilization of women (Jain 1996; Kishwar 1996b) and, interestingly, were adopted by governments across the political spectrum: the Janata Party government in Karnataka reserved 25 percent of seats for women in village and district councils in 1983; the Telugu Desam Party government in Andhra Pradesh reserved 9 percent of seats for women in the district councils in 1986; the Congress Party government of Maharastra reserved 30 percent of seats for women in urban corporations and district, block, and village councils in 1990; and the Communist Party government in Kerala reserved 30 percent of seats for women in district councils in 1991 (Lama-Rewal 2001).

In the midst of these innovations, Rajiv Gandhi became the new prime minister of India, following the assassination of his mother

Indira Gandhi in 1984, and identified women's status as a new priority issue. To this end, his government prepared a National Perspective Plan for Women in 1988, which drew on positive experiences in
Karnataka to propose 33 percent reservations for women at all levels
of local government. The report also recommended that political parties give 33 percent of their party lists to women, but dropped several items that had appeared in the first draft, including a proposal
to extend 33 percent reservations to all political assemblies, including the state legislatures and the national parliament. According to
Margaret Alva, then Minister for Women, the committee encountered
a great deal of opposition to the idea of mandating reservations at
all levels of government. In consultation with autonomous women's
groups and the women's wings of the various parties, the group therefore decided to pursue reservation at the local level first and then,
once women had gained experience in elected politics, to seek to
extend reservation to the national level (Nath 1996; Rai 1997).

Following these discussions, the government introduced a package
of reforms to create a more regulated structure of local government that
would not only devolve decision-making power to the local level but
would also provide guaranteed representation for SCs, STs, and women
(Manikyamba 1989). The 64th Amendment Bill, however, was defeated
in the upper house by the united opposition in 1989. Nonetheless, when
new elections were organized several months later, parties on both sides
of this debate incorporated a 30 percent quota for women in their party
manifestos, despite the lack of mass mobilization of women in favor of
reserved seats (Nanivadekar 2003b), even as they nominated less than
10 percent female candidates (Kishwar 1989, 6). The new National Front
government introduced a new and slightly revised version of the reservation bill in 1990, which had been modified to provide for one-third
reservation for women among the general seats and among the seats
reserved for SCs and STs (Mandal 2003; Sinha 2000). However, before
this bill could be addressed, the governing coalition collapsed and new
elections were held that returned Congress to power in 1991.

Shortly thereafter, the newly elected government introduced the
73rd and 74th Amendment Bills to provide for decentralization and
one-third reservations for women in rural and urban local government, respectively. Both bills passed relatively quickly and without
controversy through both houses of parliament, and after minor differences were reconciled, both amendments became law in December
1992. Many attributed the rapid approval of these bills to the fact
that the politicians who approved these radical amendments were

unlikely to be affected personally by their implementation (Lama-Re-wal 2001). In terms of their more specific content, the 73rd Amendment mandated one-third reservation for women in all village, block, and district level bodies; posts of chairperson and vice-chairperson across all these institutions; and seats reserved for SCs and STs in each body according to their proportion of the population. The 74th Amendment extended these same provisions to municipal corporations in large urban areas, municipal councils in smaller urban settlements, and local councils in areas in transition from rural to urban status. Under the terms of both amendments, the seats allocated to women were to be chosen by direct election and rotate across districts every five-year election cycle. The impact of these reforms was dramatic and immediate: after only one round of elections, more than one million women entered local government—and elected office—for the very first time.

The Adoption of the Women's Reservation Bill

The relatively quick passage of the 73rd and 74th Amendments inspired women's groups in India to join together to press for the immediate extension of reservations to the state assemblies and the national parliament. All the major political parties—including the Congress Party, the Janata Dal Party, the Bhartiya Janata Party (BJP), the Samata Party, and the two Communist Parties—responded, some as early as 1994,[15] by incorporating this demand in their manifestos for the 1996 elections. Although all parties presented fewer than 10 percent female candidates (Balasubrahmanyan 1998, 18–19), the United Front government, a new coalition led by Janata Dal, identified women's reservation as a priority issue in its Common Minimum Programme (CMP). While H.D. Deve Gowda, the new prime minister, pledged to pursue legislation to this end during the first session of parliament, the government in fact delayed introducing a bill until the last days of the session, a move that many women interpreted as a lack of real commitment to the issue (Kishwar 1996b; Nath 1996). Therefore, when the government finally presented the 81st Amendment Bill in September 1996, MPs had relatively little time to discuss or debate its provisions, which would reserve one-third of seats in the state assemblies and the national parliament for women, rotate reserved seats across districts after every election cycle, and include the one-third requirement among the seats already reserved for SCs and STs.

Although all the major parties had made commitments, at least in principle, to pursuing reserved seats, a large number of MPs immediately voiced opposition to the Women's Reservation Bill (WRB). Some drew on the negative experiences of women in local government to argue that women had not proven to be effective representatives (Balasubrahmanyan 1998). However, by far the most powerful objections came from OBC men, who argued that reservations for women would only strengthen upper caste dominance, because the women likely to benefit from them were likely to be those with greater social and educational opportunities. Rather than rejecting reservations altogether, they called for the policy to include a sub-reservation for OBC women. Muslim leaders soon echoed these arguments, claiming that the existing proposal would promote mainly Hindus if the policy did not specify sub-reservations for Muslim women. Other minorities followed with similar demands, including SC leaders who were apparently unaware that a sub-reservation for SC women already appeared in the bill, but who perhaps sought to garner extra seats for SCs from the women's quota, rather than yield seats to women from the existing SC quota (Kishwar 1998a; Suchinmayee 2000).

Women in parliament protested these attempts as disingenuous, noting that such objections had never been raised during debates over reservation at the local level and in fact had never been a focus of concern in the years since its implementation (Balasubrahmanyan 1998; Nath 1996). They suggested that attention to minority women was instead simply a convenient excuse for male leaders who did not want to lose their own seats in parliament, as evidenced by the fact that none of these men had taken any steps in the past to promote women within their own parties or communities. In particular, they noted that OBC men were in an excellent position to incorporate a large number of women, given that they occupied approximately 200 of the seats in the 541-member Lok Sabha.[16]

In the days leading up to the vote, several parties issued a whip instructing their MPs to vote in favor of the bill. Some openly declared their intentions to defy the whip (Kishwar 1996b), and on the day in question, a number of senior male MPs stood at the main gate of parliament instructing arriving male MPs to go home unless they wanted to lose their seats. These tactics stalled the vote due to the lack of a quorum and led the minister for parliamentary affairs to call a meeting with the female MPs to discuss the situation. Although some women themselves opposed the bill, others felt that a meeting was unnecessary because reservations already formed part of the CMP

(Nath 1996). When these women could not agree on the specifics of the amendment, the minister formed a Select Committee to consider whether the bill could be revised to incorporate sub-reservations for OBCs. To press their case, backward caste MPs from all the parties sent a common delegation to demand sub-quotas, but the chair of the committee pointed out that no quotas currently existed for OBCs in the general category of seats. For this reason, sub-reservations for OBC women could not be made until a separate constitutional amendment established such a quota. In contrast, sub-reservations for SCs and STs could be included within the bill because quotas for these groups already existed in the general category.

In its final report, therefore, the committee rejected the call for OBC sub-quotas and in addition to several small technical adjustments recommended that the bill be passed into law as soon as possible. Female supporters pressed for an immediate vote, but the speaker of parliament allowed MPs two days to review the report. Shortly thereafter, representatives from Janata Dal, the main party within the ruling coalition, announced their opposition to the bill and threatened to defy the party whip if an OBC sub-quota was not included. The opposition parties, in turn, alleged that the government was deliberately sabotaging the bill and the winter session ended without a vote (Suchinmayee 2000).

In February 1997, women's organizations and the National Commission for Women launched a new campaign calling for passage of the bill in the coming session of parliament. They argued for full acceptance of the Select Committee's recommendations and accused detractors in parliament of making demands for OBC sub-quotas simply to undermine the bill (Nath 1996). They noted that quotas were one of the few issues to bring women together across the political spectrum, because most had personally witnessed discrimination in candidate selection procedures and thus had eventually come to realize that reservations were the only way to ensure women fair access to politics. Concerned that claims for other groups threatened to divide women, these women sought to expose the true motivations of male opponents by calling attention to the large gap between the official lines taken by the parties and the actual attitudes of male members toward reservations: while parties embraced quotas publicly in order to appear progressive to win women's votes, individual men worked secretly to subvert their adoption out of reluctance to give up their seats (Gandhi 1996; Kishwar 1996a; Nath 1996).

Although reiterating many of the arguments that had already been voiced in the debates over reservations, this campaign received an unanticipated boost from a conference organized by the IPU in New Delhi that brought together 240 delegates from seventy-eight countries to discuss the theme "Partnership between Men and Women in Politics." The conference discussion revolved largely around the issue of quotas, and a great deal of news coverage in India carried comments from the various delegates on the positive impact of quotas in their own countries (Suchinmayee 2000). Several weeks later, women's groups staged a rally in front of parliament to support early passage of the bill, and at an International Women's Day function later that day, prime minister Deve Gowda pledged to seek a "consensus" on the WRB in order to reintroduce it in parliament the following month (Balasubrahmanyan 1998).

Before the bill could be introduced, however, parliament passed a motion of no confidence against Deve Gowda and he was replaced by I.K. Gujral as the new prime minister. Shortly upon coming to power, Gujral announced that his government was committed to providing reservation for women and would strive to reach a consensus among all the political parties to ensure smooth passage of the bill (Yadav 1997). Despite these intentions, the all-party meeting held to discuss the bill in May 1997 only highlighted enduring differences among various groups of MPs: some insisted on an OBC sub-quota within the women's quota, others suggested reducing the reservation from 33 percent to 10 or 15 percent, and yet others remained firm on passing the bill in its current form with no sub-quotas or dilution of its proposed provisions. When Gujral nonetheless sought to introduce the bill for debate in the Lok Sabha on May 16, he was publicly heckled by two members of his own party, Janata Dal, including its acting president Sharad Yadav, who threatened to hold up the debate unless sub-quotas for OBC and Muslim women were incorporated into the bill.

Even though the votes required to pass the amendment already existed in the chamber, the prime minister responded by calling for a national debate on the bill. Left-wing parties criticized this move, pointing out that all major parties had committed themselves publicly to 33 percent reservation for women. The government, nonetheless, continued to emphasize the need for consensus and announced in July that the WRB would receive top priority during the next session of parliament. In August, women's organizations stepped up their campaign in favor of reservation and female MPs demanded that the bill be put to a vote as soon as possible to reveal more clearly who supported reservation and who did not. Party meetings and press reports suggested that the Left and the BJP clearly endorsed quotas for women; the Shiv

Sena, Rashtriya Janata Dal (RJD), Samata, and Samajwadi (SP) parties totally opposed quotas; and Janata Dal and Congress were hopelessly divided. These splits led some to speculate that the WRB might not be addressed in this session either, and to avoid this outcome, several parties proposed amending the People's Representation Act instead of the constitution to require parties to nominate a certain proportion of women among their candidates. Six female MPs staged a walk-out to protest the Speaker's failure to take up the bill on August 14, but when the government sought to introduce the bill one week later, MPs from the ruling United Front again prevented the amendment from reaching the floor of parliament (Balasubrahmanyan 1998). At the end of the year, Congress withdrew its support from the governing coalition and new elections were announced.

Around this time, female opponents began to focus increasingly on the negative implications of the WRB. Although vocal during the early stages of debate (Gandhi 1996; Kishwar 1996a), they took advantage of male opposition to the bill to call attention to its potentially negative implications for women's social and political status in India, stressing that despite media coverage that portrayed women's organizations as unequivocally supportive of gender quotas, many feminists were in fact opposed or ambivalent toward the WRB. At the broadest level, they worried that setting aside seats for women would admit and reinforce the weakness of women by imposing an artificial solution to improve their access to politics that would undermine their legitimacy as political actors by implying that they were incapable of entering politics on their own. In particular, they were concerned that the women who would benefit from reservation would not alter existing power structures in politics or effect policy change beneficial to women at large. On the one hand, feminists argued, parties were likely to field the mothers, sisters, wives, and daughters of existing male politicians—the so-called *biwi-beti-bahu* brigade—to ensure that seats remained in their caste control. On the other hand, they noted, parties of all ideologies were likely to win elections to the reserved seats and bring progressive and fundamentalist women into parliament, with positive and negative consequences for women-friendly policy change (Balasubrahmanyan 1998; Kudva 2003).

Turning to details of the bill itself, finally, feminists suggested that the rotation requirement would prevent the emergence of an enduring corps of female politicians and, even more gravely, would reduce levels of accountability among all elected officials. Drawing on evidence from the local level, they noted that men often assumed that seats not reserved for women were reserved for men, creating a ceiling for women's representation and undermining women's opportunities to run for re-election as constituencies were de-reserved. These problems were magnified, they pointed out, by the lottery system for allocating reservations, according to which neither men nor women would know in advance which constituencies would be open to them until just before the elections. This meant that aspirants and incumbents would have little incentive to nurse particular constituencies as they could not be held accountable for their promises or their actions. Despite their specific criticisms of the WRB, however, these feminists still generally supported the goal of increasing the number of women in politics. To this end, they offered endless suggestions for improving the bill and devising alternative strategies to promote female candidates, focused mainly on multimember constituencies and centrally-mandated political party quotas. These revealed strong awareness of developments in other countries: to support the case for the party quota solution, they pointed to negative experiences with legislated quotas in Nepal, Philippines, and the Soviet Union, which they criticized as measures of co-optation, and positive experiences with party quotas in Scandinavia and Western Europe, which they viewed as mechanisms of empowerment (Dalal 2000; Narayan et al 2000).

These various debates kept the issue of reservations on the agenda through the January 1998 elections. All major parties again included a commitment to women's reservation in their respective party manifestos, and following the installation of a new BJP-led governing coalition in March 1998, the new government announced that it would seek early passage of the WRB. However, on the day that it introduced the 84th Amendment Bill in July 1998, the government was physically prevented from tabling the amendment: as M. Thambi Dorai, the union law minister, was about to present the bill, an MP from the RJD ran up to the podium, snatched the bill from Dorai's hands and, passing more copies from the Speaker's table to about fifty other MPs, tore the bill to bits on the floor of the Lok Sabha. The action was applauded by the RJD and SP party leaders, who had apparently coordinated the action the day before in cooperation with OBC and Muslim leaders of other parties. Even though surveys revealed that an overwhelmingly majority of voters, both women and men, favored reservations,[17] the Speaker announced the next day that the bill was being deferred for the time being due to lack of consensus over the amendment.

The various sides immediately blamed each other for these developments: supporters accused male MPs of sabotaging the amendment to preserve their own seats, while opponents pointed out that no OBC or Muslim women stood up to defend the bill in solidarity with the pro-reservation women's lobby (Kishwar 1998a). Several party leaders criticized the BJP for abandoning the WRB, while Prime Minister Atal Bihari Vajpayee faulted the Congress Party for his government's inability to pass the amendment, noting that his coalition lacked the two-thirds majority necessary for undertaking constitutional reform on its own (*BBC News*, 14 July 1998). In the absence of any solution to these disagreements, the bill officially lapsed in April 1999 with a no confidence vote against the government that led to the dissolution of parliament.

New elections returned the BJP to power in October 1999, and consistent with campaign promises, the new government announced in November that it would reintroduce the WRB—this time as the 85th Amendment Bill, with no changes from the 81st and 84th Amendment Bills—during the current session of parliament (Singh 1999a). On December 20, with only four days left in the parliamentary session, Congress and left-wing MPs staged a walk-out to protest the fact that the government had not yet introduced the bill, claiming that the delay proved that the government was not serious about reserving seats for women (Singh 1999b). However, when Ram Jethmalani, the law minister, presented the bill the following day, MPs from several socialist parties began to shout angrily and some ran up to the podium to snatch what they thought was the bill from the minister's hands. Demanding sub-quotas for OBCs and Muslims, they forced the Speaker to adjourn the legislature three times such that the bill could not be debated (*Information Times*, 23 December 1999).

These disruptions forced Pramod Mahajan, the minister of parliamentary affairs, to announce later that day that an all-party meeting would be convened on December 22 to work toward an agreement over introduction of the WRB (Singh 1999b). This and similar meetings over the next two years, however, produced no viable compromises, despite continuing pressure from women's groups and political parties, who both frequently took to the streets to demand reservations for women (Katyal 2000). Over time, the bill's proponents grew increasingly skeptical of attempts for "consensus," noting that few bills ever required complete agreement among the parties and that the BJP and Congress, the two parties most visibly engaged in the campaigns for reservations, together had enough votes to pass a constitutional amendment. The government responded that it would continue to explore options that might bring all parties together on the issue, including reducing the number of seats reserved for women and abandoning a constitutional amendment in favor of a centrally-mandated party quota law (Keating 2002).

After repeated delays, the government sought to introduce the WRB for the fourth time in May 2003. As with the previous two attempts, however, heated exchanges on the floor of the Lok Sabha prevented any debate on the bill, with the strongest opposition coming again from the RJD and the SP, which continued to insist that the bill be revised to include sub-quotas for OBCs and Muslims (*BBC News*, 6 May 2003). In response, the Speaker again convened a series of all-party meetings that initially failed to resolve these on-going differences but eventually achieved a breakthrough in July 2003, when representatives of four parties converged around a new proposal to create dual-member constituencies in one-third of all electoral districts, and thus increase the total number of seats in parliament by 181, to enable the election of one man and one woman from these particular constituencies. Communicating this solution to the government, the Speaker reportedly asked the government to draft a new bill, and several days later, the BJP National Executive approved a resolution to pursue a constitutional amendment along these lines.

The Congress and Left parties, however, soon began to express concerns that the new proposal would dilute the cause of women's reservation by reducing the proportion of reserved seats from 33 percent to 25 percent. Others acknowledged the advantages of a system that did not require sitting male MPs to surrender their seats, but worried about the fate of incumbent female MPs, whose districts would now reserve additional seats for men. Yet others remarked that the compromise was entirely silent on the issue of sub-reservations, the issue that had outwardly inspired the most powerful objections to the original bill (Nanivadekar 2003a). In his address to the nation on Independence Day on August 15, the prime minister regretted that no consensus had yet been reached on the bill and pressed again for the dual-member solution (*India News*, 15 August 2003).

When the parties still could not agree by March 2004, Vajpayee blamed main opposition Congress for stalling the WRB and assured voters, as elections approached, that the BJP-led National Democratic Alliance would ensure passage of the legislation if voted into power again (*Hindustan Times*, 19 April 2004). Congress leader Sonia Gandhi responded by pledging that her party, if elected, would also pass the WRB. Women's groups called both parties hypocrites, pointing out that women formed less than 10 percent of the candidates on their lists (*Hindustan Times*, 19 April 2004). After the May 2004 elections registered an increase in support for Congress, the party returned to power as part of the United Progressive Alliance (UPA). Together with its coalition partners, it issued a CMP that included a promise to introduce one-third reservation for women in state assemblies and the national parliament, as well as a pledge to earmark at least one-third of all funds provided to local governments for programs related to women and children (*Times of India*, 27 May 2004).

By February the following year, however, the government and the Congress party appeared to distance themselves from this proposal (*The Hindu*, 25 February 2005), although by spring, Shivraj Patil, the home minister, said that nineteen of the twenty parties he had spoken to had agreed to create more seats in the legislature and reserve them for women (*The Hindu*, 12 May 2005). In mid-August, the UPA held consultations in groups with various parties, and seemed to gain the support of the opposition BJP, as well as the RJD and the SP (*The Hindu*, 22 August 2005). Yet, by the end of the year two of these parties reversed their positions: the BJP decided that it would only support reservations on party lists, and not for legislative seats, while the SP returned to its demands for sub-quotas as a condition for passing the WRB (*The Hindu*, 30 August 2005). Amid growing protests from women's groups and female MPs, Prime Minister Manmohan Singh made several pledges to introduce the WRB in various sessions of parliament over the course of 2006. By the end of the year, however, the RJD reverted to its calls for sub-quotas, while Sonia Gandhi admitted that there was resistance inside her own party (*The Peninsula*, 30 October 2006), leading the UPA to decide to table the bill during the winter session of parliament (*Telegraph India*, 16 December 2006).

In early 2007, the prime minister again said that the bill would be introduced as soon as "consensus" was built on the issue. In April, the parliamentary Women's Caucus, in a rare show of unity across party lines, presented a set of joint recommendations to the Select Committee on Electoral Reforms, all of which proposed to institute legislative quotas instead of reserved seats, ranging from one-fifth to one-third of all the candidates on party lists (*Indian Muslims*, 12 April 2007). Along similar lines, the BJP proposed and approved an amendment to its party constitution that would establish a 33 percent quota for all positions inside the party (*Times of India*, 23 September 2007). Importantly, however, it stressed that this quota would not apply to elected positions unless a law was passed making one mandatory for all political parties (*The Telegraph*, 23 September 2007). In January

2008, the party reversed course and adopted a resolution supporting one-third reservations for women in parliament (*The Hindu*, 29 January 2008), and by February, it began criticizing the UPA government for not delivering on its promises with regard to the WRB (*The Hindu*, 22 February 2008). As the government moved to table the bill in May 2008, following lobbying by female MPs inside the Congress Party, the BJP reiterated its promise to back the WRB in whatever form the government might propose. Nonetheless, observers noted that key UPA allies were still opposed to reservations for women that did not include sub-quotas for OBCs, indicating that the bill was not likely pass, despite renewed support from the main opposition party (*Economic Times*, 4 May 2008).

The Implementation of the Women's Reservation Bill

As the WRB has not yet been adopted at the national level, women's representation in the Lok Sabha currently stands at only 9 percent (Inter-Parliamentary Union 2008a) (see table 4.4). Among the few female candidates selected by the parties, most come from higher castes, privileged class backgrounds, and prominent political families (Rai 2002; Srivastava 2000). Evidence from local government, where reservations have been in place for more than ten years, suggests that these selection patterns might change dramatically with one-third reservations, at the same time that it reveals the various positive and negative consequences that reservations might have on women's opportunities for influencing public policy. Following passage of the 73rd and 74th Amendments Acts, states were required to implement these laws under penalty of losing central government assistance, and thus within three years all had approved legislation reserving 33 percent of seats for women (Jain 1996). Many anticipated that women would not be found to fill all these positions, but more than one million entered local government and some councils even exceeded the quota requirement by 1996 (Nath 1996, 7). Although the women elected to the municipal councils come mainly from higher castes and have higher levels of education and higher prestige professions, women in the rural panchayats frequently come from the lower castes, and are landless, illiterate, married, and under the age of forty, with no prior political experience (Lakshmi, Jyoti, and Sharma 2000; Mehta 2002).

These patterns indicate that reservations are transforming the face of political representation in rural areas by incorporating not only

Table 4.4. Women's Legislative Representation in India

Lok Sabha		Rajya Sabha	
Year	Women (%)	Year	Women (%)
1951	4.0	1951	6.9
1957	5.5	1955	7.8
1962	6.8	1957	8.6
1967	5.9	1958	9.4
1971	4.1	1960	10.2
1977	3.3	1962	7.6
1980	5.0	1964	8.8
1984	7.8	1966	9.6
1989	5.0	1968	9.1
1991	7.2	1970	5.8
1996	6.4	1972	7.4
1999	8.8	1974	7.0
2004	9.1	1976	9.8
		1978	10.2
		1980	11.8
		1982	9.8
		1984	11.5
		1986	10.2
		1988	10.2
		1991	9.8
		1992	6.9
		1994	8.2
		1998	8.6
		2002	10.3
		2006	10.7

Source: Inter-Parliamentary Union (1995, 140-141); Inter-Parliamentary Union (1998); Inter-Parliamentary Union (2008a); Kishwar (1996b).

women, but also members of other marginalized groups. Unfortunately, these characteristics have had a range of negative implications for women's impact on rural government, as men have taken advantage of women's ignorance and lower social standing in ways that largely reinforce the existing gender and class order. At the most basic level, many women are simply not aware of their rights and duties as panchayat members and often run for office only in response to pressure from relatives, who recognize the material benefits of elected office or who seek to keep a particular seat in their family once it has been reserved for a woman. Illiterate women, especially those who are assigned to be the head of the village council due to the requirement that women occupy one-third of these positions across the state, are often the most vulnerable in this regard, because male council members ask them for their thumbprint to authorize spending without explaining why the money is being drawn, and not being able to read, they do not realize they have the right to deny such requests (Mehta 2002; Ramesh and Ali 2001).

Difficulty accepting women in positions of political power, further, often leads these women's husbands to act as if they hold the position that their wives actually occupy, to the extent that they are acknowledged as such by other council members and within the constituency at large. These men attend meetings and signal to their wives what to do, and in some cases, assume their responsibilities entirely by receiving proposals, answering questions, and overseeing policy implementation. Some women explain that this is the only way to perform their duties, as the other councilors would not take them seriously without the mediation of their husbands or male relatives, but others report that their husbands would beat them if they dared to speak during meetings (Dugger 1999; Nanivadekar 2003b). In cases where women attempt to exercise power on their own, they are subject to character assassination and even violent attacks from their relatives or political rivals for transgressing social norms that do not permit mixing with men (Jain 1996; Mandal 2003). To depose them, some male council members go so far as to initiate motions of no confidence against their female colleagues, often after they themselves refuse to cooperate with them or deliberately fail to communicate meeting times to them in an effort to "prove" their incompetence (Ramesh and Ali 2001).

Despite these troubling developments, one-third reservations for women have also had a number of positive effects on women's ability to shape local governance in ways that challenge the existing social order. Perhaps most obviously, the reservation policy creates opportunities for women who, despite their interest in politics, might otherwise never consider or dare to run for political office due to existing norms against women's political participation (Jain 1996; Raman 2002). After joining the councils, many of these women—both those who serve as proxies for their male relatives and those who come from activist backgrounds—become increasingly more effective policy-makers over time as they gain political experience and begin to assert their rights, both as women and as members of marginalized groups (Srivastava 2000). These dynamics upset traditional hierarchies in many villages, which have long been run by upper caste men, and often bring issues like education, health, domestic violence, child marriage, and child labor to the table for the very first time (Dugger 1999; Jain 1996). In

numerous cases, this leads rural women to approach female representatives regarding issues in their marital and domestic lives that they
would never bring to the attention of men (Kudva 2003), and inspires
these women to run again for political office even when their constituencies are de-reserved (Nanivadekar 2003b). Indeed, by 2006, the
government estimated that approximately 50,000 women had been
elected to general seats (*The Hindu*, 23 November 2006).

The Women's Reservation Bill and Women's Political Representation in India

Attempts to establish reservations for women in India, therefore, have
a multipart history, with the most recent chapter focused on arguments
for and against reserved seats at the state and national level. The existing literature on women and politics would expect slightly higher
levels of representation in India than in Pakistan, given the country's
relatively stable democratic history and higher levels of social and economic development, while research on gender quotas would anticipate
earlier quota adoption in India than in Pakistan, given the many groups
that support reservation and the quick passage of the constitutional
amendment for reservations at the local level. The narrative of events
presented in this chapter, however, reveals a much more complicated
relationship between coalitions of support and opposition and their
stated and unstated intentions in quota debates, with some actors
claiming strong support for reserved seats but not taking any steps to
institute them, and other actors voicing strong opposition on normative
grounds but not being consistent with these arguments in their own
behavior. A broader temporal lens thus exposes a disjointed sequence
of reforms, in which advocates are so focused on changing systemic
institutions that they ignore the practical and normative institutions
that repeatedly thwart systemic reform (see table 4.5).

The first policies to institute reserved seats appeared in India
in the 1930s, as the British government moved to include women
among a list of groups that were guaranteed representation in the
colonial regime. The nationalist movement, however, condemned
this solution as a "divide-and-rule" strategy that sought to undermine the common identity of all Indians. For this reason, after independence, the newly drafted constitution abolished special seats for
women in the interest of recognizing fundamental equality between
women and men. Nonetheless, practices at the local level introduced
a custom of co-opting women into local councils when no women

Table 4.5. Quota Reforms and Institutional Configurations in India

Systemic Institutions	Practical Institutions	Normative Institutions
Period 1 (1950–1996):		
No reserved seats *for* women FPTP *electoral system*	"Sex" as *irrelevant* criteria Placement in unwinnable *districts*	Equality before the law Representation as politics of ideas; partial politics of presence for SCs and STs
Period 2 (1996–present):		
No reserved seats *for* women FPTP *electoral system*	"Sex" as *irrelevant* criteria Placement in unwinnable districts	Equality before the law Representation as politics of ideas; partial politics of presence for SCs and STs

were elected directly. By the 1980s, several states had formalized these policies by reserving seats for women at various levels of local government. Thus, by the advent of the reservation debates in the 1990s, a variety of systemic and practical solutions mitigated the effects of these normative institutions in local politics. In contrast, the effects of systemic, practical, and normative institutions at the national level largely worked against the selection of female candidates, with the result that women formed only about 6 percent of all representatives in the Lok Sabha.

Experiments at the local level caught the eye of national leaders, who extended these policies across all states as part of decentralization package. When this bill passed, women's groups began to demand similar reservations for state assemblies and the national parliament. Parties responded to women's demands by including a commitment to reservations in their party manifestos in the run up the 1996 elections. However, when the new government sought to introduce a bill at the end of the same year, a large number of MPs voiced normative opposition, primarily on the grounds that the bill would promote upper caste Hindu women if it was not revised to incorporate sub-quotas for OBCs and Muslims. Although many women's groups suggested that sub-reservations were simply a convenient excuse for male leaders who did not want to lose their seats in parliament, they refused to consider normative reforms that would establish sub-reservations or practical reforms that would create quotas within their own parties, shifts that would not only eliminate these objections, but also pave the way for more effective institutional configurational change. Insisting that women should not be divided, and pointing out that sub-quotas for SCs and STs already existed in the provision, they continued to pursue systemic reform to the exclusion of practical and normative change. As a result, systemic, practical, and normative institutions shifted little, and women's representation in parliament remained at only 8 percent. Interestingly, however, these patterns may soon begin to move in new directions, as more and more groups call for practical and normative reforms in the shape of party and legislative quotas.

Although the WRB for state and national levels has not yet been approved, evidence from its implementation at the local level reveals that systemic reforms alone can produce dramatic changes in the numbers of women elected to political office, precisely because the mechanism of reserving seats means that seats are literally set aside for women. Insights from the local level, however, also cast light on how opponents may still draw on existing practices and norms to de-legitimize women as political actors and thus undermine their effectiveness as policy-makers. Indeed, men in several local councils have devised alternative strategies for excluding women, especially against women from underprivileged social backgrounds, to ensure that they are not present in deliberations despite the fact that seats are specifically reserved for them. These patterns suggest that systemic reforms may be extremely effective, but call attention to the need for accompanying practical and normative reforms to support the broader goal of systemic change.

Conclusions

Campaigns to establish reserved seats have thus followed two distinct paths in Pakistan and India: reform in Pakistan has been harmonizing, bringing institutions of candidate selection together in mutually reinforcing but unanticipated ways, while reform in India has been disjointed, fostering competition among institutions in a manner that undermines changes in the selection of female candidates. These patterns reveal, as predicted, that harmonizing sequences are more effective than disjointed sequences in altering patterns of political representation. The specific comparison between Pakistan and India, however, also suggests a number of special insights for countries

contemplating reservations. Perhaps most strikingly, this juxtaposition reveals that democratic regimes may in fact be an obstacle to
adoption. In Pakistan, military leaders were largely responsible for
the continuous history of reserved seats, with the only gap in these
provisions occurring between 1988 and 2000, the period when democratic regimes under the leadership of Bhutto and Sharif alternated in
power. During this time—as has been the case in India since the WRB
was introduced—both major parties repeatedly included commitments to reserved seats in their party manifestos, but never instituted
these measures while in government, using the opportunity instead
to blame the opposition for failure to approve these reforms. For nondemocratic regimes, in contrast, reserved seats provided a convenient
and easy solution for demonstrating their will to include many different groups, thus in their eyes legitimizing their rule.

Taking this last idea one step further, a second major insight generated by this comparison relates to the complex relationships between
various claims for group representation, which may result in the recognition of many groups, some groups, or no groups at all. Despite
their common colonial history, Pakistan and India adopted opposite
approaches to the question of reserved seats in the years following
independence. In Pakistan, constitutions quickly guaranteed the representation of various groups, including women, minorities, and technocrats. In India, however, the nationalist movement firmly rejected
special measures for any groups, with the exception of SCs and STs,
who were deemed so "backward" that they would not otherwise be
able to help themselves. While more recent debates register a shift in
these attitudes, they indicate that the recognition of some groups does
not automatically extend to the recognition of others and, indeed, that
competing claims by multiple groups may forestall group recognition
altogether. Comparing these two cases over time, therefore, uncovers
the multifaceted political struggles that shape the adoption and implementation of reserved seats provisions, often in strange ways: a history
of systemic reforms in Pakistan informed their later revival that, along
with other systemic reforms, inadvertently spilled over into practical
and normative reform, while a history of systemic reforms in India
first prevented and then inspired efforts at systemic reform that, due
to the success of these reforms, convinced advocates to overlook the
possibilities and importance of practical and normative change. These
patterns highlight a diversity of paths to quota reform but together
reveal the crucial importance of political action, both positive and
negative, in shaping patterns of political representation.

Party Quotas in Sweden and the United Kingdom

During the last several decades a growing number of political parties have adopted party quotas by changing their statutes to require a certain proportion of women among their parties' candidates. These policies thus attempt to revise practical institutions by establishing new criteria for candidate selection to compel elites to recognize existing biases and consider alternative spheres of political recruitment. They diverge from reserved seats in that they concern slates of candidates, rather than the final percentage of women elected, and from legislative quotas in that they constitute voluntary measures adopted by individual parties, rather than mandatory provisions applied to all political groupings. They are the most common type of gender quota, appearing in parties across the political spectrum and in all regions of the world, beginning with socialist parties in Western Europe in the early 1970s. Although party quotas continue to be the most prevalent measure employed in Europe, they frequently coexist with legislative quotas in Latin America and Africa, where party quotas often predate or accompany the adoption of more encompassing quota laws.

To understand how party quotas came to be adopted by various kinds of political parties, as well as why these policies may have diverse consequences for the numbers of women elected, this chapter examines the cases of Sweden and the United Kingdom (UK), where campaigns for party quotas emerged as early as the 1960s but gained their greatest momentum in the 1990s. Although efforts to increase women's representation began much earlier in Sweden than in the UK, both countries had relatively similar percentages of women in parliament before the first quota policies were adopted: women occupied 14 percent of the seats in the Swedish Parliament in 1970 and 9 percent of the seats in the British House of Commons in 1992 (Inter-Parliamentary Union 1995, 236, 254). By 2008, after parties in both countries had adopted and implemented quotas for a number of election cycles, these proportions increased to 47 percent in Sweden and 20 percent in the UK (Inter-Parliamentary Union 2008a). This raises the question: Why have party quotas in Sweden been more successful than those in the UK in altering existing patterns of representation?

Drawing on the theoretical concepts presented earlier, this chapter analyzes the various quota policies adopted by political parties in Sweden and the UK by tracing the actors, strategies, and institutions of candidate selection that have influenced quota adoption and implementation. The focus is on quotas in individual parties, whose effects are then pieced together to assess the overall degree of institutional configurational change. Each case study begins by situating recent reforms within the broader context of efforts in each country to increase women's political representation. Each then turns to the origins, adoption, and implementation of current quota provisions: *varannan damernas* in several Swedish parties in the early 1990s and various kinds of quota measures adopted by British parties in the 1990s and 2000s. The analysis points to a harmonizing trajectory of reform in Sweden, in which proponents initially lobbied for recommendations and targets but gradually radicalized their demands, eventually securing commitments from most parties to alternate between women and men on their candidate lists. As parties adjusted their practices and norms of candidate selection to the rules of the electoral system, institutional configurations eventually converged over time, leading to similar patterns of effective quota implementation within and across political parties. In comparison, quota reform in the UK has been largely disjointed: after a legal decision in the mid-1990s declared a particular quota policy to be illegal, supporters focused exclusively on normative institutions as the main barrier to change, causing them to overlook the possibilities for systemic and practical reform. In general, however, parsing out the effects of party quotas is more complicated than with other types of quota provisions: because these measures are adopted at the party and not the state level, their origins and outcomes are more contingent, engaging a wider array of actors and strategies with less predictable effects on institutions of candidate selection at both the party and the aggregate level. These dynamics account for the remarkable variations in the impact of party quotas across countries and political parties, at the same time that they illustrate the numerous possibilities to intervene and alter existing patterns of political representation.

Varannan Damernas in Sweden

Campaigns for the adoption and implementation of gender quotas in Sweden span a period of more than thirty years, with women in the parties first broaching the issue in the late 1960s and gaining varying degrees of commitment to these measures over the course of the 1970s, 1980s, and 1990s. Efforts to get more women elected, however, stretch back as far as the 1920s and 1930s, when women began to organize to press party officials to place more women in safe seats on their party lists. The actors in these earlier campaigns were mainly civil society actors like women's movement organizations and women inside the political parties, who framed women's increased representation as a question of normative consistency. More recent campaigns, in contrast, have engaged a much wider range of actors, including civil society groups like women's movements organizations, women's sections inside the political parties, and cross-party women's networks; state and party actors like prime ministers, party leaders, party congresses, party working groups, and state-sponsored research commissions; and, to a much lesser extent, international and transnational influences. Although both opponents and advocates expressed normative reservations toward gender quotas, advocates argued that parties that refused to take steps to increase women's representation would fail to garner women's votes and, as a result, suffer important electoral consequences. While sequences of reform have varied across the parties in terms of their timing and their content, these shifts have resulted in tight configurations of structures, practices, and norms contributing to effective quota implementation at the party level. Partial exceptions to these patterns have emerged in parties with enduring normative objections to quota adoption, yet even these parties have selected nearly equal numbers of women and men, leading to nearly 50 percent female representation overall.

Antecedents to Varannan Damernas

The principle of alternation, known in Swedish as *varannan damernas*, constitutes a relatively radical claim for equal representation by requiring that parties alternate between men and women on their candidate lists. Although other parties and national laws around the world also mandate 50 percent representation, this policy emerged in Sweden from a series of earlier efforts by women's groups to get more women nominated in positions where they were likely to be elected. After gaining the right to vote in 1921, women in Sweden engaged in a series of campaigns to persuade parties to select female candidates, precipitating a number of bitter struggles in the 1930s and 1940s over the nomination and placement of women, including those who were incumbents.[1] Because party elites hesitated to select women, especially in winnable positions, more than three-quarters of all women who sat in the lower house between 1922 and 1949 occupied "marginal" seats, which their parties would win only if they gained more mandates, or acceded to parliament during by-elections, which meant they had not originally been placed high enough on their parties' lists (Palme 1969, 65–66). This state of affairs led women to mobilize in various ways outside the parties to compel elites to select more women. The first attempt came in the late 1920s when a group of women, associated primarily with the Liberal Party, formed women's lists for local elections in 1927 and parliamentary elections in 1928. Their main goal was to elect more women, both through their own list and by creating pressures for other parties to follow suit, and thus they never developed a conventional party program. The strategy backfired, however, as female voters and party elites both distanced themselves from these actions (Torbacke 1969). Despite these failures, women's lists reappeared in 1936, 1938, 1968, 1973, 1976, 1988, and 1994, with one woman elected from such a list in 1976 (Eduards 1977).

Recognizing the need to target the existing parties, women involved in the Fredrika Bremer Association (FBF), one of the oldest nonpartisan women's organizations in Sweden, organized a meeting in 1935 with twenty-five other politically independent women's groups to discuss ways of electing more women to parliament. In the run-up to the 1936 parliamentary elections, the network encouraged women to join the existing parties and work during the nomination process to get more women placed in electable positions on party lists. The next year, the group officially established the Committee for Increased Female Representation with the goal of raising elite and public awareness on the status of women in politics through brochures, posters, newspaper articles, and public meetings (Östberg 2001), which contributed at least in part to a rise in the number of women elected at the local, provincial, and national levels in the late 1930s (Karlsson 1996, 130). When women's representation stagnated in the early 1940s, the committee initiated a second round of campaigns for the 1944 and 1948 general elections that included mass meetings, radio programs, and posters with the slogan "Without women—no democracy." The Committee ended its work after these campaigns, but the FBF continued on as a pressure group, primarily by staging hearings to question party leaders on their attitudes toward having more women in politics (Palme 1969). At meetings in 1944 and 1952, most party leaders expressed their support for increasing female representation, although they generally attributed women's absence from elected positions to women themselves by arguing that women did not participate actively enough in party work. In addition, they complained that women within their parties often had difficulties unifying around a single female candidate, complicating the task of selecting women at a time when elites generally considered one woman sufficient to represent "women" (Wistrand 1975).

Activities to bring more women into politics waned in the 1950s and 1960s but eventually gained new life in 1967, when the FBF joined women's organizations inside the parties with the politically neutral women's organizations under the umbrella of the Cooperation Committee for Increased Female Representation. As the 1968 general elections approached, the committee issued an open letter to all women to get them more interested in politics and organized a widely-attended panel with the leaders of all the parties to pressure them to select more female candidates (Palme 1969). The FBF initiated a similar campaign before the 1973 elections to call attention to women's underrepresentation by asking party leaders what they were doing to ensure that women would be elected in greater numbers at all levels of government. This campaign went further than earlier efforts by organizing mass demonstrations, distributing statistics on women's representation to the media, and holding roundtables with the leaders of the various women's organizations and seminars for girls involved in the parties' youth associations. However, the campaign stopped short of demanding that parties adopt gender quotas to ensure women's access to political office: although the board of the FBF voted by a narrow margin to support quotas, this decision was overturned at the national meeting, where delegates preferred instead to demand a 50% increase in women's representation in every election until women had attained equal representation in parliament (Gjötterberg 1975). Although the FBF continued to call on women to be more politically active and ask political parties what they were doing to nominate more women, it eventually took its first stand in favor of legislated gender quotas in 1980, when it demanded that a new law be introduced to require that party lists alternate between women and men. None of the parties picked up this proposal, however, and various women inside the FBF remained opposed to this decision.

In addition to these attempts to mobilize outside the parties, women's groups also worked inside the parties to promote the selection of female candidates. Prior to the 1960s, most of their activities revolved around the placement of individual women. The advent of the "sex role debate" at the beginning of the 1960s, however, shifted women's focus toward demanding greater access to politics for all women. Sparked by the publication of several books on women's work, this debate called for a change in assigned gender roles, with men assuming greater responsibility for child care and housework and women engaging in more work outside the home, to foster greater equality between the sexes. Due to pressure from their women's sections, parties quickly integrated these ideas into their programs, although each interpreted gender equality in line with its own political ideology: the Center Party focused on the reform of family life, the Liberal Party emphasized equal opportunities, the Social Democratic Party situated equality between women and men within the framework of class equality, and the Left Party treated gender equality as a central element in the class struggle (Eduards 1981). Interestingly, the focus on overcoming assigned sex roles also led to calls inside the parties to disband the women's sections in the name of equality, but none were abolished because women drew on the increased attention to gender issues to demonstrate the need to retain the women's sections to continue to attract female voters. This status within the parties then enabled them over the course of the 1970s and 1980s to point to the gains made by women in other parties to press for additional measures to promote women's representation. While all parties remained firmly opposed to introducing gender quotas, these demands led several parties to adopt recommendations and targets for the selection of female candidates, leading to growing differences among the parties in terms of the proportion of women elected to parliament (see tables 5.1 and 5.2).

The first party to introduce a recommendation was the Liberal Party (FP). Although women in the party had been active since the 1930s in the various campaigns organized by the FBF, elites continued to nominate only a few women in unsafe seats, to the point that women in the province of Västerbotten protested by devising their own women's list in 1968 (Drangel 1984; Wiberg 1969). These trends began to turn around in 1972, however, when party leader Gunnar

Table 5.1. Women's Legislative Representation in Sweden

Parliament	
Year	Women (%)
1970	14.0
1973	21.4
1976	22.9
1979	27.8
1982	27.5
1985	31.5
1988	38.4
1991	33.5
1994	40.4
1998	42.7
2002	45.3
2006	47.3

Sources: Inter-Parliamentary Union (1995, 236); Inter-Parliamentary Union (2002); Inter-Parliamentary Union (2004); Inter-Parliamentary Union (2008a).

Helén criticized the ruling Social Democrats for talking about gender equality but failing to fulfill this commitment with concrete actions. To this end, he proposed equal representation on all party bodies, which the party congress transformed into the goal that neither sex be represented in less than 40 percent of all internal party positions. For popularly elected bodies, however, the FP simply agreed to a resolution to seek to elect more women. In 1973, the party set up a working group on women in politics to discuss the possibility of adopting quotas. Although the group eventually rejected strict quotas in 1974, it did recommend that at least one woman be placed in a winnable position in every electoral district. If a constituency had only one safe seat, the group recommended that a woman be placed in that seat or in the next position on the party list (Gjötterberg 1975). The party increased the target to half of all electable positions in each district in 1976 and recommended, in 1978, that a 40 percent target be implemented for local elections beginning in 1979. Although the FP was still averse to the notion of quotas, the 1984 and 1988 party congresses recommended that constituencies strive for alternated lists (Freidenvall 2006). To support these efforts, the party's women's organization distributed a pamphlet in 1985 outlining strategies for ensuring that more women were nominated and elected at all levels of government.

Table 5.2. Women in Parliamentary Party Delegations in Sweden

Year	Total (%)	VPK (%)	SAP (%)	C (%)	FP (%)	M (%)	KDS (%)	MP (%)	NYD (%)
1970	14	18	17	13	9	10	...	...	...
1973	21	21	23	24	15	16	...	...	...
1976	23	24	22	28	23	16	...	...	...
1979	28	25	28	33	26	25	...	...	...
1982	28	20	30	32	14	24	...	...	...
1985	32	16	35	32	39	22	...	...	...
1988	38	38	41	38	43	27	...	45	...
1991	34	31	41	39	33	26	31	...	12
1994	41	46	48	37	35	28	33	56	...
1998	43	42	50	56	35	30	40	50	...
2002	45	47	47	50	48	40	30	59	...
2006	47	64	50	38	50	43	38	53	...

Source: Sveriges Riksdag (2003); Sveriges Riksdag (2006); Wängnerud (1999b, 35).

Key: VPK = Left Party, SAP = Social Democratic Party, C = Center Party, FP = Liberal Party, M = Conservative Party, KDS = Christian Democrats, MP = Green Party, NYD = New Democracy.

The second party to adopt measures to promote women was the Left Party (VPK). In 1972, the party congress recommended that the number of women on the party executive committee be equal to their proportion among party members. It also set up a working group with the task of studying what could be done to get women full representation in both party and elected positions (Wängnerud 2001). However, when asked by the FBF in 1973 what it was doing to promote women in politics, the party responded that quotas for elected positions were a static and unrealistic solution to solve the problem of underrepresentation (Gjötterberg 1975). At the party congress in 1976, the VPK extended its policy to recommend that women be elected to positions both inside and outside the party in proportion to their membership in the party (Eduards 1977). The party reiterated this policy in 1985, following a decline in the percentage of women in its delegation to parliament, although it softened the demand with the phrase "as far as circumstances permit" (Wängnerud 2001). The women's committee felt this solution was inadequate and organized special "women's patrols" to monitor the implementation of these recommendations at the district level for the 1985 and 1988 elections. In 1986, it called for the party to create a working group to devise a strategy for achieving a more equal division between women and men. The following year, the party congress agreed in principle to revise the party's statutes to incorporate the recommendation. Nonetheless, women continued to be selected in small numbers in some districts in 1988, spurring women in Kronoberg to protest by putting forward a women's list. Although many within the party continued to voice strong criticisms against the use of gender quotas, the party subsequently revised its statutes in 1990 to state that women should be represented as far as possible in at least 40 percent of all elected positions.

The Social Democratic Party (SAP), the dominant party in Sweden for most of the twentieth century, was the third party to establish a goal to recruit more women. The women's section inside the party (SSKF) had been active since the 1920s, seeking to ensure that female candidates were not only nominated but also placed in winnable positions on party lists. It first proposed gender quotas in 1928, but the party congress rejected the motion on the grounds that all seats should be subject to open competition. The group continued to mobilize, but succeeded only in placing one "obligatory" woman on the various party lists during the 1930s. At the time, women formed a relatively high proportion among the Social Democrats elected to parliament, but primarily won election from marginal seats (Lundblad 1962). Women made fewer gains in the 1940s, 1950s, and 1960s, despite calls from the SSKF to install quotas and efforts by party leaders to encourage the nomination of female candidates. The women's section noted that the local parties paid careful attention to occupation, geography, and age when drawing up their candidate lists, but continued to ignore "sex" as a category of representation (Karlsson 1996). When the 1968 elections brought a major victory for the SAP, but a decrease in the number of women in the party's parliamentary delegation, the SSKF renewed its efforts to increase women's representation and succeeded in getting the party to issue an official communication recognizing women's underrepresentation in electoral politics. For the 1970 elections, the SAP changed its party statutes to state that candidate lists should include women and men, older and younger people, and representatives of various occupational groups. The party still considered gender quotas too controversial, however, and therefore did not mandate any specific level of female representation. Independently, the local party in Stockholm applied a rule whereby women were placed in every third position on the list (Fagerström 1974).

Following these elections, the SSKF established a working group to get women more active in politics and attract more women to the party. When party leaders distributed a flier on candidate selection that said nothing about women's representation, the organization encouraged women to go to the nomination meetings in each district to support the women who were nominated. It also sent a letter to all constituency parties to remind them of the party congress decision, arguing that any failure to ensure women's nomination would undermine the credibility of the party on this issue. As a result of these developments, the SSKF adopted a more radical approach during its own annual meetings, when it pledged to monitor the party leadership and to initiate a serious discussion within the party on measures to elect more than a token number of women. Although the organization left the final decision up to the party congress, it suggested a temporary quota for the distribution of political positions as one way to achieve greater gender balance (Karlsson 1996). Yet, when the SSKF presented these proposals to the party congress in 1972, they proved extremely controversial, even after party leader Olof Palme made a speech in which he stressed that gender equality was a central responsibility of the labor movement. Delegates voiced strong objections to gender quotas, even suggesting that women composed a minority of all party members and thus should not impose their will on the majority (Ahlbaum 1994), leading the party congress to settle eventually on the much softer requirement that the proportion of women increase at all levels of the party by 1975. The party leadership subsequently sent a circular to all districts instructing them to make a conscious effort to place more women on the party lists before the 1973 elections.

Although the number of female candidates increased, the SAP lost the elections, resulting in an increase in the proportion of women in the party's parliamentary delegation, but no change in the actual number of women elected. The party adopted no additional measures before elections in 1976, despite efforts by women to lobby both the party leadership and the trade unions. The SSKF considered quotas again during its annual meeting in 1975, but the organization remained torn on the question of mandatory provisions. The Uppsala West women's club motioned that the only way to increase women's access to political office was through legislation guaranteeing women half of all positions, but the national organization argued that legislation was too bold and should only be used only as a last resort. Although some members were concerned that quotas were tantamount to recognizing women's failures, the group eventually agreed to pursue legislation if nothing else could be done. Consequently, they focused on getting more women nominated in the various districts, but deliberately distanced themselves from the word "quota" in favor of terms like "prioritizing" or "division," worried that the idea of quotas might frighten selection committees and voters alike (Karlsson 1996).

Slow progress over the next several years, however, led the SSKF to adopt a stronger position regarding quotas during preparations for the 1979 elections. At its annual meeting in 1978, a working group presented a report that accused the SAP of not working hard enough to recruit women. It called on the party to adopt gender quotas to guarantee women's representation, preferably in the form that neither sex could occupy more than 60 percent of the seats in all political bodies. The report stressed that such a measure did not entail promoting incompetent women over competent men, but rather aimed to foster a more representative democracy that included members of various social and economic backgrounds (Sainsbury 2004). Although many women in the SSKF agreed that "no more than 60 percent of each sex" was a good formulation, some still expressed concerns that quotas might set women back, especially in rural areas where enough qualified women might not be found. Although the SSKF did not officially support quotas *per se*, the working group report caught the attention of party leaders, who set up a committee to formulate recommendations for that year's party congress. The committee concluded that the ratio of women and men among the party's candidates should at least mirror their proportions among party members, but deliberately avoided any reference to quotas, arguing that the primary responsibility lay with women to become more involved in the party. The party congress, in turn, was averse to quotas, even in the form of "no more than 60 percent of each sex." Delegates decided instead to mandate that the proportion of women among elected officials reflect women's share of the population and the number of women in internal party positions mirror the proportion of women among party members. This formulation was not only stronger than earlier commitments, but also constituted the first time that the party officially adopted a specific goal for increasing women's representation.

In the early 1980s, the SSKF sought to promote this goal across electoral districts, but party leaders maintained that final decisions regarding candidate selection rested with each constituency organization and that, ultimately, the most important consideration for selection was competency and not sex. Finding that women's representation had stagnated, the SSKF resolved in 1984 to work for 40 percent female representation in the years leading up to the 1988 elections, although it still did not dare to place gender quotas on its list of official policy demands (Ahlbaum 1994). At its annual meeting in 1987, however, various local delegations expressed increasingly vocal support for quota provisions, with several proposing that constituency organizations strive for gender balance in candidate nominations for local, provincial, and national elections. The meeting eventually settled on a proposal that no sex be represented in less than 40 percent of all political positions, in a requirement to be inscribed in the party's statutes. They sent these demands to the 1987 party congress, which debated quotas for women in both elected and appointed positions. Although the party executive committee insisted that local organizations find their own solutions to the "representation problem," delegates agreed to revise the party statutes to include the goal that neither sex constitute less than 40 percent of all candidates. All the same, they authorized local organizations to decide for themselves how best to implement this provision (Wängnerud 2001). For appointed positions to state boards and committees, delegates adopted a more graduated approach, with a goal of 30 percent by 1992, 40 percent by 1995, and 50 percent by 1998 (Ahlbaum 1994). Delegates sharpened these policies in 1990, mandating that all nominating organizations "work" to attain "equal representation" in both direct and indirection elections (Freidenvall 2006).

The Center Party (C) considered a proposal to adopt alternated lists in 1975, but ultimately decided not to issue any specific recommendations to promote women's representation. Women in the party mobilized as early as 1939 to get women elected. They did so by sending a circular to all local women's organizations to encourage them to support female candidates and lobby for their placement in safe seats on the party's lists. Despite similar efforts in the 1940s and 1950s, however, the Center Party consistently returned the lowest proportion of women to parliament of all the political parties (Palme 1969, 75). This pattern changed dramatically in the early 1970s, around the time that the party abandoned its old name, the Agrarian Party, and shifted its profile from a farmers' party to an environmental party, a move that dramatically increased its support among women (Bergqvist 1994). Nonetheless, when asked by the FBF in 1973 what it was doing to promote women in politics, the party stressed that the key to increased representation was not gender quotas, but rather a change in women's status at home and in the labor market (Gjötterberg 1975). The party congress considered a proposal for alternated lists in 1975, but decided instead to follow the party executive's suggestion simply to work for an increase in the number of women nominated and elected. In 1977, the party again firmly distanced itself from quotas in favor of working to change voter attitudes to increase equality between women and men (Wängnerud 2001). In place of regulations, women inside the party studied nomination processes and the tactics that men used to gain access to safe seats on the party lists. They then taught these tactics to other women during subsequent election campaigns, even as the party consistently returned among the highest proportions of women to parliament of all the political parties (Andersson 1983; Ekström 1983).

The Conservative Party (M), in turn, applied a 30 percent quota for women in its party executive council from 1919 to 1964 (Eduards 1977), but generally avoided taking steps to promote women as a group. In the 1960s, the Conservatives had a relatively high proportion of women in the upper house and a relatively low proportion of women in the lower house of parliament in comparison with the other parties, but in both chambers, women were overwhelmingly placed on electoral lists as alternates and in marginal seats (Carlshamre 1969, 188–190). In the 1970s, the party began to issue general statements on the importance of having more women in politics, but it repeatedly stressed that women and men should be viewed as individuals, competing on the same grounds, rather than as collective groups (Freidenvall 2006). When asked by the FBF what it was doing to promote women's representation, the party emphasized that women should not only put women's names forward during the nomination process, but should continually pressure local party organizations to ensure that women were selected (Gjötterberg 1975). In 1978, the party congress considered devising a plan to increase women's representation, but ultimately decided to assign the party executive the task of monitoring the proportion of women in elected and internal party positions and seeking to expand women's representation whenever possible. More than a decade later, however, it authorized the party executive to investigate measures to get women more politically involved and to increase the number of women elected (Wängnerud 2001). To support these efforts, the women's organization sent a brochure to all nomination committees around the country to encourage them to nominate more women in the run-up to elections in 1991.

Parties that first gained seats in parliament in the 1980s and 1990s, namely the Christian Democrats (KDS), the Greens (MP), and New Democracy (NYD), adopted a variety of different approaches to the question of women's representation. The KDS became a political party in 1964, but first entered parliament only in 1991. In 1986, the party congress established a goal to promote women in politics by issuing a statement that a stronger representation of women was necessary in all KDS decision-making bodies. In 1987, it extended this commitment by recommending that all electoral lists and internal party bodies contain at least 40 percent of members of each sex (Frebran 1990). The MP, in contrast, wrote the principle of equal representation into its statutes when the party was first formed in 1981. This principle applied to the party leadership, which was to include one man and one woman as party spokesmen, and party committees, which were to include at least 40 percent of members of each sex. The Greens extended the 40 percent policy to electoral lists in 1987, in time to elect its first representatives to parliament in 1988 (Wängnerud 2001). Although this mirrored similar recommendations by other parties, the MP was the first to openly call this measure a "quota" (Freidenvall 2006). The NYD, finally, adopted no measures to promote women in politics when it first presented candidates to parliament in 1991, in line with its profile as an overwhelmingly male-dominated party (Wörlund 1995).

The Origins of Varannan Damernas

Efforts within the parties to promote women in politics led to substantial increases in the proportion of women elected to parliament, which surpassed 30 percent by the mid-1980s. These jumps, however, were not matched by similar increases in the number of women nominated by the parties to local and national committees, despite a recommendation by the government in 1981 that all organizations propose one man and one woman for every position to enable the government to steer the composition of these bodies toward equal representation (Eduards and Åström 1993). Recognizing that these committees played important administrative and policy-making roles, particularly at the local level, the government decided in 1985 to appoint an expert Commission on the Representation of Women to investigate existing nomination practices and propose measures for fostering gender balance. The commission published its report in 1987 and suggested that the government adopt targets to improve the proportion of women on these committees. If local parties and unions could not meet these targets on a voluntary basis, it recommended undertaking legal reform to compel the nomination of more women. These proposals energized women to demand greater access to government boards and introduced a number of new elements to the Swedish debate on women's representation that later spilled over into party policies for elected positions.

In the report, entitled *Varannan Damernas*, the commission outlined arguments for and against gender quotas. After reviewing successful experiments with quotas in Norway, it elaborated on a unique semi-quota solution devised by SAP women in Järfälla, a municipality near Stockholm, to promote the equal representation of women and men. These women set up a study circle on local politics at the end of the 1960s, which arranged debates and meetings on equality issues, worked to get women known within the labor unions, and offered women's names whenever nominations for party positions were being made. These activities eventually convinced the main union in Järfälla to agree to a long-term plan for achieving gender parity on party lists for the local council elections. To avoid conflict within the party by ousting men to replace them with women, the local SAP began electing women to positions when male representatives resigned. The party then instituted a gradual policy of alternation: for elections in 1970, the first ten names on the SAP list were men, but the rest of the list alternated between women and men; for elections in 1973, the first four names on the list were men, but the rest of the list alternated between women and men; and for elections in 1976, all names on the list alternated. For subsequent elections, the party simply devised two lists, one with women and one with men, which it then combined to ensure that equal numbers of each would be elected. The only remaining point of contention was whether a woman or a man should top the list. The report playfully dubbed this system of alternation *varannan damernas*, which literally meant "every other one for the ladies" and referred to a custom at countryside dances where every other song was women's turn to invite the men.[2]

The commission drew on these examples to illustrate the need for deliberate measures to increase women's representation, rejecting any suggestions that these outcomes occurred on their own, as the result of "natural evolution." It considered various objections to gender quotas, including charges that quotas detracted from selection on the grounds of merit, undermined voter preferences, and constituted an arbitrary recognition of one identity to the exclusion of others, but ultimately concluded that quotas were the only way to break with existing patterns of inequality. As a concession to the nominating organizations, however, the commission advocated a "softer"

approach as a sign of its confidence that they would take the necessary steps to remedy these imbalances. It proposed that women's representation in these committees reach 30 percent by 1992, 40 percent
by 1995, and 50 percent by 1998. If the first goal of 30 percent was
not accomplished by 1992, however, it recommended that parliament
introduce quotas by law. To support these efforts, the commission
further proposed that annual reports be presented to parliament to
monitor implementation of these targets and that grants be provided
for projects aimed at increasing women's representation (*Varannan
damernas* 1987). The government responded by presenting a series
of proposals for improving the proportion of women on local and
national committees. The parliament approved these measures in
1988 as part of a five-year plan of action and reiterated the recommendation that women's representation on these boards reach 30 percent
by 1992. It also authorized the payment of nine million kronor over a
three year-period to 114 projects to train women to assume leadership
roles and to teach women ways to influence nomination processes
within their own political parties (Eduards and Åström 1993).

Although these discussions revolved exclusively around women
in appointed committees, they resurfaced and became relevant for
elected positions several years later, when the proportion of women
in parliament decreased for the first time since 1928, from 38 percent
in 1988 to 34 percent in 1991 (Eduards 1992, 86). While this percentage was still high in comparison with other countries, the election
sent shockwaves throughout Sweden, because many had believed the
upward trend to be irreversible. The decline reflected the fact that the
election was a victory for the right-wing parties, those with the weakest policies regarding female representation, but it also highlighted
shortcomings across all the parties in terms of their recruitment of
women (Maillé and Wängnerud 1999). Reacting to these developments, women in the Center Party called on women to be placed as
substitutes for cabinet members who were required to give up their
seats in parliament, while women in the Center and Social Democratic parties insisted that women be elected to important posts in
parliamentary standing committees (Eduards 1992; Sainsbury 1993).
At the same time, a small group of women began to meet to discuss
why the proportion of women had decreased during the elections
and to find ways of influencing the established parties to place more
women in safe seats on party lists. They agreed to work in secret, but
their activities soon spread throughout the country by word of mouth,
until the network was eventually exposed during a news broadcast

several months later. The group soon took the name Support Stockings,[3] and although its original intent was to serve as a pressure group on the existing parties, rumors soon circulated in the media that women might form an entirely new political party.

While a women's party already existed Sweden,[4] and women's parties had proven nonviable electoral alternatives in the past, these speculations sparked a vivid debate that continued throughout 1992. Throughout these discussions, the Support Stockings maintained that their goal was simply to get more women into politics by altering existing recruitment practices. Opponents did not contest this aim, but instead criticized the group for its secret organizing, absence of a membership roll, and lack of a policy program, all of which they used to characterize the network as undemocratic and unprofessional and as a potential source of chaos to the party system (Rönnblom 1997; Sangregorio 1994). Others expressed concerns that the Support Stockings were organizing as women against men, overlooking the need to work together for the common good, as well as the importance of ideology in defining political priorities.[5] Nonetheless, many women inside the parties openly unified around the goal of *varannan damernas*, lending credibility to the threat that women might break away in a new political formation if the established parties did not take stronger steps to select more female candidates.

The Adoption of Varannan Damernas

These events triggered debates across the political spectrum on the need to adopt stronger measures to ensure equal representation. Over the next several years, women pressed the parties to revisit their existing policies to incorporate the principle of *varannan damernas*, which many argued was not a quota, but rather a method for achieving gender balance. The FBF supported this view and encouraged all parties to consider this principle when composing their electoral lists. These efforts met with great success, as by the late 1990s, most parties agreed to alternate between women and men. Yet, parties differed to the degree that they characterized this policy as a recommendation or as a quota, reflecting not only their commitment to gender balance but also their beliefs regarding the legitimacy of positive action. The FP did not need to consider a new selection policy, because it had already recommended alternated lists at its party congress in 1984. However, following women's widespread mobilization, it revisited the issue at its party congress in 1993, where delegates decided to strengthen this provision by suggesting that a woman top every other district list to improve women's overall chances of getting elected (Wängnerud 2001). The VPK, for its part, reacted to these developments by proposing constitutional reform to guarantee the equal representation of women and men in all elected bodies (Eduards 1992). Although this reform never materialized, the party revised its statutes in 1993 to mandate that at least 50 percent of all positions be filled by women, as far as circumstances allowed. Three years later, the party congress decreed that exceptions to this rule could only be made once. After that, all nominating organizations had to ensure that candidates for all internal and elected organs included at least 50 percent women (Wängnerud 2001).

The SAP, in turn, initiated discussions on *varannan damernas* almost immediately following the elections. In early 1992, party leader Ingvar Carlsson called a meeting to evaluate the challenge posed by the Support Stockings. He learned that women inside the party strongly sympathized with calls for equal representation, to the extent that the SSKF was considering launching a separate women's list in the next parliamentary elections. Concerned that such a list would split the vote and work to the benefit of the right-wing parties, the party responded by appointing a woman to fill the post of party secretary (Eduards 1992). Carlsson, nonetheless, objected to the demand to adopt alternated lists, arguing that such a policy should come from the grassroots rather than from party leaders. As calls for *varannan damernas* grew, however, the party executive committee eventually decided that all lists for local, provincial, and parliamentary elections in 1994 should alternate between women and men. To convince the broader party of this goal, the leadership commissioned a working group to study women's representation in the party and produce a debate piece on the issue for the party congress in 1993. The group noted that women were already well-represented within the party, and thus only a few minor steps were necessary to ensure that women's proportion in party and elected positions mirrored women's share of the population. To this end, it proposed alternated lists as the best measure for promoting the equal nomination of women and their equal placement in list positions where they were likely to be elected (Socialdemokraterna 1993).

The SSKF supported these calls and, for the first time, unequivocally supported quotas for women in all political positions, arguing that the conflict over women's representation could not be resolved any other way (Ahlbaum 1994). Some women actively opposed this decision, however, including one of the leaders of the Social

Democratic Youth Association,[6] sparking a debate within the party at large over the choice of the word "quota." Many felt that the term *varannan damernas* was more desirable because it alluded to equal division between women and men, whereas quotas implied that the women selected might not otherwise be qualified (Freidenvall 2005). As a result of these discussions, the party congress received more motions than ever before on quotas and alternated lists. Delegates ultimately approved six bills to revise the party statutes to require alternation between women and men on all party lists, as well as the appointment of women to half of all party positions, seats in local and national committees, and chairmanships within and outside the party. Although some inside the party continued to express concerns that gender would be prioritized over merit (Eduards 2002), the party's brochure on gender equality for the 1994 elections noted that men and women were still not entirely equal, and thus policies were necessary to ensure the equal representation of women and men in all political decision-making (Socialdemokraterna 1994).

The Center Party did not take any immediate steps to change its party policies following the 1991 elections, although it did respond to demands by women inside the party to insert women as substitutes for cabinet members who were required to relinquish their seats in parliament. In 1995, however, the party congress noted that the party was attracting more female voters and that it could only retain their support by promoting more women to leading positions both within and outside the party. Upon further consideration, the party congress announced in 1996 that its goal was to nominate women to half of all these positions (Wängnerud 2001).

In contrast, the Conservatives were much more hesitant to revise their selection procedures following the 1991 elections. Those inside the party argued that equality between women and men meant equal chances in political life and that any discussion of quotas simply went against this goal. All the same, the party's women's organization remained dissatisfied with the proportion of women in positions both in the party and in parliament. In 1992, they succeeded in gaining a commitment from party leaders to get more women involved in politics through special training and education programs. However, this pledge did not prevent the issue from resurfacing at the party congress in 1993, when delegates addressed several motions on women's representation. Advocates noted that female voters would no longer accept lists composed primarily of men, and that in order to garner more votes, the party needed to increase the number of women on its electoral lists (Freidenvall 2006). Concerned that the left-wing parties had monopolized feminism, but careful to respect the right of constituency parties to select their own candidates, delegates agreed to adopt a goal of equal representation for all internal party positions and to support the nomination of more women on party lists (Wängnerud 2001). All the same, they offered no concrete strategies except to reject quotas in favor of training, networking, and mentoring programs that would enable women to compete on equal terms with men.

Similar to the established parties, the newest parties reacted in a variety of different ways to the decline in women's representation in 1991. Christian Democratic women were the most active, producing a manifesto for the party congress in 1992 that called on the party to recruit more women, prioritize women when making political appointments, and alternate between women and men on candidate lists, ensuring in addition that women topped at least half of all these lists. Rather than approving this manifesto, the KDS decided instead to set up a working group to study ways of achieving gender balance within the party. The women's organization felt that this was not sufficient and presented a special women's list for parliamentary elections in 1994. Although the list did not elect any candidates (Kristdemokratiska Kvinnoförbundet 2002), this action led the party congress that year to declare that the KDS would strive for the equal representation of women and men in all political positions. To implement this principle effectively, the party congress in 1995 requested that all district and local party organizations devise their own equality plans. The Greens, for their part, had already made extensive commitments to women's representation in the 1980s. The party reaffirmed its policies in 1995 to state that all internal party positions would consist of at least 40 percent of members of each sex, but that the party would strive as far as possible for at least 50 percent female representation. The party changed this policy in 1997 to require 50 percent of each sex, plus or minus one person, for all internal and elected positions (Wängnerud 2001). The NYD, finally, did not consider adopting any measures to promote women in politics, but it also did not win any seats in parliament after 1991.

The Implementation of Varannan Damernas

In the years following the 1991 elections, women gained varying degrees of commitment to the principle of *varannan damernas*. The

impact of these measures was immediate, as those parties with alternated lists—the VPK, the SAP, and the MP—registered strong gains
in voter support in 1994, leading to a major increase in the number of women elected to parliament, from 34 percent in 1991 to
41 percent in 1994 (Wängnerud 1999b, 35). These elections set a new
record worldwide and brought more young women into parliament
than ever before, due largely to policies adopted by the SAP, the MP,
and the Conservatives to promote more candidates under the age
of thirty. This fostered the impression among some, however, that
younger women had won office at the expense of younger men and
older women, at the same time that older men remained on as incumbents (Burness 2000). Aware that voters might view the new policy
as empty political opportunism, the SAP sought to demonstrate that
they were serious about equal representation, so when they were
invited to form a new government, they extended the principle of
varannan damernas to the cabinet by appointing women to half of all
ministerial positions.

By the time elections took place again in 1998, several parties
had strengthened their policies regarding women's representation,
notably the Center, Conservative, and Christian Democratic parties.
Although most continued to prefer goals and targets over quotas,
all parties elected more than 30 percent women, five more than
40 percent women, and three more than 50 percent women, leading
to an overall increase from 41 percent in 1994 to 43 percent in 1998
(Wängnerud 1999a, 301). Despite their official stands on gender quotas, some parties were more successful than others in meeting their
stated goals. The VPK, for example, returned 42 percent women,
despite its commitment to alternation, because it still tended to top
its lists with men and often won an odd number of mandates (Genberg
2002, 31). The Center Party, in contrast, elected 56 percent women to
parliament, although it had never adopted an official quota policy.
Some attributed this success to a campaign by women inside the party
to convince supporters to cast personal votes for women,[7] in light of
the change in the electoral system that introduced a limited degree of
voluntary personal voting for parliamentary elections beginning in
1998. This reform enabled voters to register a vote for a specific person while also casting a vote for a particular party, as part of an effort
to cultivate a stronger relationship between voters and representatives (Holmberg and Möller 1999). Because a sufficient number of voters must opt to exercise the personal vote, and candidates must win a
certain threshold of votes, only twelve members of parliament gained

seats through this system. This enabled one more woman to be elected than would have been elected, given the parties' placement of male and female candidates.[8] The slight increase in women's representation overall, however, was partly overshadowed by negative media attention to the decrease in young women elected to parliament. Although all the parties paid less attention to younger candidates in 1998 than in 1994, the three youngest women elected in 1994—aged 21, 21, and 22 at the time—decided to leave parliament after only one mandate, fueling speculation that young women were more likely than young men to abandon a political career (Burness 2000).

Despite gains in 1994 and 1998, women continued to lobby the parties to adjust their selection practices to achieve greater gender balance in elected positions. The SAP remained committed to the principle of alternated lists and, following a campaign by the women's and youth organizations inside the party, openly declared themselves a "feminist" party in 2001 (Brink 2002). The VPK also agreed to alternate its lists, but was less enthusiastic about this measure than the SAP, because it was concerned that too much focus on gender quotas in politics overshadowed other substantive issues important to women (Genberg 2002). The Center Party still hesitated to adopt strict quotas for the selection of female candidates, but it did become the only right-wing party to label itself "feminist" in 2001 (Westerlund 2002). The FP expressed continuing ambivalence toward quotas, arguing that quotas were sometimes necessary in exceptional circumstances, but were never legitimate when they promoted less qualified candidates at the expense of more qualified ones (Udovic 2002). The Conservatives, finally, maintained that quotas were simply not the solution to women's underrepresentation (Lorentzi 2002). Although parties did not radically overhaul their existing policies, ongoing attention to the issue of candidate recruitment contributed to further increases in the number of women in parliament in 2002: all parties elected more than 30 percent women, six more than 40 percent women, and two more than 50 percent women, resulting in the election of 45 percent women overall (Inter-Parliamentary Union 2004). Part of this increase, however, stemmed from the effects of personal voting, which enabled six women and six men to win seats in parliament who otherwise would not have been elected. Four of the six women elected in this way were from the Conservative Party, revealing that voters were more likely than party selectors to choose women over the men who had been placed higher on the party list (Rundkvist 2002).

Some of these patterns were replicated in the elections that took place in 2006, although with one important alteration to the political environment. In spring 2005, a new feminist political party was launched called Feminist Initiative (FI), which early polls forecast might win as much as 20–25 percent of all votes cast (*New York Times*, 6 April 2005). As most of this support threatened to come through defections from parties on the left, prime minister Göran Persson (SAP) suggested that the new feminist group could allow a right-wing coalition into power "through the back door" (Castle 2005). The first party conference organized by FI, however, led to large-scale defections from the party, as well as steep decline in voter support, given that many framed FI as a platform for radical feminist ideas that did not resonate with the larger public (Simonsson 2005). In the end, the party garnered less than 1 percent of the popular vote and won no seats in the new parliament. All the same, women's representation increased two more percentage points to 47 percent (Inter-Parliamentary Union 2008a), with all parties electing more than 30 percent women, five parties more than 40 percent and four parties 50 percent or more (Sveriges Riksdag 2006). This roughly equal divide was mirrored among those who won seats through personal votes, who consisted of three women and three men (Svensson 2006). Taken together, these various patterns indicate that while some parties in Sweden are still more willing than others to promote women, these differences have narrowed substantially over time.

Varannan Damernas *and Women's Political Representation in Sweden*

Efforts to promote women's representation in Sweden, therefore, have occurred primarily at the party level, with women's groups inside and outside the parties pressing for increasingly stronger measures to ensure the selection of female candidates. Existing research, particularly by non-Swedish scholars, frequently attributes these successes to women's relatively high social and economic status or to the presence of gender quotas (cf. Bystydzienski 1995; Phillips 1995). The narrative of events presented here, however, reveals that women began to mobilize for increased representation as early as the 1920s, when women enjoyed few of the benefits associated with the Swedish welfare state and, in fact, the state actively reinforced the distinction between public roles for men and private roles for women through public policy (Hirdman 1990). Further, until the 1980s, most parties—and most women—rejected gender quotas as a measure to improve women's access to political office. Many preferred instead to adopt more informal policies establishing goals or targets for the selection of female candidates, with the threat to institute formal quotas if these goals and targets were not met. When quotas were adopted by some parties in the 1980s and 1990s, consequently, they served more to consolidate women's gains, rather than to motivate them (Dahlerup and Freidenvall 2005). A broader temporal lens thus uncovers a relatively continuous process of mobilization on the part of women from the 1920s to the 1990s to ensure that political parties not only nominated women, but also placed women in winnable positions on the party lists. Women radicalized these demands in some parties, but not in others, leading to varying degrees of practical and normative reform and, in turn, slightly uneven progress across the parties in terms of the proportion of women elected to parliament. Notwithstanding these differences, recruitment patterns across the Swedish parties have converged increasingly over time, with parties undergoing similar sequences of harmonizing reform that have adjusted the practices and norms of candidate selection to the features of the electoral system to produce one of the most gender equal parliaments in the world today (see table 5.3).

When proposals to institute a policy of alternation first appeared in Sweden in the early 1990s, they emerged in a context in which women had long mobilized for increased representation, but hesitated to demand formal quotas out of the belief that such measures were unnecessary and even counterproductive. As a result, in the period leading up to 1991, systemic institutions did not change but practical institutions shifted dramatically, as women politicized "sex" as a central criterion of candidate selection. Women's campaigns also succeeded in reshaping normative institutions to a certain degree by improving the proportion of women each party considered necessary for "women" to be adequately "represented," from one woman per list to at least 40 percent. However, they continued to struggle with reigning normative perceptions regarding "quotas," which many parties—and women's sections—continued to view as undemocratic and as implying the selection of unqualified women. All the same, the combination of favorable systemic institutions with new practical institutions and partially reformed normative institutions led to a dramatic increase in women's representation from 1 percent in 1921 to 38 percent in 1988 (Inter-Parliamentary Union 1995, 236).

Table 5.3. Quota Reforms and Institutional Configurations in Sweden

Systemic Institutions	Practical Institutions	Normative Institutions
Period 1 (1921–1972):		
PR electoral system	"Sex" as relevant criteria Placement in winnable and unwinnable positions on party lists	Equality before the law and partial equality of results Representation as politics of ideas and partial politics of presence
Period 2 (1972–1993):		
PR electoral system	"Sex" as central organizing principle of candidate lists Placement in more winnable positions on party lists	Equality before the law and equality of results Representation as politics of presence
Period 3 (1993–present):		
PR electoral system Some personal voting	"Sex" as central organizing principle of candidate lists Placement in winnable positions on party lists	Equality before the law and equality of results Representation as politics of presence

The decline in the number of women elected to parliament after elections in 1991, however, led women across the political spectrum to organize in new ways to pressure parties to place more female candidates in safe seats on party lists. Given the strong normative aversion to "quotas" in all the parties, they pressed elites to adopt the principle of *varannan damernas*, which they stressed was not so much a quota as a method for achieving gender balance by alternating between women and men. By the late 1990s, most parties applied alternation, but differed to the extent that they treated this policy as a recommendation or as a quota. These reforms refined existing practical institutions by designating "sex" as a central organizing principle for the entire candidate list, above more traditional considerations like class, age, geography, and occupation. At the same time, they altered reigning normative institutions by transforming calls for proportionate representation to demands for equal representation. Lingering ambivalence over the term "quota," nonetheless, reflected continued normative resistance among many elites to any sort of positive action that might create unfair advantages for one sex over the other. The light-hearted reference to a dance floor tradition, however, enabled supporters to frame a policy that was essentially a 50 percent quota as a measure aimed only at equal division and sharing of political power, a more radical claim for equal representation but one more consistent with reigning normative institutions.

Parties made varying degrees of commitment to the principle of *varannan damernas* during elections in 1994, 1998, 2002, and 2006. While some were more successful than others in meeting their stated goals, most parties elected equal numbers of women and men by 2006, with the only major exceptions being various right-wing parties that continue to resist strict gender quotas. However, a slight change in the electoral system to allow a limited degree of personal voting enabled voters to compensate for some of these shortcomings in several elections by casting personal votes for women, resulting in their election despite being placed quite far down their respective party lists. Together, these patterns indicate varying degrees of practical and normative reform across political formations, although all parties to a certain extent have revised their criteria for candidate selection and their willingness to intervene in local selection processes. In interaction with existing systemic institutions, these shifts have enabled most parties to make relatively similar progress in promoting women's representation, such that women now make up more than 47 percent of the Swedish parliament. These successes have attracted a great deal of international attention and, in turn, have assumed an important role in world wide discussions on women and politics. Indeed, misconceptions about the role of gender quotas in Sweden have sparked and informed quota debates in regions around the world, leading proponents to point to Sweden—nonetheless accurately—as an example of the power of political action in promoting equal representation.

All-Women Shortlists, Twinning, and Zipping in the United Kingdom

Campaigns for the adoption and implementation of gender quotas in the UK reach back more than twenty years, as the first attempts to require women on constituency shortlists surfaced in the early 1980s and the most recent reforms were integrated into party practices in 2007. During this time, the actors involved in quota campaigns have included civil society actors like social movement organizations, women's movement organizations, women inside the parties, cross-party women's networks, and individual male aspirants; state and party actors like members of parliament (MPs), party leaders, party congresses, trade unions, and the courts; and international and trans-national actors like international organizations and transnational political party networks. Involved at various points in these campaigns, these actors have pursued or rejected quotas for a range of different reasons, including normative consistency with party ideology, attempts to make electoral gains among female voters, and concerns to defend particular normative definitions of the principle of equality. Following a court decision in 1996 that declared a specific type of party quota—known as 'all-women shortlists'—to be illegal, both advocates and opponents focused on the normative dimensions of reform to bolster their arguments for and against positive action. This legal atmosphere constrained but also created opportunities for parties in the run-up to elections for the new devolved assemblies in Scotland and Wales in the late 1990s, whose quota strategies—known as "twinning" and "zipping"—not only conformed to reigning principles of equality, but were also tailored by individual parties to particular aspects of the mixed electoral system, producing high numbers of female representatives. Continuing debates over norms at the UK level, however, led national campaigners to concentrate exclusively on amending the terms of the Sex Discrimination Act to allow positive action in candidate selection. Combined with enduring systemic and practical barriers, this permissive normative reform has enabled parties to exercise a great deal of discretion with regard to candidate selection, with mixed results across the various political parties.

Antecedents to All-Women Shortlists, Twinning, and Zipping

All-women shortlists emerged in the UK in the early 1990s as a unique solution for ensuring the selection of female candidates in a first-past-the-post (FPTP) electoral system by requiring that final lists of candidates—or "shortlists"—in certain electoral districts be composed entirely of women. This policy, as well as later solutions known as twinning and zipping, grew out of earlier efforts by feminists to get parties to pay more attention to female voters by promoting female candidates. For most of the twentieth century, women were active in the two main political parties, Labour and Conservative, but were rarely given the opportunity to run for political office. Various efforts by women inside the Labour Party to mobilize for the selection of more female candidates in the mid-1970s did not get very far. Rather, both parties continued to nominate very few women and place them in districts where they were unlikely to be elected (Rasmussen 1983; Vallance 1984). The situation shifted in the early 1980s, however, as several new parties emerged and Labour experienced successive electoral defeats, leading it to revise its image as a working man's party.

The first party in the UK to pass a measure to promote women's representation was the Social Democratic Party (SDP). Formed in 1980, the SDP portrayed itself as a new type of party, concerned with promoting the interests of women, as opposed to Labour, which it claimed sought only to protect the interests of organized male workers (Perrigo 1996). In 1981, the party congress approved a resolution that at least one woman be included on every candidate shortlist. This policy was then increased to at least two women per shortlist in the run-up to elections in 1983. Two years later, another new party, the Liberal Party, emerged and passed a similar resolution that at least one woman be included on every candidate shortlist (Coote and Pattullo 1990). When the two parties merged to form the Liberal Democrats in 1988, they agreed—when reconciling their respective party programs—to retain the compulsory shortlisting policy (Lovenduski and Randall 1993).

The Labour Party was the third to establish a goal to nominate more female candidates, when its party conference decided in 1987 that in districts where a woman had been nominated, at least one woman had to be included on the shortlist for constituency selection. The issue had first been raised inside the party in the early 1970s. At the time, however, the party concluded that the primary responsibility for women's underrepresentation lay not in the party structure but in the organization and traditions of society at large (Brooks, Eagle, and Short 1990). Nonetheless, the issue resurfaced in the late 1970s as more and more feminists became active in the party and formed the Women's Action Committee (WAC) to press for changes in the party constitution to promote women in positions of power both inside and outside the party. The party's traditional women's organization, the Labour Women's Conference, agreed in principle with these goals but initially opposed any attempts to require the inclusion of women on candidate shortlists. In 1982, however, it joined the WAC in supporting this proposal, contributing to a growing lobby within the party in favor of limited positive action for women in candidate selection. As Labour was in the midst of efforts to remodel both its policy positions and its internal organization, its National Executive Committee (NEC) responded to these demands in 1983 by establishing a goal to increase women's involvement at all levels of the party through various kinds of voluntary measures.

While the NEC continued to support an approach based on discretion, the party conference discussed and approved the compulsory shortlisting rule four years later. In cases where a woman was not shortlisted, the policy specified that the final name on the shortlist was to be dropped and a ballot held to determine which of the women nominated during the first phase should be included on the list. Although modest, it was adopted against the express wishes of the NEC, in large part because most of the trade unions, a large and powerful segment of the party organization, threw their support behind the measure. In 1989, the conference revisited the question and took the policy one step further by approving Composite 54, which accepted in principle that quotas were the only way to ensure the equal representation of women and men at all levels of the party. Delegates called on the NEC to present proposals for how such quotas might be applied for party committees, local delegations, the NEC, and the Shadow Cabinet, in time for the next party conference (Brooks, Eagle, and Short 1990). Despite support for quotas for internal party positions, however, delegates strongly opposed the use of quotas for the selection of candidates to parliament, preferring instead to retain the existing compulsory shortlisting rule, which guaranteed the nomination but not the election of more women (Russell 2003).

The Conservative Party, in contrast, did not consider any proposals to nominate or select more female candidates during this period. As the political party that traditionally attracted a high proportion of female voters, it felt little need to make special appeals to women. Nonetheless, at a more informal level, party selectors generally sought to include at least 10 percent women on the party's approved list of candidates (Vallance 1984).

The Origins and Adoption of All-Women Shortlists

These tentative efforts to ensure the nomination of more female candidates produced a slight increase in the number of women elected to parliament in all the parties over the course of the 1980s. All the same, these proportions remained extremely low in international perspective and thus compelled Labour women to look abroad for examples of successful efforts to increase women's representation. Through their participation in meetings of the Socialist International (SI), a worldwide association of socialist, social democratic, and labor parties, they learned of a series of recommendations within the organization in support of gender quotas. They became acquainted with the dramatic gains made by women in the Nordic countries as a result of positive action, and contacts with women in other socialist and social democratic parties in Western Europe revealed to them that many of these parties had already adopted gender quotas, often leading to major changes in the proportions of women elected to national parliaments (McDougall 1998; Short 1996). In light of these experiences, several women began to lobby for similar measures in the Labour Party. They distributed a pamphlet at the party conference in 1990, which recognized the need for internal party quotas but also stressed the importance of introducing all-women shortlists (AWS) for the selection of candidates to parliament, a demand that the party conference had rejected in 1989. To strengthen their case, they pointed to the results of a consultation carried out by the NEC a year earlier, which uncovered strong support for quotas in all sectors of the party. They also outlined the findings of a poll conducted by the Shadow Communications Agency, which found that British women identified strongly with many of the party's women-friendly policy positions, but associated these positions with the Conservatives, as they regarded Labour as a party more oriented around male concerns (Brooks, Eagle, and Short 1990).

Although some inside the party remained convinced that a switch to a one-member-one-vote system (OMOV) was the solution to women's underrepresentation, the conference that year agreed to a set of concrete goals, following a process of consultation with all party organizations and affiliates, that established a 40 percent quota for women in all positions inside the party and set a target of 50 percent women in the party's delegation to parliament within ten years or three general elections. Although the party conference did not recommend any specific strategies for achieving this target, the NEC urged constituency parties to adopt AWS, particularly in those seats where a Labour MP was retiring. However, because most of the local parties had already selected the candidates to contest safe seats, only one AWS was considered before the 1992 elections, and it was in a marginal seat (Eagle and Lovenduski 1998). At the same time, several local party organizations expressed strong opposition to any changes in the existing selection procedures (Lovenduski 1999). For this reason, delegates to the party conference in 1991 spent a considerable amount of time discussing rule changes for achieving internal party quotas, but remained undecided on the issue of selecting female candidates to parliament (Eagle and Lovenduski 1998).

The consequences of a stated commitment to recruit more female candidates, combined with the lack of a formal quota policy, became obvious during elections the following year. Labour fielded a relatively high number of female candidates, 138 compared with 38 among Conservatives and 143 among Liberal Democrats, but registered only a minor increase in the number of women actually elected, as local parties had placed most of these women in unwinnable seats (Russell 2003, 69). Perhaps more shocking to the party was its fourth consecutive loss to the Conservatives, despite predictions that it might finally return to power after thirteen years in opposition. Initial analyses of the elections revealed a significant gender gap in support, with women remaining more likely than men to vote for the Conservatives (Perrigo 1999). The reason for this gap became apparent in focus groups, which showed that women continued to view Labour as the most male-dominated party, despite its efforts to foster a more women-friendly policy image. The party leadership therefore resolved to step up its efforts by following the advice of the Shadow Communications Agency, whose research suggested that the best means for expanding support among female voters was to give women more power inside the party, especially through nominating more female candidates. Women inside the party stressed that any new policy had to target the seats that Labour was likely to win, since the proportion of women elected to parliament in 1992 had increased only slightly from 6 percent to 9 percent, despite a major increase in the overall number of female candidates (Eagle and Lovenduski 1998).

In search of concrete proposals, the party leadership turned to Clare Short, then chair of the NEC Women's Committee, to devise a policy for the selection of female candidates. After conferring with a number of senior women within the party, she concluded that the only realistic policy was to group constituencies regionally and to require that, within each group, AWS be used to select candidates in half of all vacant seats that the party was likely to win, including seats where a Labour MP was retiring. A number of party feminists had wanted the leadership to require AWS in all vacant and winnable seats until gender balance was achieved. However, aware of the importance of local party autonomy and the interests of popular male candidates, Short offered the 50 percent policy as a compromise solution that would increase the number of women in safe seats at the same time that it would preserve some discretion for local parties, as well as opportunities for men to contest safe seats. The recommendation was supported by the party leader and the chair of the Organisation Committee, who presented it to the 1993 party conference as part of a broader package of proposed changes to the party constitution.

Despite concerns to increase women's representation, the main subject of debate at the conference revolved around whether or not to OMOV, a system that would do away with collective voting at party conferences and thus transform relations between the trade unions and the party at large. As such, the proposal to adopt AWS did not receive very much public attention at the conference.[9] Behind the scenes, however, women mobilized to get various unions behind the measure. For reasons specific to each organization, some unions backed OMOV but not AWS, while others supported AWS but not OMOV. Yet, the presence of both in the same package of reforms required unions to vote in favor of—or against—both policies. By the morning of the vote, only the Manufacturing, Science, and Finance Trade Union (MSF) was undecided. Realizing that the vote might go either way, two other unions presented a last minute resolution to enable a second vote on AWS in case the overall package was rejected. The MSF eventually decided to abstain because it did not want to impede AWS, although it strongly opposed OMOV. As a result, the package passed by a narrow margin and both reforms were instituted (McDougall 1998).

With most eyes focused on OMOV, the decision on AWS went almost unnoticed at the time by the party and the public at large. Once passed, however, it attracted strong criticism from many prominent party and union leaders, who argued that AWS would be difficult to implement at the grassroots level and would raise serious legal and procedural issues within the party (Lovenduski 1997). Indeed, some portrayed the adoption of AWS as the work of a small radical faction that had achieved its goals at the expense of the moderate majority, a view refuted by a number of studies showing strong support for quotas across all sections of the party (Norris 1997a). Despite this evidence, a small group, including some senior party officials and several MPs, campaigned against the policy and sought to reverse it at the party conference in 1994, arguing that the policy might cost the party the next elections. However, the most hostile reactions came from opposition parties and tabloid newspapers, which criticized AWS as a superficial solution that would have a perverse effect on women's status by privileging special treatment over equal treatment (Russell 2003; Squires 1996). A number of high profile lawyers stated publicly, furthermore, that they believed that AWS might be incompatible with the terms of the Sex Discrimination Act (SDA) of 1975. Aware of these objections, as well as the need to be sensitive to the autonomy of local parties in the process of candidate selection, the NEC asked party officers from the relevant constituencies in each region to organize "consensus meetings" to decide which seats would be subject to AWS (Studlar and McAllister 1998). While AWS remained controversial, most of these meetings managed to comply voluntarily with the provision, although the NEC did force one constituency to adopt an AWS when the regional meeting failed to agree (Russell 2003). As might be expected, resistance to the policy was strongest in cases where the previous candidate had been a man, who could no longer be shortlisted under the new rules (Norris 1997a). Nonetheless, by January 1996, thirty-three women had been selected to key target seats and two had been chosen to replace retiring Labour MPs (Eagle and Lovenduski 1998).

At that time, however, the party was forced to abandon the policy in light of a successful court challenge by Peter Jepson and Roger Dyas-Elliott, two male party members who had sought nomination in districts designated for AWS. Although earlier legal complaints had been dismissed by the Equal Opportunities Commission (EOC) on the grounds that it had no jurisdiction over the Labour Party, Jepson and Dyas-Elliott brought their case to the Industrial Tribunal in Leeds. In *Jepson and Dyas-Elliott v. The Labour Party and Others*, they argued that their exclusion from the process of candidate selection violated the terms of the SDA, which prohibited discrimination in the fields of employment, education, and goods, services, and premises. Representing their case, Jepson argued that the selection of candidates by parties was governed by Section 13 of the SDA, which prohibited sex discrimination in professional bodies in judging qualifications for employment. The defense lawyer for Labour responded that candidates for parliament were office-holders, not employees, and thus were not governed by Section 13. Rather, regulations regarding candidate selection fell under Section 33, which allowed parties to make special provisions for one sex in the constitution, organization, and administration of the party.[10] This clause, the party maintained, permitted it to exclude potential male candidates from consideration from certain seats, an interpretation confirmed by the EOC (Russell 2000). As such, candidate selection was not subject to employment legislation and thus could not be judged by an industrial tribunal, but only by parliament and the system of electoral and high courts.

In giving its judgment, the Tribunal agreed that members of parliament did not have employment contracts, because they were ultimately chosen by the voters and not the parties. However, it argued that candidate selection did constitute a qualification for becoming an MP, since endorsement from a major party was essentially a prerequisite for winning political office. For that reason, the policy of AWS did violate the employment provisions of the SDA, since it did not allow men to be considered as candidates in districts designated for AWS. Supporters urged the party to appeal the decision to a higher court, but the party leadership decided that an appeal might not be worth the risk. This was because the judgment applied only to the two constituencies where Jepson and Dyas-Elliott had sought selection as candidates and, as such, did not affect the status of the thirty-five women who had already been selected elsewhere in the country on the basis of AWS. An appeal to a higher court would have applied to all constituencies and thus issued a binding decision for all of England and Wales. Given that the legal process might not conclude before the elections, the party decided simply to abandon the policy rather than foster an atmosphere of uncertainty surrounding all candidate selections, especially considering the high profile of the case and the largely negative attitude of the press toward AWS (Russell 2000; Russell 2003).

The Origins and Adoption of Twinning and Zipping

Despite these controversies, Labour came to power in May 1997 with an ambitious set of policy proposals to modernize British politics. In line with the party's campaign promises, one of the first items to reach the policy agenda was the establishment of a Scottish Parliament and a National Assembly for Wales. After voters approved these plans in referendums in September 1997, debates began in parliament regarding the specific details of these new institutions. In light of the ruling on AWS, female Labour MPs voiced concerns that women might be excluded, unless guarantees for women's representation were explicitly incorporated into the bills on the devolved assemblies. With the

support of her colleagues, one of these MPs introduced an amendment to the Government of Wales Bill in March 1998, proposing
that parties be exempt from the SDA when selecting candidates to
the National Assembly for Wales. Although the amendment gained
support from Plaid Cymru and the Liberal Democrats, it was soon
withdrawn by the MP who had submitted it on the request of the government. Several weeks later, another female Labour MP presented
a similar amendment to the Scotland Bill that referenced the United
Nations' Convention on the Elimination of All Forms of Discrimination Against Women (CEDAW) as a justification for positive action.
This proposal was supported by the Scottish National Party and the
Liberal Democrats, but was strongly opposed by the government,
which pointed to the European Court of Justice and the European
Union (EU) Equal Treatment Directive (ETD) to argue that it could not
guarantee that parties would be free from legal challenge, even if an
exemption could be made under British law. A memo leaked to *The
Guardian* suggested, further, that various members of government
believed that any change to accommodate quotas might violate the
European Convention on Human Rights, in addition to EU equality
law, although the secretary of state for Scotland did favor using the
Scotland Bill to introduce a broader amendment to the SDA (Russell
2000; Russell 2003). Despite these setbacks, women in both Scotland
and Wales persevered with their demands for representation, leading
several parties to reconsider quotas in candidate selection, even in
the face of legal uncertainty.

   In Scotland, a range of state and civil society groups had been
engaged in a cross-partisan campaign for a Scottish Assembly since
1988. After a small proportion of women were included in early deliberations set up to discuss and plan a future government of Scotland,
an internal working group was formed and proposed that one man
and one woman be elected from each constituency in order to guarantee equal representation in the new legislature. This "50:50 system" was embraced by women across the political spectrum, quickly
gained the support of most of the major unions, and was passed by a
large margin at the Scottish Labour Party conference in 1990. All the
same, early constitutional discussions ultimately could not agree on a
specific mechanism for achieving gender balance, as parties disagreed
among themselves regarding which electoral system to espouse. To
ensure that this commitment was not forgotten, women established
an extensive network known as the Scottish Women's Coordination Group. Stressing the need to include gender equality in future

Scottish institutions, they drew special attention to the relatively low level of female representation in Scotland as compared with many other countries in Western Europe, where positive action had led to dramatic improvements in the numbers of women elected to national parliaments (Brown 1996). To this end, they lobbied the parties and the Scottish Constitutional Convention to consider electoral arrangements and candidate selection procedures that would favor the election of women.

Following the referendum on devolution, an additional member (AMS) electoral system was approved for Scotland, which entailed seventy-three members being elected from single-member constituencies and fifty-six members being elected from party lists. Voters would cast two votes, one for a constituency seat and one for a party list, with the party list vote being used to improve the proportionality of the vote-to-seat ratio (Galatas 2004). To address concerns regarding women's representation, the EOC encouraged all parties to apply positive action, despite lingering ambiguities regarding the scope of the SDA, and contacted all parties for a meeting to discuss their candidate selection procedures. Although the EOC only met with the Scottish Labour Party and the Scottish Liberal Democrats, all parties—apart from the Conservatives—considered positive action, with many inside the parties wondering publicly whether quotas would violate national and EU antidiscrimination legislation (McDonald, Alexander, and Sutherland 2001).

In the end, only Scottish Labour adopted an explicit policy. Realizing that it would win most of its seats in constituency elections, the party focused on devising a mechanism to facilitate the election of women in single-member seats. Although women inside the party initially believed this measure would be AWS, the *Jepson* decision required them to search for an alternative scheme. Working around these legal constraints, they proposed "twinning" pairs of constituencies according to geography and winnability and then selecting a woman as the candidate for one of the constituencies and a man as the candidate for the other. They argued that this system would produce the same results as AWS, but would be more difficult to challenge on the basis of the SDA, as men would not be excluded from selection contests. Indeed, to prove he was a victim of sex discrimination, a man would need to pass through a series of hurdles to make it to the final shortlist and then lose out to a woman (Brown et al 2002; Russell, Mackay, and McAllister 2002). The party agreed to adopt this policy on a one-time basis, on the grounds that incumbency in subsequent elections would make twinning virtually impossible to apply (Squires 2004). Despite some tensions in practice as to how candidate selection should occur, the twinning policy was relatively uncontroversial within the party and faced no overt legal challenges in the run-up to the first Scottish Parliament elections in 1999 (Bradbury et al 2000).

The Scottish National Party (SNP) made various commitments to women's representation during the devolution campaign. Nonetheless, it did not discuss any specific mechanisms for gender balance until 1998, in the midst of preparations for the first elections to the new Scottish Parliament. In contrast to Labour, the SNP expected to win most of its seats through the regional lists. For this reason, the party's women's organization suggested "zipping" the party lists to alternate between women and men. Although it had the support of a number of influential figures inside the party, this proposal was rejected by a narrow margin at a party conference held in May 1998. Interestingly, opponents pointed less to potential legal obstacles to zipping than to the need to select candidates solely on the basis of merit, going so far as to ridicule suggestions that the SNP was compelled to respond to Labour's twinning policy with a positive action measure of its own. The party leadership, however, privately expressed concerns about the SNP's public image if the party failed to elect a substantial proportion of women, especially given its relative lack of support among female voters. Consequently, the party's National Election Committee wrote a letter to all local parties encouraging them to select female candidates by including at least one woman on every shortlist for constituency elections and by placing a number of women near the top of all party lists for regional elections (Bradbury et al 2000).

The other parties adopted more limited measures to promote women in the new parliament. While the Scottish Liberal Democrats publicly supported the principle of equal representation, most inside the party opposed any statutory restriction on the freedom of local parties to select their own candidates (Brown 1996). Aware that the party was likely to win seats in constituency elections and regional lists, leaders initially proposed that all shortlists for constituency seats be composed of two men and two women and all regional lists be "zipped" in order to compensate for any imbalances in the constituency selection and election process (Bradbury et al 2000). At the party conference in 1998, delegates approved the balanced shortlist provision for constituency elections but rejected the proposal to "zip" the regional lists, despite the support given to this measure by the party leader, on the grounds that such a policy might be vulnerable to a legal challenge under the terms of the SDA (Brown et al 2002). The Scottish Green Party considered quotas as early as 1989, when the party conference approved an emergency motion to apply a 33 percent quota for women during the next general elections. However, because many local parties later opposed central interference in their candidate selection procedures, the party conference the following year agreed to a "trigger" policy, whereby local parties would inform the Party Council any time the proportion of women fell below 40 percent in the party membership, its local executive, or its choice of candidates. In these instances, the local party in question would be required to analyze the reasons behind the relative absence of women, as well as present plans for remedying the imbalance (Collie, Hoare, and Roddick 1991). The Scottish Conservative Party, for its part, remained opposed to any kind of positive action. It resolved not to devise any rules or procedures that would create an "artificial gender balance" among the candidates selected (Bradbury et al 2000).

In Wales, various state and civil society groups had been mobilizing for constitutional reform since 1987, but the devolution campaign was much less extensive than it had been in Scotland. Early declarations did not include any references to gender equality, leading a small group of women in the parties and in the state equality agencies to argue for a commitment to gender balance among those elected to a future Welsh assembly (Chaney 2003). In 1997, following the voter referendum, an AMS electoral system was also approved for Wales, with forty members being elected from single-member constituencies and twenty members being elected from regional lists. As in Scotland, all parties except the Conservatives debated positive action in relation to the aspect of the electoral system where they expected to win the most seats, with two parties—the Welsh Labour Party and Plaid Cymru—ultimately deciding to adopt formal policies to promote the election of women.

The leaders of Welsh Labour, in contrast to their British and Scottish counterparts, initially expressed strong hostility toward any form of positive action in candidate selection. When the new electoral system was introduced, some in the party suggested a compromise solution that would use the regional lists to compensate for under-representation of women in constituency seats. However, this proposal was quickly dismissed, given that the party expected to win few of the list-based seats. Given this impasse, the issue passed to the British Labour Party conference in 1997, where mostly English delegates, who were not to be affected at all by the decision, endorsed twinning as the only feasible option in Wales. Despite this pressure, the party executive in Wales was not willing to impose twinning and decided to defer the decision to the Welsh party conference in 1998, where delegates approved the measure by a narrow margin, with as many as nineteen of the forty constituency parties and several important trade unions opposing the policy (Russell, Mackay, and McAllister 2002). Although twinning would apply only to the first elections to the National Assembly for Wales, opponents sought to undermine the policy by threatening legal action and refusing to cooperate at the constituency level. To facilitate compliance, party leaders asked local parties to make their own suggestions for implementation, a tactic that resulted in a number of pairings that were geographically dis-perse and not equally winnable. When six local parties refused to cooperate, however, the leadership imposed twinning pairs against local opposition (Bradbury et al 2000; Edwards and McAllister 2002). Despite these struggles, legal challenges never materialized, although opponents expressed some hostility toward the women who were selected through the twinning policy (Russell, Mackay, and McAllister 2002).

Plaid Cymru, the Party for Wales, had never elected a single female MP to the House of Commons (Russell 2000, 11), but pressure from the women's section led to recommendations that the party adopt the goal of 50 percent female candidates to a future Welsh Assembly. Uncertain about the outcome of the referendum on devolution, how-ever, the party did not address candidate selection as an issue at its annual conference, shifting the responsibility for devising the selec-tion procedures to the party's National Council. Witnessing the sharp divisions inside Labour, and concerned about a possible conservative reaction within Plaid Cymru itself (Russell, Mackay, and McAllister 2002), the Council rejected twinning but accepted the need to use the regional lists to compensate for any shortcomings in the elec-tion of women to the constituency seats. Nonetheless, it could not reach a consensus regarding the exact placement of female candidates on these lists and referred the final decision to the NEC. Anticipat-ing that four constituency seats were likely to be won by men, the NEC decided that women would occupy the first and third places on the five regional lists so that at least five women would be elected to balance out the four men. This proposal attracted criticism, but the underrepresentation of women among constituency candidates appeared to persuade many that it was necessary, if not desirable

(Bradbury et al 2000). Entirely absent from these discussions, interestingly, were any threats or concerns about legal action, as few party members were inclined to challenge the party through the "English" legal system (Russell 2000).

Following the referendum, the Welsh Liberal Democrats debated a number of options for promoting women's participation in the new Welsh Assembly. The proposals presented to the party conference in 1998 included "constituency zipping" in the single-member seats, with every other seat assigned to a female candidate, and "list zipping" on the regional lists, with every other member of the list being a woman. Delegates rejected both suggestions by an overwhelming margin, however, in favor of balanced shortlists for constituency elections only, the same solution adopted by the Liberal Democrats in Scotland. The Welsh Conservatives, in contrast, remained firmly opposed to positive action of any type, stressing the need to select candidates solely on the basis of merit (Bradbury et al 2000; Russell, Mackay, and McAllister 2002).

The Implementation of All-Women Shortlists, Twinning, and Zipping

Although the British Labour Party leadership chose not to appeal the decision in *Jepson*, it did establish a working group to identify other ways of promoting the nomination and selection of women to the remaining vacant seats (Norris 1997a). The effects of this strategy were limited, since most selection committees simply reverted to the candidate who had fought the seat in 1992, who was usually a man (Lovenduski 1997). However, because the party did not alter any of the selections that took place before January 1996, women formed 25 percent of all Labour candidates and, following the party's landslide victory, made up 24 percent of all elected Labour MPs (Eagle and Lovenduski 1998, 7). As a result, the proportion of women in the House of Commons increased from 9 percent in 1992 to 18 percent in 1997 (see table 5.4), although the Conservatives and the Liberal Democrats both registered decreases in the number of women elected (Russell 2003, 71–72) (see table 5.5). This aggregate change sprang partly from the use of AWS, as all thirty-five women selected in this way won their seats. Five other women had been selected to replace sitting Labour MPs after the intervention of the national party, while eleven women won unexpectedly in marginal seats (Eagle and Lovenduski 1998; Russell 2003, 72). These results were met with great

Table 5.4. Women's Legislative Representation in the UK

House of Commons	
Year	Women (%)
1970	4.1
1974	3.6
1974	4.3
1979	3.0
1983	3.5
1987	6.3
1992	9.2
1997	18.2
2001	17.9
2005	19.5

Sources: Childs, Lovenduski, and Campbell (2005, 19); Inter-Parliamentary Union (1995, 254).

celebration around the country, thanks to efforts by various feminist groups to raise the profile of women during the elections. The women elected also became a central symbol of Tony Blair's campaign to modernize Labour—indeed, the British media referred to them as "Blair's Babes"—although Blair himself had never been a strong supporter of AWS.

The twinning and zipping policies adopted for Scottish and Welsh elections produced even more striking results. Although women constituted only 17 percent of Scottish MPs to Westminster in 1997,

Table 5.5. Women in Parliamentary Party Delegations in the UK

Year	Total (%)	Labour (%)	Conservative (%)	Liberal Democrat (%)	Others (%)
1983	3.5	4.8	3.3	0[a]	0
1987	6.3	9.2	4.5	4.5	8.7
1992	9.2	13.7	6.0	10.0	12.5
1997	18.2	24.2	7.9	6.5	10.0
2002	17.9	23.1	8.4	11.3	16.0
2005	19.8	27.7	8.6	16.1	9.7

Source: Childs, Lovenduski, and Campbell (2005, 19).

[a]Liberal Party and Social Democratic Party combined.

women won more than 37 percent of the seats in the first Scottish Parliament in 1999, 41 percent of all constituency seats and 32 percent of all regional list seats (Busby and MacLeod 2002, 32; Squires 2004, 10). Twinning was used to select Scottish Labour candidates for all constituencies with the exception of the four Highlands and Islands constituencies, leading to the election of twenty-eight women and twenty-eight men to the new Scottish Parliament (Lovenduski 2002, 21). Although the SNP did not adopt any formal measures, the informal suggestions made by party leaders resulted in women forming nearly one-third of all constituency candidates and being placed at the upper end of all regional lists (Brown et al 2002), producing 43 percent women among SNP delegates to the new Scottish Parliament. The three other parties selected very few female candidates, and most that were chosen were not placed in winnable seats and positions (Bradbury et al 2000). As a result, women constituted only a small proportion of Liberal Democrats, Conservatives, and Greens elected to the Scottish Parliament (see table 5.6).

Similar patterns emerged in Wales. Although women constituted only 3 percent of Welsh MPs to the House of Commons in 1997, they won 40 percent of the seats in the first National Assembly for Wales in 1999, 48 percent of all constituency seats and 25 percent of all regional list seats (Russell 2003, 73; Squires 2004, 11). The twinning strategy used by Welsh Labour, despite greater struggles in implementation than in Scotland, led to the election of women to more than 57 percent of the seats won by Labour in the new Welsh Assembly. Plaid Cymru applied a zipping policy for the first three positions on the regional lists, starting with a woman (Bradbury et al 2000). However, the party did better than anticipated in the constituency-based elections, where the party did not have a quota policy, thus resulting in the election of only 35 percent women overall. In contrast, the

Table 5.6. Women's Representation in the Scottish Parliament

Year	Total (%)	Labour (%)	Conservative (%)	Liberal Democrat (%)	SNP (%)
1999	37.0	50.0	17.0	12.0	43.0
2003	39.0	50.0	22.2	11.8	25.7
2007	34.1	50.0	29.4	12.5	27.7

Sources: Russell (2003, 76); Scottish Parliament (2007a); Scottish Parliament (2007b); Squires (2004, 11).

Table 5.7. Women's Representation in the National Assembly for Wales

Year	Total (%)	Labour (%)	Conservative (%)	Liberal Democrat (%)	Plaid Cymru (%)
1999	40.0	57.1	0	50.0	35.3
2003	50.0	63.3	18.2	50.0	50.0
2007	46.7	61.5	8.3	50.0	46.7

Sources: National Assembly for Wales (2007); Squires (2004, 11, 12).

Liberal Democrats—who had not adopted a full quota, but instead balanced shortlists for constituency-based elections—elected equal numbers of women and men, while the Conservatives elected no women at all (see table 5.7).

These various election results, combined with broader discussions of legal and constitutional reform, sparked a series of discussions starting in 1998 as to whether or not the government should amend the SDA to allow parties to pursue positive action in candidate selection. In addition to the *Jepson* decision, which raised the specter of legal challenges to any party that sought to implement policies to recruit more women, voices within the various parties expressed concerns that positive action might violate the EU's ETD, which mandated equal treatment in access to employment and promotion. However, after seeking the views of a range of different organizations, the EOC announced that developments in EU law regarding positive action, most notably in the Treaty of Amsterdam,[11] might open the way for measures to be introduced in the UK. Despite this opening, as well as some support from the Liberal Democrats and the leader of the Conservatives, the government's proposal to reform SDA was ultimately rejected by Labour Party officials on the grounds that an amendment might place the country in breach of European and human rights law. The following year, the interpretation of British nondiscrimination law put forward in the *Jepson* decision was reaffirmed by a second case, *Sawyer v. Ahsan*, which addressed racial discrimination in the process of candidate selection and hinged on the question of whether or not the selection of candidates was covered by employment legislation according to Section 12 of the Race Relations Act 1976. The appeals court agreed that being a local councilor was indeed a profession, binding all future employment tribunals to apply the Race Relations Act, and by extension the SDA, to the selection of candidates to all levels of political office (Russell 2000).

In this legal environment, few parties were able to agree on any form of positive action for women during preparations for general elections in 2001. Without AWS, many inside Labour began to worry that local parties would select only men in the seats where sitting Labour MPs were retiring, leading to a drop in the number of Labour women in the House of Commons. To avoid this, the party's General Secretary wrote to all constituencies to remind them of the party's goal from 1990 to select 50 percent female candidates within three general elections (Ward 2000b; Wintour 2000). Although many candidates had already been selected by early 2000, Joan Ruddock—an MP and Labour's ex-minister for women—initiated an Early Day Motion, signed by more than 100 MPs of all parties, and a Private Member's Bill, backed by a number of Labour MPs and several Liberal Democrats and Conservatives, calling for reform of the SDA to allow parties to pursue positive action in candidate selection (Russell 2003). While party leader Blair had earlier been skeptical regarding the use of AWS, these developments persuaded him to take a different approach, and he announced that he would be willing to seek legal change after the general elections if the constituencies continued to select mostly men (Ward 2000a; Ward 2000b).

Several months later, a report by the Constitution Unit at University College London, authored by Meg Russell (2000), analyzed a variety of proposals and concluded that reform of the SDA to allow parties to apply special measures for women would not in fact violate international law. Indeed, it found substantial support for positive action in human rights legislation, including the European Convention on Human Rights, the International Labor Organization Convention, and CEDAW. The report also noted that the EU had repeatedly supported the concept of positive action in its treaties, action programs, and court decisions. In fact, the European Commission had on two occasions explicitly stated that the selection of candidates did not fall under the purview of the ETD. If opponents continued to insist that candidate selection was covered under the terms of the ETD, however, the report highlighted a recent decision by the European Court of Justice in *Hellmut Marschall v. Land Nordrhein-Westfalen* to allow positive action in cases where women were underrepresented and no reasons specific to an individual male candidate tilted the balance in his favor. This decision in effect overturned *Eckhard Kalanke v. Freie Hansestadt Bremen*, which had restricted the scope of positive action permissible under the ETD by declaring that women could not be given absolute and unconditional priority over equally qualified men. If that was still not enough to convince opponents of the position of EU legislation on positive action, the report pointed to Article 141 of the Treaty of Amsterdam, which explicitly stated that the principle of "equal treatment" did not prohibit states from maintaining or adopting measures to enable members of the underrepresented sex to pursue a particular vocational activity. As treaties were primary legislation, and directives were a form of secondary legislation, this article had legal precedence over all interpretations of the ETD. However, while international and EU law permitted positive action, the report noted, it did not require positive action and in this sense overrule domestic law.

The British Labour Party addressed these findings at its annual conference in October 2000, where delegates endorsed a plan to allow parties to introduce measures to guarantee the selection of women and ethnic minorities in winnable seats. Although they included this commitment in their party manifesto, they simply required gender balanced shortlists for all vacant seats for elections in 2001, a policy that resulted in the selection of only four women among the thirty-nine candidates chosen to replace sitting Labour MPs (Russell 2003, 77). This meant that the proportion of new candidates who were women was lower in 2001 than in 1992 and 1997, leading some to conclude that balanced shortlists might in fact have been counterproductive, as they enabled constituency parties to comply fully with the quota while still selecting men (Fawcett Society 2001a; Squires 2004). The only other party to consider positive action was the Liberal Democrats, who ultimately decided only to require women on shortlists without any restrictions on actual candidate selection (Fawcett Society 2001b; Russell 2000). Although very few seats changed between parties, these patterns led to the first drop in women's representation in the UK since 1979, from slightly more than 18 percent in 1997 to slightly less than 18 percent in 2001 (Russell 2003, 77). In response, the Queen's Speech outlining the new Labour government's policy program included a promise to introduce reforms to the SDA to allow parties to take steps to increase women's representation, despite attempts by a number of important figures inside the party to exclude this commitment from the speech (Childs 2004; Russell 2003).

Shortly thereafter, the government submitted the Sex Discrimination (Election Candidates) Bill for debate in the newly elected House of Commons. This bill did not seek to compel parties to adopt positive action, but to exclude from the purview of the SDA any act taken by a political party to reduce inequality in the numbers of women and men elected at any level of political office. In spite of the bitter controversies that had emerged over the earlier policy of AWS, both opposition parties consciously decided not to object to the reform, a consensus that was made possible by the permissive, and not prescriptive, nature of the bill. The proposal thus passed all stages in both houses of parliament without a vote, a type of expedited passage normally reserved for entirely noncontroversial bills on topics of low public salience (Childs 2002a; Childs 2002b; Russell 2003). All the same, some MPs did question whether the reform was compatible with EU equality legislation, while some Conservatives tried unsuccessfully to introduce an amendment that would require individual male candidates with local connections to be considered even when parties sought to implement positive action strategies.[12] For the most part, however, the bill met with broad cross-party agreement, with most arguments for and against the bill being voiced by female MPs (Childs 2002b). With little media attention, the bill passed virtually unnoticed into law in February 2002, amending both the SDA and the Sex Discrimination (Northern Ireland) Order 1976 to allow parties to introduce positive action measures without any risk of legal challenge when selecting candidates for the House of Commons, the European Parliament, the Scottish Parliament, the National Assembly for Wales, and local government. Unusually, however, the bill contained a "sunset clause" stating that the Act would expire at the end of 2015—in time for at least three general elections to have taken place—unless a specific order was made to the contrary.

These reforms occurred as parties began to select candidates for the second elections to the Scottish Parliament and the National Assembly for Wales, creating new opportunities for parties to consider positive action. In Scotland, the Labour Party did not repeat its twinning strategy, as it expected few vacancies or changes in patterns of electoral support, but it did introduce a limited amount of positive action in its list selections by picking women to head its lists in the two areas where it stood the best chances of gaining new seats (MacDonnell 2003). The SNP, the Scottish Liberal Democrats, and the Scottish Conservatives, in contrast, all rejected positive action (Russell, Mackay, and McAllister 2002). Nonetheless, the percentage of women elected increased slightly, from 37 percent in 1999 to 39 percent in 2003, due largely to the effects of incumbency: the number of women elected to single-member constituencies remained stable, while the number of women elected to list seats increased by three (Squires 2004, 11). In Wales, Labour also did not repeat its twinning policy, but the party did decide to apply AWS in half of its vacant constituency seats. Plaid Cymru, for its part, strengthened its requirements for list elections by reserving the top two seats on all regional lists for women, rather than simply the first and third positions (Russell, Mackay, and McAllister 2002). Although no other parties changed their candidate selection policies, these shifts contributed to an increase in the proportion of women elected to the National Assembly for Wales, from 40 percent in 1999 to 50 percent in 2003 (Squires 2004, 12).

For parliamentary elections that took place in 2005, however, reform of the SDA caused all three major parties to initiate discussions as to whether or not to adopt any measures to recruit more female candidates. Labour agreed to apply AWS in at least half of all seats where incumbent Labour MPs were retiring, with the goal of electing at least 35 percent women. To facilitate implementation, the party asked all sitting MPs to indicate whether or not they planned to step down by the end of 2002. Their constituencies could then volunteer for an AWS, but if only a small number of constituencies complied, the NEC would impose AWS on unwilling districts in order to fulfill the party target. The constituencies where sitting MPs decided to retire after the deadline would automatically be assigned AWS (Childs 2004; Russell 2003). The Liberal Democrats considered AWS at their party conference in 2001, but rejected this measure in favor of a target of 40 percent female candidates in districts where sitting MPs were standing down and seats requiring a swing of less than 7.5 percent to win (Strickland et al 2001). Opponents of quotas viewed the decision as a victory and claimed that more training and support for female candidates would resolve the problem of underrepresentation, but some senior female MPs warned that the party might lose votes if it did not select enough female candidates as a result of this policy (Childs 2004; Ward 2001b). The Conservatives, finally, remained much more divided on the question of positive action. Some members called on the party to adopt quotas to ensure the election of more women to parliament, but even the milder efforts of the party chairman to persuade constituency parties to select women in winnable seats met with little or no response from local officials, who continued to select mainly men (Childs 2004; Russell 2003; Ward 2001a). The result was that 20 percent women were elected overall, with marked differences across the political parties: Labour elected close to 28 percent in its parliamentary delegation, the Liberal Democrats elected around 16 percent, and the Conservatives only 9 percent (Childs, Lovenduski, and Campbell 2005, 19).

Six months after these elections, which had entailed the third consecutive electoral defeat for the Conservatives, the party chose David Cameron as its new leader. Only minutes into his speech accepting the position, Cameron noted that it was important to change patterns of representation in the party (Campbell, Childs, and Lovenduski 2006). Although he was not the first Conservative leader to argue that the party would continue to lose female voters if they did not elect more women,[13] his efforts were distinct in that they were able to build on a campaign called Women2Win that had been launched by women inside the party the month before. As an alternative to AWS, these women proposed that the Conservatives create a list of fifty men and fifty women to stand in the one hundred most winnable seats, recognizing that while 118 female candidates had been fielded by the party in 2005, ninety-three of these were in seats the party was unlikely to win (*The Independent*, 24 November 2005). Less than a week after his election, Cameron therefore set out a plan that involved adoption of a "priority list" of aspirant candidates—to consist of at least 50 percent women and a "significant" proportion of black, minority ethnic, and disabled candidates—from which Conservative-held and target constituencies would be required to select their candidates (Campbell, Childs, and Lovenduski 2006).

By August 2006, the central party executive had drawn up an "A-list" of 150 candidates—including nearly 60 percent women—but many constituency parties continued to chose local candidates instead. For this reason, Cameron announced new plans to require associations in the party's target seats to include at least two women on the final shortlists of four candidates considered in their constituencies. This policy involved an important change to the process of candidate selection itself: whereas the local party executive previously drew up a shortlist which members voted on, members were now allowed only to choose the final four names on the shortlist, two of whom needed to be women, before the executive alone selected the candidate (*Daily Telegraph*, 21 August 2006). In January 2007, Cameron officially dropped the A-list policy in favor a general list of six hundred candidates approved to stand for the party, but still required local parties to make certain that half the candidates that they were considering at every stage were women, producing gender balanced shortlists of two men and two women. The party declared, nonetheless, that the A-list had been a success as it had helped ensure that nearly 40 percent of the candidates selected thus far were women (*The Times*, 24 January 2007).

In elections to the Scottish Parliament and National Assembly for Wales held later that same year, women's representation declined slightly in both assemblies. In Scotland, the proportion of women fell from 39 percent in 2003 to 34 percent in 2007. Interestingly, all parties elected a higher percentage of women to their parliamentary delegations than they had in 2003 (Scottish Parliament 2007a; Scottish Parliament 2007b). However, the distribution of these seats shifted in significant ways, with the SNP—a party that elected only 28 percent women—gaining twenty seats, while Labour—which had the highest proportion of women elected, 50 percent—lost four. Similar patterns prevailed in Wales, as women's representation dropped from 50 percent to 47 percent, at the same time that Labour lost three seats, and Plaid Cymru and the Conservatives gained three seats and one seat, respectively. While both Labour and Plaid Cymru elected fewer women than before, moving from 63 percent to 62 percent and 50 percent to 47 percent, the most significant drop was among Conservatives, from 18 percent to 8 percent (National Assembly for Wales 2007). These dynamics, viewed together with developments for Westminster, indicate ongoing efforts to promote women's representation in the UK, even amongst those parties most resistant to positive action strategies. At the same time, however, they suggest that, due to important variations among parties' commitments, the numbers of women elected to various political bodies continue to be subject to changing electoral fortunes, as parties on opposite sides of quota debates win or lose in relation to their opponents.

All-Women Shortlists, Twinning, and Zipping and Women's Political Representation in the United Kingdom

Campaigns to promote women's representation in the UK have thus unfolded at a number of different levels, with varying degrees of success in the adoption and implementation of quota policies. Comparative research generally focuses on the electoral system as a primary reason for the low numbers of women in British politics, in part due to the complicated nature of applying positive action measures in single-member districts (Caul 1999). The narrative of events outlined in this chapter, however, reveals that parties in Westminster and the devolved assemblies have devised a series of creative solutions in light of these constraints in order to increase the number of women placed in winnable districts and safe seats on party lists. These tactics, nonetheless, sparked intense debate among various groups, which supported or opposed quotas on a range of different grounds. At the UK level, a successful legal challenge led quota advocates to identify the normative definition of equality and equal treatment as the main barrier to change, causing them to overlook possibilities for systemic and practical reform. In Scotland and Wales, in contrast, debates over the legal status of quotas intersected with campaigns for devolution, which presented an opportunity for supporters to frame quota policies as a crucial element of democratic innovation, leading several parties to adapt their practices and norms of candidate selection to features of the new electoral system. These distinct responses to normative ambiguity point to the unpredictable nature of disjointed sequences of reform, which typically entail competition and discord across institutions, but in some cases prove to be a catalyst for subsequent institutional configurational change, explaining the low percentage of women in the House of Commons (see table 5.8) in

Table 5.8. Quota Reforms and Institutional Configurations in the UK

Systemic Institutions	Practical Institutions	Normative Institutions
Period 1 (1918–1993):		
FPTP electoral system	"Sex" as irrelevant criteria Placement in unwinnable districts	Equality before the law Representation as politics of ideas
Period 2 (1993–2002):		
FPTP electoral system	"Sex" as irrelevant and relevant criteria Placement in winnable and unwinnable districts	Equality before the law and partial equality of results Representation as politics of ideas and partial politics of presence
Period 3 (2002–present):		
FPTP electoral system	"Sex" as irrelevant and relevant criteria Placement in winnable and unwinnable districts	Equality before the law and equality of results Representation as politics of ideas and partial politics of presence

Table 5.9. Quota Reforms and Institutional Configurations in Scotland and Wales

Systemic Institutions	Practical Institutions	Normative Institutions
Period 1 (1998–2002):		
AMS electoral system	"Sex" as irrelevant and relevant criteria Placement in winnable and unwinnable districts and winnable and unwinnable positions on party lists	Equality before the law and equality of results Representation as politics of ideas and politics of presence
Period 2 (2002–present):		
AMS electoral system	"Sex" relevant criteria Placement in winnable districts and winnable positions on party lists	Equality of results Representation as politics of presence

comparison to the high proportions of women in the Scottish Parliament and National Assembly for Wales (see table 5.9).

Proposals to establish a policy of AWS were first voiced in the Labour Party in the late 1980s, at a time when all institutions of candidate recruitment militated strongly against the selection of women: unfavorable systemic institutions, namely a first-past-the-post electoral system organized around single-member districts, combined with practices and norms that did not recognize "sex" as a central category of political representation. As a consequence, the percentage of women in the House of Commons remained far below the world average, around 6 percent in the late 1980s. Through contacts with women in other socialist parties, women inside the party grew familiar with successful quota policies elsewhere in Europe. While they gained a string of concessions from the party, they were initially unable to gain any concrete practical reforms given strong normative resistance within certain sectors of the party. However, consecutive electoral defeats in the early 1990s led the party to rethink its approach, eventually culminating in the adoption of AWS in half of all vacant seats that the party was likely to win, a strategy that women inside the party had suggested in light of features of the electoral system that made other kinds of quota policies impossible to apply. Once

passed, the policy became controversial on both practical and normative grounds, leading some local parties to resist AWS and other
party members to challenge the policy in court. When AWS were
overturned, a number of experts claimed that the decision was based
on an incorrect interpretation of the law, but party leaders agreed to
discontinue the policy, leading to reversals with regard to both practical and normative institutions.

The normative controversy over AWS continued to loom after the
elections, with opponents of quotas responding to all efforts to institute them by pointing to various articles of national and international
law. Despite this atmosphere of legal uncertainty, parties in both
Scotland and Wales took steps to promote women's representation
in the new assemblies, yet with great care to remain within the letter of
the law. At the same time, they adapted their quota strategies to the
aspect of the new electoral systems where they were likely to garner
the most seats: the Labour parties employed a twinning strategy to
ensure that equal numbers of women and men would be elected to
constituency seats, while the SNP and Plaid Cymru considered mechanisms that would maximize the election of women from party lists.
Although both sets of decisions reflected efforts to bring systemic,
practical, and normative institutions together in mutual reinforcing
ways, the resulting configurations explain why the election of women
in both assemblies was higher in single-member districts: the winner-
take-all structure of these contests, combined with the electoral
strength of Labour, enabled party selectors to predict with greater
confidence which districts the party was likely to win, and thus
better pinpoint where female candidates should be placed to meet
the goal of equal representation. Regional list contests, in contrast,
entailed some unanticipated victories or losses, leading smaller parties to under- or over-estimate the number of candidates they would
elect, leading to greater or lesser degrees of gender imbalance despite
policies of alternation. Over the course of three election cycles, these
patterns have endured, despite small fluctuations in the numbers of
women elected.

At the UK level, in contrast, the successful legal challenge to quotas
caused supporters to identify the interpretation of certain articles of
the SDA as the main barrier to positive action in candidate selection,
and by extension, to further increases in the number of women elected
to the House of Commons. The government considered amending the
SDA as early as 1998, but doubts over the legality of positive action
ultimately persuaded it to abandon these plans. A decrease in the

number of women elected to parliament in 2001, combined with a series of new legal arguments, however, convinced the government to introduce a new bill that would allow, but not compel, parties to adopt measures to reduce inequalities in representation. While the focus on normative reform stemmed from a desire to clarify the legal ambiguities informing discussions on positive action, the need to approve the bill in both houses of parliament forced advocates to settle for this more permissive formulation, in effect limiting the scope for normative change. At the same time, the debate bracketed the issue of systemic and practical reform, opening the way for parties to react as they saw fit to the new provision. As such, all three major parties have responded in distinct ways: Labour has engaged in full practical reform by reintroducing AWS; Liberal Democrats have pursued partial practical reform by establishing targets for the election of women; and Conservatives initially avoided but have now begun to implement limited practical reforms by requiring equal numbers of men and women on candidate shortlists. These variations indicate the ongoing presence of multiple institutional configurations with the British party system, suggesting that patterns of candidate selection are likely to continue to diverge across parties in the next general elections.

Conclusions

Campaigns to establish party quotas have thus followed two distinct trajectories in Sweden and the UK: reforms in Sweden have been harmonizing, adjusting institutions of candidate selection to the goal of equal representation, while reforms in the UK have been disjointed, engendering conflict across institutions with unpredictable results across parties and levels of government. These patterns confirm the argument made in the previous chapter that harmonizing sequences are more effective than disjointed sequences in increasing women's representation. However, the comparison of these two cases also provides several more specific insights for parties and grassroots campaigns contemplating quota reform. Most obviously, it reveals that party quotas rarely have uniform effects on women's representation. Indeed, analyzing the origins and impact of party quotas requires two distinct levels of analysis—the party level and the party-system level—that together explain why particular policies have a greater or lesser impact on the overall numbers of women elected to parliament.

In Sweden, almost all parties have adopted quotas or quota-like measures that privilege "sex" as a criteria for candidate selection, provisions that have gradually expanded over the last twenty years through dynamics of party competition. In the UK, in contrast, only a single party has consistently adopted quotas at all levels of government. As a result, the increase in the number of women elected to the House of Commons is due almost entirely to changes in the recruitment patterns of the Labour Party. In the devolved assemblies, these patterns are quite different: several parties have adopted quotas or quota-like measures such that women now constitute nearly one-half of all members of the Scottish Parliament and the National Assembly for Wales.

These divergent paths of reform, in turn, offer a second important insight for parties that have experienced setbacks in their efforts to institute gender quotas. While disjointed sequences of reform typically lead advocates to focus on single institutions in an attempt to overcome an earlier defeat, they also present opportunities to pursue broader institutional configurational change. The cases of Scotland and Wales indicate that new campaigns may have a strong positive impact on the number of women elected. Although reform of the SDA provided a similar opportunity for parties at the UK level, only Labour has pledged to revise its selection procedures to any significant degree. These developments suggest that disjointed sequences may eventually become harmonizing at the system or the party level, with a range of different effects on women's representation. Comparing these various campaigns over time, therefore, uncovers several possible relationships between institutional reform and the impact of gender quotas: tentative practical reforms in some parties in Sweden gave way to increasingly stronger practical and normative reforms across all parties, producing nearly equal representation, while limited practical reforms in one party in the UK provoked normative resistance and reform, leading to decreases and increases in women's representation. These patterns highlight the multifaceted struggles behind the adoption, implementation, and impact of quota provisions, pointing again to the central role of political action in achieving and subverting quota reform.

Legislative Quotas in Argentina and France

In recent years an increasing number of national parliaments have adopted legislative quotas by reforming constitutions and electoral laws to state or require that political parties nominate a certain percentage of women among their candidates. These measures thus aim to change normative institutions by revising the meanings of equality and representation underlying processes of candidate selection to permit positive action, foster more equal results, and recognize "sex" as a political identity. In this way, they differ from reserved seats in that they address party selection practices, rather than the final proportion of women in parliament, and from party quotas in that they apply to all parties within a given country, rather than simply those that choose to adopt quotas. They are also the newest type of candidate gender quota, appearing first only in the 1990s as a measure for promoting women's access to political office. With some exceptions, legislative quotas tend to be found in developing countries, particularly in Latin America, and post-conflict societies, primarily in Southeastern Europe, the Middle East, and Africa. They are increasingly preferred by countries currently debating quota adoption, many of whom are seeking a "fast track" to more balanced numbers of women and men in parliament (cf. Dahlerup and Freidenvall 2005).

To explore how quota laws have reached the political agenda in various countries, as well as possible reasons for variations in their effects, this chapter compares the cases of Argentina and France, where campaigns for legislative quotas began in the late 1980s and early 1990s. In 1990, before quotas were adopted, these two countries had almost identical proportions of women in parliament: women constituted 6 percent of the Argentine Chamber of Deputies and 7 percent of the French National Assembly (Inter-Parliamentary Union 1995, 58, 121). By 2008, after both countries had adopted quotas and applied them in several electoral cycles, these proportions had grown to 40 percent in Argentina but only to 18 percent in France (Inter-Parliamentary Union 2008a). These patterns similarly defy predictions in the gender quotas literature with regard to the details of quota laws. Argentina adopted a 30 percent quota, which amended only the national electoral code and did not specify how the quota would be implemented or monitored, while France adopted a 50 percent quota, which changed both the constitution and the electoral law and outlined how the quota would apply in various elections, as well as the sanctions that would be imposed on parties that did not comply with these requirements. The question thus emerges: despite seemingly unfavorable conditions, as well as a much less radical quota regulation, why has Argentina been more successful than France in altering existing patterns of political representation?

Applying the framework developed previously, this chapter examines the 1991 *ley de cupos* in Argentina and the 1999–2000 *loi sur la parité* in France in order to identify the actors, strategies, and institutions of candidate selection that have played a role in quota adoption and implementation. As both countries have experienced several distinct efforts at quota reform, each case study begins by outlining historical antecedents to the present quota provisions: the extremely successful Justicialist Party quota in Argentina in the 1950s and abortive attempts to establish a 25 percent quota for municipal elections in France in 1982. The analysis then traces the origins, passage, and application of the present quota laws. It finds that reform processes in Argentina have been harmonizing: supporters of the quota law occasionally drew connections to the earlier party quota as means for advocating reform and, upon adoption, continually refined the provisions of the law to ensure effective implementation by adjusting the rules, practices, and norms of candidate selection. In contrast, dynamics in France have largely been disjointed: proponents constantly sought to overcome the legacy of the earlier regulation for local elections, which had culminated in its rejection on the grounds that it was unconstitutional. This setback required advocates to pursue normative reform as a first order of business, leading them to overlook, or at least bracket, the importance of systemic and practical change. These distinct sequences explain the enormous variations in the impact of these measures on women's representation, at the same time that they shed crucial light on the multidimensional political struggles necessary for ensuring women's equal political presence.

The *Ley de Cupos* in Argentina

Campaigns for the adoption and implementation of gender quotas in Argentina span roughly fifteen years, with the first calls to adopt quotas being voiced in the late 1980s and the final reforms on quota implementation taking place in 2001. During this time period, the actors involved in these campaigns have included civil society actors like women's movement organizations and women in the political parties; state actors like parliamentary representatives, government officials, women's policy agencies, and courts; and international and transnational actors like international organizations and transnational networks. Involved in different ways at various stages of these campaigns, these actors have promoted or contested the quota law for diverse reasons, ranging from normative consistency and electoral concerns to transnational learning and international pressure. As various actors have sought to facilitate or subvert quota implementation, they have exposed the institutional shortcomings of the original quota provision, prompting supporters to pursue additional systemic, practical, and normative reform. Over time, these efforts have resulted in a dense network of mutually reinforcing rules, practices, and norms contributing to effective quota implementation in both houses of congress.

Antecedents to the Ley de Cupos

When the *ley de cupos* was passed in Argentina in 1991, several observers noted its uniqueness, as Argentina was the first country in the world to use legal means to ensure women's political representation (Jones 1996). However, recent case studies identify important continuities between this law and earlier party quotas, while also locating the roots of this specific reform in women's experiences following the democratic transition. Before the 1990s, the highest numbers of women in parliament were elected in the early 1950s, when the governing Justicialist Party (PJ) applied a 30 percent quota for women in party organs and elective positions. Lead by General Juan Domingo Perón, the PJ emerged initially as a platform for promoting labor union demands, but soon sought to expand its base by appealing to women. Upon coming to power in 1946, Perón proposed that the military government grant voting rights to women by executive decree, without waiting for Congress to establish this right through law

(Molinelli 1994). Because many traditional feminist groups opposed this strategy as authoritarian, the government held back until Congress granted women the right to vote and to be elected in 1947. Soon after, Perón organized the PJ into three sectors—the "political branch," the women's branch, and the trade unions branch—and allotted each sector one-third of all party offices and electoral candidacies.

The women's branch[1] was led by Perón's wife, María Eva Duarte de Perón, who not only organized local women's units around the country, but also insisted that women be placed in districts where they were likely to be elected (Chama 2001). Indeed, she personally selected all the female Peronist candidates in 1951, making her directly responsible for the relatively high proportion of women in parliament, given that all female members of parliament in the period 1952–1955 were from the PJ (Molinelli 1994). Other parties ran female candidates in 1951, but none were elected, mainly because these parties did not consider "sex" to be central to their electoral calculations (dos Santos 1983). After Eva Perón's death in 1952, the PJ continued its efforts to recruit women, bringing women's representation in the Chamber of Deputies from 16 percent to 22 percent in 1955 (Inter-Parliamentary Union 1995, 58) (see table 6.1). With this jump, Argentina ranked fourth in the world in terms of the percentage of women in parliament, behind only the Communist countries of East Germany, the Soviet Union, and Mongolia (Htun and Jones 2002, 43).

Soon afterward, however, Juan Perón's government was overthrown in a coup, provoking a dramatic decline in the number of women in both houses of parliament. Although unions continued to be strong within the Peronist movement, the coup combined with the death of Eva Perón contributed to radical changes within the party's women's branch, which not only lost power but also quickly became one of the most conservative sectors of the movement (Feijoó 1994). Fewer women appeared on the PJ lists, with even fewer in positions where they were likely to be elected. When a democratic government was again elected in 1963, only one woman was elected to the Chamber of Deputies, constituting 1 percent of all parliamentary seats. With the return of the Peronists in 1973, women's representation began to increase again, although these gains did not match the earlier successes, reaching only 8 percent (Feijoó 1998, 31). When Perón died in 1974, his third wife, María Estela Perón, became the first female president of Argentina, but her government was also overthrown by a coup in 1976, leading to another military regime lasting until 1983.

Table 6.1. Women's Legislative Representation in Argentina

Chamber of Deputies		Senate	
Year	Women (%)	Year	Women (%)
1946	0.0	1946	0.0
1948	0.0	1951	20.0
1951	15.5	1958	0.0
1955	21.7	1963	0.0
1958	2.2	1973	4.3
1960	1.1	1983	6.5
1963	0.5	1986	6.5
1965	2.1	1989	8.7
1973	7.8	1992	4.2
1983	3.9	1995	6.1
1985	3.9	1999	3.0
1987	4.7	2001	35.2
1989	6.3	2003	43.7
1991	5.8	2005	42.3
1993	14.4	2007	38.9
1995	21.8		
1997	27.6		
1999	27.2		
2001	30.0		
2003	33.9		
2005	35.8		
2007	40.0		

Sources: Carrio (2002, 3); Inter-Parliamentary Union (1995, 58); Inter-Parliamentary Union (2008a); Marx, Borner, and Caminotti (2007, 81–83).

During this last military dictatorship, women began to organize collectively and established their legitimacy as political actors through activities identified with femininity, like soup kitchens, mothers' clubs, production cooperatives, and community health centers. The most well-known of these groups was the Mothers of the Plaza de Mayo, who met every Thursday in front of the presidential palace in Buenos Aires to demand information on their "disappeared" children. Through such activities, women came to play a central role in the democratic transition. However, the later resurgence of political parties largely marginalized women as political actors (Feijoó 1998; Marx 1994). Although women participated in campaigns and public meetings, and most of the parties organized women's sections to facilitate women's involvement in party activities, no party leaders took any steps to actively recruit female candidates. As a result, the first democratic elections in

1983 revealed that democracy itself was not enough to bring about any substantial changes in women's representation: at just over 4 percent of all deputies, there were not only fewer women elected than during the earlier Peronist period, but also lower numbers of women than during the previous democratic government (Bonder and Nari 1995, 186). These outcomes surprised many women and led them to look abroad for new strategies to promote women's representation.

The Origins of the Ley de Cupos

The return to democracy in Argentina brought a decrease in the percentage of women in parliament, but it also created new opportunities for women to connect with other women's groups around the world (Lubertino Beltrán 1992). Through contacts with women from kindred political parties, as well as at national, regional, and international women's conferences, they soon became familiar with attempts in Europe and elsewhere in Latin America to institute quotas for women in politics. These examples inspired women inside the parties and across civil society to lobby for a gender quota law, which eventually passed due to combined pressure from women's groups and from then-President Carlos Saúl Menem. Despite its origins in transnational information sharing, however, this particular law was in fact unusual in international perspective in that it was a national quota law, rather than a quota embedded in political party statutes. In this sense, it represented a homegrown solution that emerged in the course of transnational exchange, as activists sought to "translate" insights from other countries into their own (cf. Krook 2006b).

Information on gender quotas came to Argentina via two distinct venues. Women in the political parties—for reasons of language, ideological affinity, and financial support—learned about quotas through contacts in Europe with women in the Spanish Socialist Party (PSOE), German Social Democratic Party (SPD), and Italian ex-Communist Party, and in Latin America with women in the Uruguay Broad Front, Chilean Socialist Party, and Brazilian Workers' Party. They were particularly interested in discussions that took place inside the PSOE between 1987 and 1990, which led to the adoption of a 25 percent party quota in 1988. Indeed, they circulated a mimeographed account of these debates which passed from person to person until it was eventually published by the Friedrich Ebert Foundation in 1991 (Fundación Friedrich Ebert 1991b). This same foundation also published information on quota debates inside the German

SPD (Fundación Friedrich Ebert 1991a), but this brochure appeared after many women in Argentina had already grown convinced of the importance of quotas. Women in the political parties were then able to draw on these papers as a guide for convincing both women and men of the merits and need for gender quotas, as well as for drafting bills to modify party charters and statutes (Lubertino Beltrán 1992).

Women in civil society, who overlapped to a certain extent with women inside the parties, learned about quotas in other ways, through the Argentine delegation to the United Nations (UN) Third World Conference on Women in Nairobi in 1985, personal contacts with Spanish Socialist women on their visits to Argentina during the first years of the transition, discussions with women in Costa Rica about their proposed bill on real equality for women in 1988, and the meetings of the Socialist International (SI) in Stockholm in 1989. Both the UN and SI conferences were central to providing international normative support for gender quotas, although the central antecedent to the Argentine quota bill was the debate surrounding the proposed Bill on Real Equality for Women in Costa Rica. In its original form, this bill established that over the course of the next five elections, the lists of candidates must be proportional to the number of women and men on the list of registered voters, which was essentially a demand for 50 percent female candidates. According to a central participant in these exchanges (Lubertino Beltrán 1992), this bill was the first time that women in Argentina had heard of the imposition of quotas via legal means, although this aspect of the bill was largely ignored by Costa Rican women. Indeed, the final text of the bill eliminated the quota demand when the new Costa Rican law was promulgated in 1990 (Saint-Germain and Morgan 1991).

These various contacts facilitated and informed a series of internal debates within the political parties concerning the adoption of gender quotas. These discussions initially occurred in a parallel fashion across the various parties, without much previous contact and without a cross-party strategy. Women in the PJ broached the topic of gender quotas as early as 1983, mainly by seeking to revive the historical 30 percent quota associated with the women's branch, while women in other socialist parties, the Popular Socialist Party and the Democratic Socialist Party, imported discussions on quotas within the SI to their own parties beginning in the mid-1980s. Women in the Civic Radical Union (UCR) initiated quota debates slightly later in 1988, the same year that a contact group was established among female activists in the various parties. These developments coincided with increased activism among women's groups around the country, which began organizing national meetings (*encuentros*) in 1986. Although political differences initially precluded cooperation among women in the contact group and at the feminist conferences, women from nearly all political persuasions eventually came out in support of gender quotas.[2] At the end of 1989, they formed a cross-party network to press for the passage of national quota law (Gómez 1998), a decision that marked a significant change in tactics among many Argentine feminists, who had long rejected politics as a male arena (Craske 1999).

The Adoption of the Ley de Cupos

Inspired by these developments, as well as authorized by women inside her party (Bonder and Nari 1995), a female Senator from the UCR, Margarita Malharro de Torres, submitted a bill to the Senate in November 1989 calling for a revision of Article 60 of the National Electoral Code to establish a minimum of 30 percent women on all candidate lists, placed in positions with real possibilities of being elected. The proposal, however, was not accompanied by the broader support of the UCR (Durrieu 1999). Several days later, a group of female legislators from several parties presented a similar bill in the Chamber of Deputies proposing that electoral lists not include more than 70 percent candidates of the same sex and that for every two candidates of the same sex, a third be of the opposite sex, alternating in this way all the way down electoral lists (Gallo and Giacabone 2001). Although quota initiatives were not new, as other bills appeared as early as 1983 (Reynoso 1992), these proposals were novel in that they came with the support of women across all the major political parties (Bonder and Nari 1995).

The Senate bill was not addressed until September 1990, but during this time, Malharro de Torres lobbied other women inside the Senate so that when the bill finally received parliamentary attention, female legislators worked together to convince their male counterparts to vote in favor of the proposal (Chama 2001). When the bill finally came up for debate, some male Senators voiced their opposition by characterizing quotas as demagogic, high-handed, and anti-democratic (Reynoso 1992). For the most part, however, the vote took place in near silence, according to one insider, because most senators were certain that the bill would be rejected or would expire before it could be addressed in the Chamber of Deputies (Durrieu 1999).[3] As a consequence, the quota was approved by an overwhelming majority, with the explicit opposition of only two male senators from the PJ.

Despite the empty gesture by Argentine senators to contain the effects of the quota proposal, approval of the bill in the Senate inspired women inside all the parties to organize across party lines to ensure the bill's passage in the Chamber of Deputies. They mobilized women around the country to lobby their own representatives, while they themselves set out to convince their male colleagues by sending one woman to speak with each man, taking advantage of existing political links like having worked together in the same committees or having shared the same political and professional experiences (Chama 2001). To reinforce these efforts, they further initiated a campaign to sensitize journalists and radio and television reporters about the need for quotas. Pursuing a parallel party-based strategy, women in the majority PJ organized a series of women's meetings to discuss the law with prominent male politicians, a tactic which led many of the men to express enthusiastic public support for gender quotas. A small group of these women also approached President Menem, who pledged his support and encouraged women to continue mobilizing before evaluating whether or not he should intervene directly in the debate (Bonder and Nari 1995).

The quota bill eventually came up for consideration in the Chamber in November 1991.[4] In the days leading up to the debate, feminist organizations in Buenos Aires sent every deputy a letter calling on them to vote in favor of the proposal (Reynoso 1992). On the day of the vote, women descended on the capital from all over the country to conduct a "vigil for the quota" until the bill became law (Chama 2001, 65). They filled not only the parliamentary galleries and hallways, but also spilled out into the surrounding streets, standing firm from 4 p.m., when the session started, until the early hours of the following morning when the debate finally came to a close. As the session got underway, deputies opposed to the bill argued against gender quotas and, met with jeers from women sitting in the galleries, several sought to prolong the debate indefinitely in the hope that the women would eventually leave. As the hours passed, female deputies who had not previously been supporters of the quota began to manifest their support for the measure (Durrieu 1999). Even with this change, however, many still anticipated a negative vote. Indeed, confident that the measure would not pass, none of the parties had developed a common position either for or against the quota (Chama 2001).

Despite these expectations, the situation shifted dramatically at 2 a.m. At that time, President Menem placed a phone call to José Luis Manzano, the minister of the interior, asking him to address the deputies on his behalf and to tell the PJ legislators, the majority members of the Chamber, to vote in favor of the bill. Observers have given several different explanations to account for this last minute intervention. To some, Menem's support for the quota bill was consistent with his party's historical commitment to women. To others, it represented a relatively transparent attempt to close the gender gap in support for the PJ by catering to women's demands (Bonder and Nari 1995; Jones 1996). In either case, it was an unusual step by Menem who, both before and after the quota law, sided decisively with conservative groups on issues related to women's status (Feijoó 1998). In his speech before the Chamber, Manzano expressed the president's support for the bill and appealed, among other arguments, to the legacy of Eva Perón and the party's earlier quota for women (Durrieu 1999).[5] These remarks unified the Peronist legislators behind the bill and, in effect, dragged along many of the deputies from the other parties who were no longer comfortable opposing the measure on their own (Chama 2001; Durrieu 1999). At 3 a.m., the measure passed nearly unanimously with the support of all the party blocs except the Union of the Democratic Center and the Movement toward Socialism.

The Implementation of the Ley de Cupos

The final version of the bill passed in both houses of parliament followed the text submitted by Senator Malharro de Torres, which was a slightly milder version of the bill initially presented in the Chamber of Deputies. As a consequence, Law 24.012 amended Article 60 of the Electoral Code to stipulate that lists of candidates must include 30 percent women, in proportions which make their election possible, and that lists that do not comply with this requirement would not be approved. This provision, in contrast to the earlier Chamber proposal, did not specify where female candidates should be placed on party lists but only that they should be included "in proportions which make their election possible." Almost immediately, debate began over the meaning of this phrase, with some interpreting it to cover the entire party list and others to apply only to the seats that the party expected to win. In light of these disagreements, President Menem sought to clarify the provision by issuing Executive Decree 379/93 on International Women's Day in March 1993. This decree established that 30 percent should be understood as a minimum percentage of female candidates that should apply to the whole list, as well as to the number of seats that any given political grouping expected to win in a particular election. To ensure proper application of this principle, an annex to the decree outlined exactly how many women should be included depending on the number of party seats up for reelection. In cases of noncompliance, an article of the decree mandated that parties had only forty-eight hours to rectify their lists before these were definitively rejected by the electoral courts.

Despite these clarifications, many of the lists compiled for the October 1993 parliamentary elections violated these provisions. More specifically, most lists included 30 percent women among their candidates, but not 30 percent women among their candidates who were likely to be elected (Durrieu 1999), a pattern that many party leaders justified according their own interpretations of the law (Minyerski 2001). Most were in fact quite open regarding their intentions not to implement the placement provision. Many made rude comments to female deputies in the hallways of parliament, and all informed the Ministry of the Interior that they would not enforce the decree (Durrieu 1999), resulting in systematic violations across all parties and all provinces (Lubertino 2000). Further, many of the women being placed on lists were closely tied to their party leadership, often through a personal connection, meaning that women associated with feminist issues were rarely selected as candidates. Confronted with the zero-sum nature of the quota, party leaders thus actively sought to undermine the impact of the law on women's descriptive and substantive representation, in spite of the nearly unanimous vote in favor of the measure just two years before. For their part, many women inside the parties resigned themselves to the fact that the quota simply would not be implemented to its fullest extent (Durrieu 1999; Marx and Sampaolesi 1993).

At this juncture, groups of women in the Cabinet of Female Presidential Advisors,[6] the National Council of Women,[7] and the various parties began a legal campaign to ensure that all political groupings complied with the law (Durrieu 1999; Jones 1996). To spread information rapidly on the composition of the lists in each electoral district, they organized a communication network that often relied on help from female candidates in the parties whose lists did not conform to the law. They also identified female lawyers who would agree to represent them on a pro bono basis to challenge these violations in the electoral courts. Working simultaneously in all twenty-four electoral districts, they examined more than 200 lists and quickly distributed details on every violation to their sponsors in each province. To ensure media coverage, they further established a network of female journalists in almost all the provinces who publicized cases of non-compliance, as well as the work of the women who sought the rejection of the illegal lists (Chama 2001; Durrieu 1999). Although this legal campaign resulted in more than thirty lawsuits (Jones 1996),[8] these efforts faced resistance from electoral court judges, who argued that the quota law was not a law affecting public order and thus the only person who could contest noncompliance was the particular victim, or the specific female candidate, who had been placed too far down on her own party's list. For reasons of party loyalty and even intimidation, many women declined to pursue these types of legal challenges. This procedural obstacle, however, sparked creativity among supporters of the law, who presented fictitious victims to attract media attention for their cause. Although all judges deemed these cases inadmissible, some still did not approve the candidate lists and sent them back to the parties so that they could be redone in conformity with the law (Chama 2001; Durrieu 1999).

In several cases, efforts to ensure compliance with the quota provision entailed significant political and economic costs for the women involved. In the province of Santiago del Estero, one female candidate was placed third on the UCR list when, by her interpretation of the law, she should have been placed at least second. She informed the provincial leader of the UCR that the party was in violation of the law and risked having its list rejected. He responded by revoking her party membership and removing her name from the party list for her "anti-party activities" (Durrieu 1999; Jones 1996). In the province of Entre Ríos, a female deputy in the PJ came to a similar conclusion that, according to the law, she should have been placed at least third, rather than fourth, on her party's list. She was forced to draw on her own resources to finance a nine-month court battle, but her case eventually reached the Supreme Court, which confirmed her interpretation of the law. This decision, known popularly as the Darci Sampietro case,[9] also concluded that Law 24.012 was a public order law, meaning that federal judges had an obligation to apply it, despite whatever conflicts might exist between the law and individual party charters and other internal party decisions.

In series of other cases, the National Electoral Chamber established a number of other important legal clarifications. These included the meaning of the phrase "in proportions which make their election possible," which was to be understood as equal to the number of seats that a party had up for reelection; the applicability of the quota law to all parliamentary elections, regardless of the specific electoral system employed; and the legality of the quota with regard to the constitutional principle of equality before the law.[10] These victories not only legitimized the quota law, but also inspired more and more female candidates to challenge partial implementation (Minyerski 2001). Although the campaign did experience some setbacks, as in cases where favorable judgments were reversed on appeal (Durrieu 1999), the various legal battles resulted in the quota being implemented correctly in more than 90 percent of all electoral districts and by the majority of political parties (Chama 2001). The five party lists that failed to comply with the law were deemed admissible either because the lists had been created prior to the executive decree, or because district-level judges had accepted them based on an incorrect interpretation of the law (Jones 1996, 91, n. 5). As a result of these changes in candidate selection, the percentage of women in the Chamber of Deputies increased from 6 percent in 1991 to 14 percent in 1993 (Inter-Parliamentary Union 1995, 58). The modest nature of this increase can be explained in part by the fact that the law applied to only the half of the chamber's 257 seats that were up for election in 1993. The law would apply to the other seats for the first time in 1995, when the other half of the chamber was renewed.

Among the obstacles faced by the campaign in 1993 was the issue of competing juridical interpretations of the law (Chama 2001). Much of the contradictory jurisprudence stemmed from the question of whether affirmative action was constitutional, with many judges maintaining that quotas violated the principle of equality before the law (Lubertino 2000; Rodríguez 1994). An opportunity to settle these doubts emerged in 1994 when both houses of parliaments decided to reform the Argentine Constitution, for reasons largely unrelated to the quota law. Working together, the National Women's Council and women in the various political parties lobbied members of the Constitutional Assembly to incorporate international treaties and conventions on human rights into Argentine law, including several international provisions regarding women's political participation (Chama 2001). Their task was facilitated by the relatively high proportion of women (26 percent) in the Constitutional Assembly, which was also governed by the quota provision (Bonder and Nari 1995, 191).[11] As a result of their combined efforts, the new Constitution incorporated the United Nations Convention on the Elimination of

All Forms of Discrimination Against Women (CEDAW), as well as several articles establishing the legitimacy of positive action with regard to the quota law. Article 37 states that real equality of opportunities between men and women regarding access to political office will be guaranteed through positive action measures adopted by the political parties and the electoral system, while the Second Transitory Clause clarifies that the measures alluded to in Article 37 can never be less than those in effect at the time that the Constitution is approved (that is, 30 percent). Together, these reforms brought the debate on unconstitutionality to an end and prevented any future backtracking on the percentage mandated by the quota law (Carrio 2002).

In addition to these reforms, the Constitutional Assembly established a new system for elections to the Senate, to begin in 2001 once all existing Senate mandates had come to an end. In place of indirect elections, each province would directly elect a group of three senators comprised of two representatives from the party winning the most votes and one representative from the party winning the second highest number of votes. These reforms inspired a new set of debates regarding the applicability of the quota law to Senate elections, given the practical issue of translating the 30 percent regulation to groups of one or two seats. Women's groups organized a new legal campaign to ensure the implementation of quotas in these elections, but they were much less successful than in their other campaigns in gaining support among female candidates, lawyers, and politicians. Further, they were not able to elicit a response from the Ministry of the Interior, the Ministry of Justice, or even the president of the Supreme Court. Indeed, when they sought to gain a favorable judgment from the National Electoral Chamber that would serve as a precedent for all other provinces, the same court prevented their case from being heard. This legal vacuum allowed local parliaments to interpret the constitutional mandate according to their own interests, leaving the matter unresolved for several years, with the result that the Senate continued to have only about 4 percent women, in comparison with almost 30 percent women in the Chamber of Deputies (Durrieu 1999).

As parties began to prepare for the 1995 parliamentary elections, women's groups again waged a legal campaign to ensure compliance with the quota. The earlier lawsuits, combined with the various constitutional reforms, created a more favorable environment than in 1993. All of the lists had at least one woman in the third position, and thus the campaign had to dispute only 8 percent of the lists because they did not conform to the law in other ways. For this reason, women's groups concentrated their efforts in only a few provinces where parties continued to present 30 percent female candidates but not in positions where there were likely to be elected. In a case originating in the province of Tucumán,[12] the National Women's Council secured an important victory when the provincial court rejected its petition on the grounds that the council did not have legal standing to challenge any of these party lists. When it appealed this decision to the National Electoral Chamber, this court declared the legitimacy of the council, as well as any member of the party in question, to contest party lists in any given electoral district.[13] In justifying this decision, the National Electoral Chamber argued that when parties did not present lists that conform to the law, voters suffered a harm that deprived them of voting for their preferred party lists, and thus could not be denied legal standing to require that this right be respected (Minyerski 2001). Around this same time, the National Electoral Chamber rendered judgments on two other cases which not only reinforced the double condition of the quota law—proportion and placement— but also specified the placement of women when parties anticipate winning only one or two seats.[14] It decided that placing a woman in the third position did not satisfy the provisions of the law because it resulted in 100 percent male representation. Although placing a woman second when a party won two seats would lead to the election of 50 percent women, the court noted that the 30 percent requirement set by the quota law constituted a minimum percentage. To comply with the law, therefore, parties were obligated to place a woman in one of the first two spots if they were likely to win fewer than three seats.

Supporters of the quota law obtained further support for their cause when the National Ombudsman requested that the National Electoral Chamber and the attorney general ensure that electoral court judges verify that all lists of candidates comply with the law, the Constitution, and the presidential decree. The attorney general responded by instructing federal prosecutors to take all actions necessary to guarantee that the law was not violated, as well as by monitoring electoral court judges and replacing those who did not respect these orders. As a consequence, various parties were compelled to redo their lists, meaning that many more complied with the law in 1995 than in 1993. Most parties still placed women in the lowest positions allowed by the law (Jones 1996), but the proportion of women elected to the Chamber of Deputies increased from 14 percent in 1993 to 22 percent in 1995, finally equaling the 22 percent attained in 1955 (Inter-Parliamentary Union 1995, 58).

The National Women's Council built on these gains in the months leading up to the 1997 elections by reminding the relevant judicial authorities of their obligation to guarantee quota implementation. Discovering eleven lists to be in violation of the quota law, the courts ordered these parties to rectify their lists on the grounds that they were unconstitutional and a breach of effective rights (Chama 2001). As a result, the percentage of women in the Chamber of Deputies rose to 28 percent. To consolidate these gains, at the end of 1997 the Women in Equality Foundation established a multiparty database of women in politics, complete with information on leadership abilities and level of education, so that elites in all parties could no longer claim that they could not find enough capable women to put on their candidate lists. Before the 1999 elections, however, some parties continued to ignore the requirement to place women at least second in cases where the party anticipated winning only one or two seats. As a result, the UCR-Frepaso alliance—which did particularly well that year—increased its representation with two men in numerous constituencies, while the new party Action for the Republic obtained single seats in various districts with all its lists headed by men. Because the election brought fewer women into the Chamber of Deputies in 1999 (33/130) than in 1997 (37/127), the elections resulted in a slight drop in the percentage of women in the Chamber to 27 percent (Carrio 2002, 137; Chama 2001, 112–13).

These patterns, combined with the impending Senate elections in 2001, led to renewed discussion in Argentina regarding the placement of female candidates when parties expect to win only one or two seats in a given electoral district. Although this requirement affected elections to the Chamber of Deputies, especially in the case of smaller parties, it had crucial implications for the applicability of the quota law to Senate elections. Reforms in 1994 had not only made these elections direct beginning in 2001, but had also established that the party with the most votes in each district would win two seats, while the party with the second highest number of votes would gain one seat.

As this debate got underway, the Inter-American Commission of Human Rights (IACHR) agreed to hear a petition submitted by an Argentine woman with regard to the specific placement of female candidates on party lists. First waged within the national electoral courts, this case revolved around the specific questions of placement and the meaning of the phrase "in proportions which make their election possible."[15] The claimant, María Teresa Merciadri de Morini, challenged the UCR in the province of Córdoba in 1993 for placing women fourth and sixth on a list of six candidates. Because the UCR was likely to return only five deputies, she argued, two women should have been placed in the first five list positions as outlined by Executive Decree 379/93. As her case moved through the judicial system, it was rejected on several grounds: she was a member of the UCR in Córdoba, but not the particular candidate affected by the implementation decision; she confused "probability" with "possibility" of being elected; and she misinterpreted the quota provision and the presidential decree, which calculated the proportion according to the number of seats being elected in each province, not by each party (Minyerski 2001). Although other cases had established legal precedents to the contrary, Merciadri de Morini lacked any further recourse within the national court system. She therefore appealed the decision to the IACHR on the grounds that her rights to due process, participation in government, equality before the law, and effective recourse, as set forth in the American Convention on Human Rights, had been violated by the Argentine Republic (Inter-American Commission on Human Rights 1999).

After the IACHR declared itself competent to hear this case, the government engaged in a series of communications with the commission in 2000 (Carrio 2002; Inter-American Commission on Human Rights 2001). Despite its earlier claims that the IACHR lacked authority to challenge the composition of electoral lists, the government of Fernando de la Rúa eventually issued Executive Decree 1.246 in December 2000 clarifying the provisions for implementing Law 24.012. This decree recognized that despite the regulations established by Decree 379/93, political parties continued to interpret the law in different ways, a problem that was exacerbated by inconsistent rulings by the various local and national courts. The new decree reiterated that the 30 percent quota applied to the number of seats that each party had up for reelection, as well as the right of any person registered to vote in a particular electoral district to challenge lists they judged to be in violation of the law. To resolve issues of candidate placement, it outlined detailed regulations regarding the list positions of female candidates and alternates: while the first person on the list may be a man or a woman, the second person on the list must be someone of the opposite sex; when two seats were up for re-election, one of the nominees must be a woman; when one or two seats are up for re-election, placing a woman third is not in compliance with the law; overall, lists must include at least one woman for every two men in order to meet the minimum percentage; until the 30 percent requirement is met, no three consecutive slots may be filled by members of the same sex; and should women on the list drop out of the race for any reason, they must be replaced by other women, while men in the same situation may be replaced by men or women.

The decree mandated that parties amend their bylaws to incorporate these provisions before the 2001 elections. In addition, it established a common procedure for rectifying lists that did not comply: when parties come to register their lists, electoral court judges must verify whether women are placed on party lists below where they should have been; in cases of violation, judges must notify parties to reorder their lists; parties must comply within forty-eight hours of this decision; and, if the ruling is not obeyed, judges themselves must move the women to higher positions on the lists. In response to these changes, a friendly settlement was reached between Merciadri de Morini and the government in March 2001. As a result of these negotiations, the October 2001 elections witnessed the full application of the quota provision for elections to the Chamber of Deputies, where women's representation increased from 28 percent to 30 percent, and to the Senate, where the proportion of women jumped from 3 percent to 35 percent (Carrio 2002, 137). These figures shifted, respectively to 34 percent and 44 percent in 2003, 36 percent and 42 percent in 2005, and 40 percent and 39 percent in 2007 (Inter-Parliamentary Union 2008a; Marx, Borner, and Caminotti 2007, 81–83).

The Ley de Cupos and Women's Political Representation in Argentina

Campaigns to promote women's political representation in Argentina have thus resulted in more than perfect implementation of the 30 percent quota law. The existing literature attempts to explain this success by focusing on single actors and motivations, or specific details of quota policies and the contexts in which they operate, observed over relatively short periods of time (cf. Htun and Jones 2002). The narrative of events presented in this chapter, however, reveals that this outcome evolved in steps over the course of fifteen years through a series of smaller institutional reforms, initiated by variable coalitions of actors supporting or opposing these changes for different, and often conflicting, reasons. Indeed, analyzing the three stages of these campaigns—origins, adoption, and implementation—indicates that distinct combinations of actors, strategies, and institutions are relevant to explaining outcomes at various points in the campaign. A broader temporal lens thus not only reveals the limits of universalizing causal claims, but it also casts light on the harmonizing sequence of reforms that has adjusted the rules, practices, and norms of candidate selection in Argentina to ensure women's greater presence in parliament (see table 6.2).

When proposals to institute a quota law first appeared in Argentina in the late 1980s, the only institution of candidate selection ostensibly favorable to women was the proportional representation (PR) list electoral system. Because existing practical and normative institutions did not treat "sex" as a central category for candidate selection, however, women's representation remained below 6 percent in both houses of parliament. Looking for means to alter the status quo, feminist organizations and women inside the political parties looked for lessons abroad, and through transnational learning, became familiar

Table 6.2. Quota Reforms and Institutional Configurations in Argentina

Systemic Institutions	Practical Institutions	Normative Institutions
Period 1 (1947–1991):		
PR electoral system	"Sex" as irrelevant criteria Placement in unwinnable positions on party lists	Equality before the law Representation as politics of ideas
Period 2 (1991–2000):		
PR electoral system	"Sex" as relevant criteria Placement in winnable and unwinnable positions on party lists	Equality before the law, and equality of results Representation as politics of presence
Period 3 (2000–present):		
PR electoral system	"Sex" as relevant criteria Placement in winnable positions on party lists	Equality of results Representation as politics of presence

with attempts to institute quotas elsewhere in the world. Drawing on these experiences, as well as international documents establishing the normative legitimacy of quotas, they organized within and across party lines to press for the passage of a national quota law.

To this end, a female senator and several female deputies presented slightly different bills proposing to amend Article 60 of the National Electoral Code to require a minimum of 30 percent women on all candidate lists. Senators deliberated the bill in late 1990 and voted overwhelmingly in favor of the measure. However, many supported the law as an empty gesture, confident that the measure would not be approved by the Chamber of Deputies. When the bill reached the chamber one year later, it looked certain not to pass until the last minute intervention of the president, who pressed his party's deputies to vote in favor of the measure. Although he made arguments about normative consistency by drawing parallels with the PJ's earlier party quota, many suggested that he was also guided by electoral considerations to close a gender gap in support for the PJ. In approving the law, legislators reformed systemic and normative institutions by amending an article of the electoral law to redefine the existing principle of representation. The statement that all lists must include a minimum of 30 percent women, however, did not specify how parties should translate this provision in their selection practices, leaving practical institutions largely untouched.

The lack of a specific placement mandate for female candidates sparked an almost decade-long battle among women to ensure that the 30 percent female candidate requirement translated into the election of at least 30 percent female representatives. The executive decree issued in 1993 stressed that the principle of representation contained in the law referred to a minimum quantity and introduced the first practical reforms by introducing broad placement mandates indicating the number of female candidates that parties must include among their total number of candidates up for reelection. Despite these attempts to change norms and practices, however, many party elites continued to apply multiple interpretations of the law to avoid placing women in spots where they were likely to be elected. At this juncture, women's policy agencies at the state level, together with women in the political parties, initiated a legal campaign to ensure compliance with the quota law and the executive decree. In addition to some limited practical change, their legal battles helped to specify various systemic and normative aspects of the quota law by clarifying that it applied to all parliamentary elections, regardless of electoral system, and that it did not contravene the constitutional principle of equality before the law.

Many judges, however, continued to maintain that the *ley de cupos* violated the principle of equality before the law. When both houses of parliament agreed to reform the Constitution in 1994, the women's groups seized the opportunity to settle this normative debate. They succeeded in incorporating several new articles that together redefined the existing constitutional principle of equality to legitimate the use of positive action in efforts to increase women's representation. Systemic reforms with regard to Senate elections emerged parallel to these discussions, although the applicability of the quota to these elections was left largely unresolved, leaving local male-dominated assemblies to interpret the quota provision according to their own interests. Campaigns to ensure quota implementation in the Chamber of Deputies continued throughout the late 1990s and entailed efforts to institute further practical reform by refining and enforcing placement mandates, as well as to confirm the normative principles of equality and representation established through earlier legislation. By the end of the decade, all federal prosecutors and judges were required to enforce the law, if necessary by redoing the lists themselves, while courts increasingly referenced the Constitution to justify rejecting lists that did not comply with the law, evidence of a clear shift in legal norms.

Despite these changes in systemic and normative institutions, however, parties continued to undermine the goals of quota law in their selection practices. The main issue lay in situations where parties were renewing one or two seats, which was gaining relevance in light of upcoming Senate elections that would revolve entirely around the distribution of one or two seats. These concerns, combined with an ongoing lawsuit waged within the framework of the Organization of American States, led the president to issue a new presidential decree at the end of 2000. This decree offered the final word on the placement of female candidates in absolutely all situations and required judges to rectify lists if parties did not do so themselves. These procedures solidified the reform of party selection practices, culminating in complete institutional configurational change and, consequently, perfect implementation of the quota law beginning with the 2001 chamber and Senate elections. Further increases in the numbers of women elected to both houses provides compelling evidence for the enduring nature of these shifts in rules, practices, and norms, which have now largely been internalized and no longer generate major controversy (cf. Marx, Borner, and Caminotti 2007).

The *Loi sur la Parité* in France

Campaigns for the adoption and implementation of gender quotas in France cover a period of almost thirty years, with initial calls to adopt quotas emerging in the early 1970s and the most recent reforms on implementation being introduced in 2007. During this time, the actors involved in these campaigns have included civil society actors such as social movement organizations, women's movement organizations, women inside the parties, and scholars; state actors such as parliamentary representatives, government officials, women's policy agencies, and the courts; and international and transnational actors such as international organizations and transnational networks. Involved in different ways, these actors have pursued or opposed quotas for diverse reasons, including defending distinct normative definitions of equality and representation, responding to specific electoral motivations, or engaging in empty gestures of support for quota reform. After a court decision in the early 1980s declared quotas to be unconstitutional, both sides of these debates have focused primarily on the normative implications of quota adoption, with opponents bolstering their position with reference to this legal precedent and advocates highlighting the need for constitutional reform. In identifying normative institutions as the main barrier to women's increased representation, however, supporters have paid much less attention to systemic and practical obstacles to change. Consequently, quota reform has proceeded in a relatively diffuse fashion, with varying combinations of rules, practices, and norms resulting in uneven implementation across parties and across levels of government.

Antecedents to the Loi sur la Parité

The law on parity in France has garnered a great deal of international attention among scholars, activists, and politicians. Their fascination with parity springs not only from the demand for equal representation of women and men, but also from the unique set of theoretical arguments developed during the course of this campaign. Importantly, these innovations did not emerge as a simple response to the question of women's underrepresentation in French politics, but rather as a reaction to earlier failed attempts to promote women's political presence through quotas and other types of electoral reform. As in Argentina, women's movements in France avoided electoral politics until relatively recently, preferring to focus instead on issues related to daily life like domestic labor, reproductive choice, and sexuality (Jenson and Sineau 1994).

Until the 1990s, therefore, most work to increase women's representation came from women inside the various political parties, with little or no input from women's movements in civil society. Most of these efforts were concentrated inside the Socialist Party (PS), where party feminists first began to demand gender quotas in the early 1970s. At the national party convention in 1974, two female party members proposed that the PS statutes be amended to include a 10 percent quota for women, both in party leadership positions and among the party's candidates for political office. They argued that the adoption of quotas was consistent with socialist ideology and would demonstrate the party's commitment to achieving equality between women and men. The proposal received unanimous support from the party committees responsible for statutory reform and was subsequently approved by a majority of the delegates to the party convention. Before voting in favor of the provision, however, delegates changed the requirement slightly so that the quota would apply only to elections governed by PR, thus excluding elections to the National Assembly which are decided by a two-round majoritarian vote (Appleton and Mazur 1993; Opello 2006).

Women sought to expand these provisions at subsequent party conventions with the goal of eventually increasing the quota to reflect the proportion of women among party members. Delegates voted to raise the quota to 15 percent in 1977, and then in 1979, they agreed to a 30 percent quota for European Parliament (EP) elections, a 20 percent quota for women in the party leadership, and the nomination of as many women as possible to "winnable" districts in two-round majoritarian elections. Following these gains, Véronique Neiertz, the national secretary for women's rights, proposed in 1981 to increase the quota to 30 percent for the party leadership and the party's candidates in PR elections, as well as to extend the 30 percent quota to elections run by majoritarian vote. Party leaders postponed discussion of this proposal, however, until the next party convention in 1982, where it was never presented or voted on by party delegates. While Martine Buron, the new national secretary for women's rights, repeatedly called for party quotas to be increased to 30 percent at the next three national congresses in 1983, 1985, and 1987, all her proposals were rejected by party delegates. A number of women inside the PS reiterated these demands in 1990, while others proposed a 40 percent quota with a plan to increase to 50 percent by 2000, along with the creation of a commission to oversee quota implementation. While party delegates did vote to raise the quota to 30 percent, they still made no provisions to extend such measures to majoritarian elections (Opello 2006). Despite the extended attention given to quotas during the 1970s and 1980s, the PS rarely implemented any of these policies to their fullest extent, in part because the party never established any enforcement mechanisms to ensure their application. In the few cases where the percentage of female candidates did approximate the quota, as in the 1986 regional and legislative elections, most women were placed in positions where they were unlikely to be elected, thus undermining the impact of these quotas.

At the same time that these debates got underway in the PS, several women in parliament pursued a parallel strategy to increase women's representation through quotas for local elections. In 1975, the secretary of state for women's status, Françoise Giroud, proposed limiting to 85 percent the percentage of candidates of the same sex who could appear on lists for municipal elections, a provision that essentially amounted to a 15 percent quota for women. In 1979, the new minister of women's status and the family, Monique Pelletier, changed this demand to 80 percent in an amendment to a bill on municipal election reform. The measure was approved almost unanimously in the National Assembly, but the measure never reached the Senate, in part because the government preferred not to pursue such a controversial reform during the 1980–81 presidential campaign (Bird 2003). When the PS came to power following these elections, the new government decided not to include quotas for women in a bill that would introduce semi-PR for municipal elections, despite the party's apparent commitment to gender quotas. Instead, an independent deputy affiliated with the PS, Gisèle Halimi, proposed in 1982 that lists of candidates not include more than 70 percent of candidates of the same sex, applied to every three positions on the list.

While the PS group in parliament reduced her proposal to 75 percent with no restrictions on the ordering of male and female candidates, the government remained unconvinced and argued publicly that the political parties, not the National Assembly, should decide the ratio of male and female candidates. Indeed, during the parliamentary debates, the minister of the interior, Gaston Defferre, requested that the measure appear as a separate article so that, if the Constitutional Council should annul it, the broader law might still be applied (Bird 2003). Because Defferre was speaking on the government's behalf, this suggestion fed rumors that the high court would declare the quota unconstitutional, creating an opportunity for deputies to appeal to female voters by supporting the quota, while secure in the knowledge that it would never actually be applied (Mazur 2001; Mossuz-Lavau 1998). Thus, after separating the quota provision from the main legislation, legislators voted nearly unanimously in favor of the measure. Several months later, as expected, the court reviewed the bill on municipal electoral reform. While its attention focused initially on articles other than the one providing for quotas (Gaspard 1998; Mossuz-Lavau 1998), the Constitutional Council eventually took up the quota article and declared it unconstitutional on the grounds that Article 3 of the Constitution and Article 6 of the Declaration of the Rights of Man and the Citizen together affirmed the principle of equality before the law, which precluded all types of division of voters and candidates into categories for all types of political voting.[16]

Although feminists paid little attention to this verdict at the time, it had an enormous impact on future campaigns to increase women's representation in France. Most crucially, the decision affirmed an interpretation of "equality" as equality before the law, a principle that all Constitutional Council decisions, jurisprudence, and works of authority on the Constitution had treated as sex-neutral (Mazur 2001). The Constitutional Council decision in 1982 reinforced this view, precluding attempts to institute equal outcomes through sex-specific policies. The verdict, further, cast doubt on the possibility of using legal means to compel parties to promote women's access to political office, forcing advocates of quotas to focus on developing a more fundamental critique of the existing principle of equality as a root cause of sex-based differences in political representation.

The Origins of the Loi sur la Parité

Following the 1982 Constitutional Council decision, efforts to increase quotas inside the PS lost momentum, and for several years little progress was made at either the national or the party level to promote women's representation. In 1986, however, feminists became more optimistic when the electoral system for parliamentary elections was changed from two-round majoritarian to PR. Because many female activists anticipated that this shift would substantially increase the number of women elected, they did not mobilize extensively within the parties to ensure that women were placed high on the candidate lists (Jenson 1996). As a result, women comprised 25 percent of all candidates, but the proportion of women elected rose only marginally, from 5 percent to 6 percent. Although the PS roughly met its 20 percent party quota by including 19 percent female candidates, party selectors had placed most women quite far down on the candidate lists, such that in the end they constituted only 10 percent of the Socialist deputies in parliament (Mossuz-Lavau 1998, 24–25).

After this disappointment, French women interested in promoting women's representation began to look for inspiration in movements outside the established parties and beyond their own national borders. Between 1986 and 1988, various women became active in the Rainbow movement, which insisted on parity, or the equal involvement of women and men, in all group decision-making. When the group was dissolved in 1988, many adherents joined the Greens and, similar to Green parties elsewhere in Europe, inscribed the principle of parity in the party's statutes (Lipietz 1994). They have subsequently applied this principle to all party lists since the 1989 EP elections (Guigou 1998). Around the same time, the Council of Europe (COE) began a series of debates on the deepening and strengthening of democracy in Europe. In contrast to the European Union (EU), which in the late 1980s focused mainly on the rights of individuals as economic actors, the COE has long worked to promote the rights of individuals as political actors. In 1986, it organized the first European Ministerial Conference on Equality Between Women and Men, where member states identified the increased presence and participation of women in public life as a central feature of democracy. In 1988, they signed the Declaration of Equality of Women and Men calling on the COE to devise policies and strategies for integrating women into all levels of political life.

To this end, the European Committee for Equality between Women and Men convened a seminar of experts in Strasbourg in 1989 to share and develop mechanisms for promoting women's access to political office. The two main contributions to these debates were papers by Marit Halvorsen, outlining Norwegian experiences in bringing more women into politics, and Élisabeth Sledziewski, elaborating new normative arguments for increasing women's political presence based on ontological differences between women and men (Steering Committee For Equality between Women and Men 1992, 17–27, 29–43). Although the debates reflected a wider array of positions regarding party versus statutory quotas, most subsequent accounts equate this meeting with the first definitive statement on "parity democracy," not only as a new concept in European politics but also as a set of innovative arguments for justifying positive action to promote women in politics (Mossuz-Lavau 1998; Scott 1998). Many of the ideas formulated by Sledziewski provided inspiration for women in France, who not only perceived new ways of overcoming the 1982 decision, but also recognized that COE support for parity democracy could lend important legitimacy to their efforts to increase women's political representation.

The rise of parity democracy in Europe coincided with a series of developments within France involving more critical examination of the principles and goals underlying the theory and practice of democracy in France. The bicentennial of the French Revolution in 1989, in particular, sparked a flood of books attributing women's absence from politics and other spheres of power to the Revolution itself and, especially, its core principle of the universal citizen. As scholars began to revive the history of French feminism, they focused on exclusions inherent in French republicanism and rehabilitated work by earlier feminists calling for the equal representation of women and men in politics (Fraisse 1989; Gaspard 1994). In 1990, the first parity association was formed by Régine Saint-Criq, a former regional councilor who had left the PS because of its persistent failure to implement its own party quota (Praud 2001). A number of similar organizations appeared in rapid succession several years later, following the 1992 publication of *Au pouvoir citoyennes! Liberté, égalité, parité*,[17] a self-proclaimed manifesto for the parity movement in France. In addition to introducing the term parity, the book addressed reasons why women were underrepresented in electoral politics and, to rectify the situation, proposed that parity be inscribed in the law with the phrase: "Elected assemblies, at the regional as well as the national level, are composed of as many women as men." To implement parity, the authors suggested alternating between women and men on lists for elections governed by PR, and joining current districts to create two-member slates, each with one woman and one man, for majoritarian elections (Gaspard, Servan-Schreiber, and Le Gall 1992).

Almost immediately, women around the country began to establish new parity associations, as well as to make parity a goal of many existing women's organizations. When elections in 1993 returned only 6 percent women to the National Assembly (Inter-Parliamentary Union 1995, 121), activities in favor of parity multiplied with debates, roundtables, conferences, newsletters, and demonstrations in front of the National Assembly. By the end of the year, women's organizations drafted the Manifesto of the 577 for Parity Democracy—a reference to the number of deputies in the National Assembly—signed

by 289 women and 288 men from all points on the political spectrum, demanding the incorporation of parity into the national constitution. Soon after the publication of the manifesto in *Le Monde* (19
November 1993), one of the largest newspapers in France, a number
of left-wing parties announced they would apply parity to their lists
for the upcoming EP elections in 1994.

Over the course of the next year, various deputies submitted proposals in the National Assembly to institute parity or, at least, to
ensure greater political representation for women. Although President François Mitterrand expressed reservations about quotas, he
agreed that dramatic increases were unlikely to occur on their own. To
increase their influence in these debates, parity associations—including women's groups in civil society and the political parties that had
adopted the goal of parity—created an umbrella organization, Tomor-
row Parity, with the goal of collecting a million signatures in favor of
constitutional reform (Mossuz-Lavau 1998). These various developments enabled parity advocates to place the issue at the forefront of
political debate during the 1995 presidential elections and to gain a
commitment from all the major candidates for some type of political
reform. Édouard Balladur (Rally for the Republic, or RPR) proposed a
30 percent quota for women on lists for PR elections; Jacques Chirac
(RPR) supported parity, but not legal quotas, and promised to create a
state agency responsible for overseeing its implementation; and Lio-
nel Jospin (PS) came out in favor of parity, the use of financial penalties to ensure compliance with parity, and a change in all electoral
systems to PR (Mossuz-Lavau 1998; Sineau 2001).

Upon being elected, Jacques Chirac appointed Alain Juppé as
prime minister and oversaw the nomination of a record number of
women to the cabinet.[18] Together they commissioned the Observatory for Parity, a state-level agency, to study and develop strategies
concerning women in politics. Although the proportion of women
in the cabinet soon dropped precipitously from 28 percent to 13
percent (Mossuz-Lavau 1998, 21–22), parity advocates continued to
lobby for legal reform. In 1996, ten prominent female politicians from
both the left and the right came together to outline their own proposals for attaining equal representation, which were published in
L'Express, a major weekly news magazine, as the Manifesto of the Ten
for Parity (6 June 1996). Much less radical than the Manifesto of the
577, this document called for voluntary measures within the parties
rather than a parity law, expansion in the use of PR, drastic reduction
in multiple office-holding, public financing for parties that respect

parity, and a referendum on a constitutional amendment to introduce positive action. In the same edition, *L'Express* revealed the results of a nationwide poll showing that 71 percent of the French population would support a law or constitutional amendment establishing equal representation. The paper also included interviews with Juppé and Jospin, both of whom endorsed a constitutional amendment and a referendum to establish measures to promote women in politics.

These public declarations in favor of parity are notable, and somewhat unusual, in that calls for parity entail a much more radical demand—equal representation for women and men—than campaigns for quotas elsewhere in the world. Nonetheless, parity gained a broad base of support, spanning women in civil society, the political parties, and the state; new and established women's groups; feminist activists and academics; left-wing and right-wing politicians; and male and female voters. These patterns reflected the unique nature of the parity solution, which sought to redefine the principles used by the Constitutional Council to reject quotas—equality before the law and representation of the whole, rather than its parts—to devise a new normative justification for quotas consistent with the broader framework of French republicanism. To accomplish this task, advocates argued that current understandings of equality and representation—as well as their subject, the "universal citizen"—were originally deemed to apply only to men.

Rather than abandon these concepts entirely, they proposed reforming the Constitution to provide for the equal representation of women and men in political life, on the grounds that this was the only way to recognize explicitly the two sexes of the abstract universal citizen. Instituting parity was crucial to the general welfare of society, they claimed, because "sex" was the universal difference among human beings, a division that cut across all other groups, categories, and communities. This policy differed fundamentally from establishing quotas, because while quotas implied special representation rights for minorities, parity simply called for equitable sharing of power between women and men, the two halves of the human race. As a consequence, the inclusion of women would provide for a more accurate reflection of the whole people and the common interest, and not the representation of a distinct social category with viewpoints and interests consistently different from those of men. Inscribing parity in the Constitution, they argued, would therefore not reverse the accomplishments of the French Revolution, but rather would finally fully realize them.[19]

The concept of parity thus embodied a series of moves to reframe demands to promote women's political representation by establishing "sex" as the universal division among human beings, the logic of parity as distinct from the logic of quotas, and the goal of parity as changes in patterns of participation and not in the content of public policies. These formulations, importantly, contained a number of ambiguities that not only accounted for the broad coalitions in favor of parity, but also for the particular groups opposed to including it in the Constitution. The argument that "sex" is the universal difference, for example, presented advocates with a means to justify their focus on women, while also reducing the impact of criticism that recognizing parity would escalate claim-making by other underrepresented groups. This solution appealed to those who sought measures to tackle sex discrimination, as well as those concerned that parity would open the way to multiculturalism and thus the erosion of cultural assimilation at the heart of French republicanism.

Feminist critics of parity, however, argued that giving political value to sexual difference was invariably reactionary, not only because it reduced women to their ovaries, but also because reifying sexual difference made it impossible to see commonalities between women and men (Badinter 1996; Varikas 1995). Various intellectuals and politicians, for their part, refused to accept the distinction between sex and other types of political cleavage. They insisted that a concession for women would spur "differentialism" and "communitarianism" among other groups, with fatal consequences for the secular and universal republic. In their view, any shortcomings in the founding principles of the French republic were a legacy of their historical implementation, a situation that would evolve naturally over time until women and men were as equal in practice as they were in theory (Ozouf 1995).

In a similar vein, the claim that parity was not a quota enabled supporters to rationalize their pursuit of special measures to increase women's representation and thus overcome the negative impact of the earlier Constitutional Council decision. This argument was attractive to feminists and nonfeminists who recognized the importance of taking action to promote women's access to political office, but who rejected the negative connotations of quotas or recognized the need for a semantic shift to implement a measure that for all intents and purposes was functionally equivalent to a quota. Feminist opponents continually sought to demystify this distinction, asserting that parity was simply a stricter form of quota and, as such, threatened to turn women into victims who needed special help to succeed, reinforcing the same prejudices that misogynists had long used to keep women out of politics (Pisier 1995; Trat 1995). Other critics emphasized that exclusion was not simply about numbers and ridiculed attempts to institute quotas as a misplaced desire to imitate the United States, pointing out that the countries with the highest levels of female representation had never mandated such measures by law (Badinter 1996; cf. Scott 1998).[20]

The focus of parity on policy-makers, rather than on the content of public policies, finally, allowed advocates to remain agnostic as to the expected policy outcomes of the parity provision. This position appealed to male politicians concerned that parity might benefit women at the expense of men, because women in office would represent women's interests, and to feminists worried that parity falsely assumed essential differences between women and men, because not all women in office pursued women's issues. Various feminists responded that supporting female candidates simply because they were women would draw attention away from substantive policy questions affecting women, as well as risk advancing women who were already co-opted by male leaders, thus increasing the distance between elite and regular women (Le Dœuff 1995). Other opponents asserted that politics should revolve around ideas, not around people, and that sexual differences had nothing to do with political ideology (Badinter 1996). Despite the many efforts to reduce the appeal of parity, however, the concept remained sufficiently ambiguous to garner the support of groups that otherwise disagreed on other political issues. Indeed, one critic observed that parity was like a chameleon, able to accommodate all publics and all sensibilities (Varikas 1995). This led others to worry that not enough attention was being paid to the arguments against parity, preventing a truly democratic debate from taking place (Amar 1999).

The Adoption of the Loi sur la Parité

The public debate on parity, combined with pressures from women inside the PS, led Jospin to announce in May 1996 that at least 30 percent of the party's candidates for parliament would be women, the first time that the quota would apply to two-round majoritarian elections. Although several male leaders inside the party argued that they would not be able to find enough suitable women, the party approved a list of 167 female candidates in February 1997, slightly more than 30 percent (Gaspard 1998). Despite their declarations in favor of parity, President Chirac and Prime Minister Juppé took no concrete initiatives in this direction. Indeed, Juppé became more reticent about his support following a 1997 survey showing that 75 percent of all deputies in the National Assembly opposed inscribing parity in the Constitution, with most of this opposition coming from the conservative majority of the RPR and Union for a Democratic France (UDF) (Sineau 2001, 176). Consequently, in the first parliamentary debate on parity in March 1997, Juppé stressed that he continued to support measures to promote women's representation, but he suggested reducing the demand for parity in the Constitution to some form of temporary measure to encourage female candidates (Bird 2003). A vote never took place, however, and shortly thereafter Chirac dissolved the Assembly and called for new elections, one year ahead of schedule. Although caught off-guard by this announcement, many of the parties on the left presented relatively high proportions of female candidates, ranging between 27 percent and 33 percent. The right-wing parties, in contrast, nominated only 8 percent to 12 percent women among their parties' candidates, choosing instead to stand behind their incumbents, who were overwhelmingly male. As a result, 42 of the 63 women elected, a record 11 percent of the National Assembly, were from the PS (Mossuz-Lavau 1998, 61–62) (see table 6.3).

Although Chirac had anticipated that early elections would help consolidate the power of the UDF-RPR alliance, his strategy backfired when a majority of voters chose the Socialists, leading to the appointment of Jospin as the new prime minister. Within a matter of days, Jospin named more than 30 percent women to his new cabinet and announced that he planned to pursue an amendment to incorporate parity into the Constitution (*Le Monde*, 21 June 1997).[21] Chirac responded a month later that he too would support constitutional reform, if nothing else could be done to ensure women's access to political office (Mossuz-Lavau 1998). Over the next two years, the issue of parity became part of broader discussions in the media on reforms to modernize French politics, like strengthening local democracy, bringing an end to multiple-office holding, and introducing limited electoral system reform. Although some right-wing officials claimed that the government was using parity as an excuse to change the electoral system for National Assembly elections (Ramsay 2003), public awareness of women's under-representation in politics began to grow as journalists compared the situation in France with other countries in the EU. Many were shocked to learn that France had

Table 6.3. Women's Legislative Representation in France

National Assembly		Senate	
Year	Women (%)	Year	Women (%)
1945	5.6	1946	6.7
1946	5.1	1948	3.8
1946	7.0	1951	2.8
1951	3.7	1955	2.8
1956	3.2	1958	1.9
1958	1.5	1959	1.6
1962	1.9	1962	1.8
1967	2.3	1964	1.8
1968	2.1	1968	1.8
1973	2.7	1971	1.4
1978	4.3	1974	2.5
1981	7.1	1977	1.7
1986	6.6	1980	2.3
1988	6.9	1983	2.8
1993	6.4	1986	2.8
1997	10.9	1989	3.1
2002	12.2	1992	5.0
2007	18.2	1995	5.6
		1998	5.9
		2001	10.9
		2004	18.2

Source: Inter-Parliamentary Union (1995, 121); Sineau (2002, 4); Inter-Parliamentary Union 2008a.

the lowest percentage of women in parliament, ahead of only Greece, and that the percentage of women elected to the National Assembly had barely changed since 1945, when women were first eligible to run for political office (Lovecy 2000). These developments spurred both leaders to reaffirm their commitments to parity on International Women's Day in March 1998.

One month later, Jospin announced his plans to pursue a constitutional amendment for parity in positions of political, economic, and social responsibility. He argued that the best place to introduce this amendment was Article 1, which affirms the principles of the French republic and guarantees equality before the law. Because the president has the power to initiate constitutional amendments, along with individual members of parliament, Chirac considered Jospin's proposals and, despite his earlier statements, rejected the term "parity" in favor of the term "equal access," and reform of Article 1 in favor of Article 34, which simply lists the policy areas in which the legislature may make law. After the two men reached a compromise to support a law guaranteeing equal access to positions of political, economic, and social responsibility, however, the Council of State argued that economic and social equality were already included in the Preamble of the Constitution. Upon further negotiation, Chirac agreed to reform Article 3, which outlines the basic rights of citizens in relation to national sovereignty, on the condition that Jospin drop his demand to introduce a new electoral system for the National Assembly, one of his long-standing political commitments (Giraud and Jenson 2001; Sineau 2001). Conservatives in the Senate, further, insisted that the verb "guarantees" be replaced with "favors" (*favoriser*) equal access, thus reducing the claim for equal representation of women and men to the milder goal of increasing the number of female candidates.

With these changes, the amendment was submitted for its first reading in the National Assembly in December 1998. Élisabeth Guigou, the minister of justice, opened the debate by reviewing the history of the parity concept. On these grounds, she argued that reform of Article 3 would not introduce a sexual cleavage into politics, but would bring an end to political exclusion, and thus finally fully realize the goals of the French Revolution. To make her case, she criticized the 1982 Constitutional Council decision for ignoring the Preamble of the Constitution, which guarantees equal rights for men and women in all domains, and presented the current bill not as redundant but as a means for giving concrete content to this principle of equality. She pointed out that the Constitutional Council itself had cleared the way for such a measure, given its judgment in January 1997 that legislators had a duty to take the appropriate steps to prevent any departures from this principle of equality.[22] She also noted that Article 141 of the new Treaty of Amsterdam, which has constitutional status in all EU member states and would come into force in May 1999, permitted member states to adopt positive action measures to promote women's participation in professional life. In her judgment, therefore, both national and international law supported and even obligated legislators to pass a measure to facilitate women's access to political office (Guigou 1998). Although some female politicians continued to lobby against parity, arguing that a good cause had taken the wrong path (*L'Express*, 11 February 1999), the measure was adopted unanimously by the National Assembly in March 1999. The Senate, in contrast, rejected the measure on its first reading, but under heavy pressure from Chirac, eventually adopted it by an overwhelming majority. As per the procedure for ratifying a constitutional amendment, both houses of parliament then met in a special session at Versailles in July 1999 and approved the provision as Constitutional Law 99-569.

Passage of the constitutional amendment, in turn, set in motion a second round of debates regarding reform of the electoral law to specify and enforce equal access to electoral mandates and elective functions. In December 1999, Jean-Pierre Chevènement, the minister of the interior, submitted the government's proposals for the specific types of elections to which the parity principle would be applied, moments when compliance would be monitored, and sanctions that would be imposed on parties for not fully complying with these requirements. To the disappointment of many parity advocates, the bill focused on the nomination of female candidates, rather than on the proportion of women elected, and made the weakest provisions for elections to the National Assembly, whose low percentage of women had inspired the parity campaign in the first place (Giraud and Jenson 2001). More specifically, the bill mandated distinct requirements for different types of elections, according to the particular electoral system used. For elections held under PR, the bill required that lists alternate between women and men in elections with only one round (European, regional, and Senate elections in departments with three or more Senate seats), and achieve parity per group of six candidates, with three men and three women in any order, in elections with two rounds (regional and municipal elections in towns with more than 3500 inhabitants). In these elections, the penalty for noncompliance would be rejection of the list, such that parties would not be able to participate in elections unless they complied with the law.

For elections using two-round majoritarian voting, the bill mandated that parties present 50 percent male and 50 percent female candidates across all electoral districts, with no requirement as to in which districts female candidates should be placed. In these elections, the penalty for noncompliance would be financial, with parties losing a percentage of their state funding equal to half the difference in percentages of male and female candidates. By this arrangement, parties would still be guaranteed 50 percent of their financing, even if 100 percent of their candidates were men. This text was adopted almost unanimously in the National Assembly, with only one vote cast against it, in January 2000. The Senate adopted a slightly different version in March, leading to additional votes in the Assembly in March, the Senate in April, and the Assembly again in May 2000.

Upon final approval in the National Assembly, a group of sixty senators referred the bill to the Constitutional Council on the grounds that the measure instituted quotas by constraining and penalizing means, broke a constitutional tradition of not changing the electoral law less than a year before the next elections, prevented incumbents from being reelected on their original lists, and limited the free choice of voters. Although the council had upheld the unconstitutionality of quotas as late as January 1999 in a decision concerning provisions for regional elections (Lenoir 2001, 244, n. 98), it revised this view and confirmed the constitutionality of quotas at the end of May 2000,[23] leading to the promulgation of a new electoral law in June 2000.

The Implementation of the Loi sur la Parité

The parity law—as it is known, despite the fact that the word "parity" appears nowhere in the legislation—witnessed a sharp reversal of support once it passed in both houses of parliament and was explicitly sanctioned by the Constitutional Council. On the one hand, many parity advocates expressed their disappointment with the reform, voicing concerns that the law had been justified with reference to biological differences between the sexes, parity groups had not been included in the process of formulating the new law, and the Ministry of the Interior had been put in charge of monitoring implementation, rather than an independent watchdog group or state agency (Gaspard 2001; Giraud and Jenson 2001). On the other hand, vocal philosophical objections to parity virtually disappeared, being replaced by more subtle and insidious opposition from sitting deputies and political party elites (Bird 2003). The fears and hopes of both groups were vindicated across the first three elections governed by parity in 2001 and 2002, which revealed enormous variations in the impact of quotas at different levels of government.

For local elections in March 2001, parties were required to present equal numbers of women and men, placing three women and three men in any order for every six candidates. Although lists that did not conform would be declared ineligible, several male politicians predicted publicly that the parties would not be able to find enough female candidates. According to a poll commissioned by the Observatory for Parity, however, 78 percent of the list leaders reported that it was easy to apply the parity law when drawing up their lists (Sineau 2001). Indeed, the requirement to include women provided a welcome pretext for some leaders to eliminate male councilors they did not like (Bird 2003). As a result, the percentage of women in local councils in towns and cities with more than 3500 inhabitants increased from 26 percent in 1995 to 48 percent in 2001. This outcome reflected more than minimal compliance with the parity provision: if parties had placed three men followed by three women all the way down their party lists, the percentage of women elected would have been 43 percent. Importantly, the proportion of women elected across all local councils was only 33 percent, given that the parity law did not apply to towns with fewer than 3500 inhabitants, which comprise 93 percent of all municipalities and 85 percent of all local councilors in France.[24] All the same, women's representation increased in these towns as well, from 21 percent in 1995 to 30 percent in 2001 (Sineau 2002, 3).

For Senate elections in September 2001, parties contested 102 seats, seventy-four determined through list-based elections governed by parity and twenty-eight selected by majoritarian elections exempt from the parity requirement.[25] For list-based elections, parties were required to alternate between women and men from the top to the bottom of the list. As a result, many male incumbent senators were moved to lower positions on party lists. Rather than risk not being elected, many decided to set up alternative lists where they appeared in the first position. In at least four cases, these dissident lists split the right-wing vote, contributing to the election of four Communist Party (PCF) women ranked second after Socialist men. Twenty of the twenty-two women elected won their seats in the list-based elections, increasing women's total representation in the Senate from 6 percent in 1998 to 11 percent in 2001 (Sineau 2002, 4).

For National Assembly elections in June 2002 parties were required to present 50 percent male and 50 percent female candidates across all electoral districts, with no particular placement mandates and relatively mild financial penalties for those parties that did not comply. The financial regulations created distinct incentives for parties of different sizes (Murray 2004). The smaller parties generally respected parity in their nominations, both because they did not have many incumbents to unseat and because they were under pressure to maximize the amount of state subsidy they could claim. Some of these parties had long practiced parity, like the Greens and the PCF, because it was consistent with their party ideologies. Others, like the National Front (FN) and the Hunting-Fishing-Nature Party, were extremely male-dominated parties that mainly applied parity to avoid drastic cuts in their state subsidies and, at least in the case of the FN, to cultivate a more favorable image among women.

The larger parties, in contrast, opted not to apply strict parity in their nominations, both because they were unwilling to sacrifice male incumbents and because they had the financial resources to absorb losses in state funding. Indeed, these parties were able to recoup some of their financial losses during the second round, as the penalty assessed on the first round could be compensated by an increase in the number of deputies elected, a factor that raised the amount of state subsidy (Remy 2002). Consequently, the two main parties on the right, the Union for a Popular Movement (UMP)[26] and the UDF, presented less than 20 percent female candidates, while the main party on the left, the PS, nominated 36 percent (Green 2003, 5). These problems were exacerbated by the lack of a placement mandate, as the law created no disincentives for parties to place their female candidates in unwinnable districts. As a consequence, parties yielded record numbers of female candidates, 39 percent, but women's representation in the National Assembly increased only a fraction from 11 percent in 1997 to 12 percent in 2002 (Inter-Parliamentary Union 2004). As several analysts pointed out, however, these results might not have been as disappointing had it not been for the outcome of the presidential elections in April-May 2002, when Jospin was eliminated in the first round in favor of FN leader Jean-Marie Le Pen. This situation sowed panic in all the parties, but especially the PS, and led the mainstream parties to reverse many of their selections in April 2002, withdrawing many female candidates in favor of more experienced male politicians (Huret 2002; Remy 2002).

In the wake of these various elections, legislators pursued a number of reforms related to the parity provision. On the one hand, the new right-wing government initiated discussion on a number of electoral reforms that would, in essence, undo several of the most effective aspects of the parity law. In December 2002, the government proposed changes to the electoral system for regional and European elections beginning in 2004. Although retaining one-round PR, they created departmental sections for regional elections and eight large inter-regional districts instead of one national district for EP elections. These changes affected the impact of the parity law because, although parties are required to alternate between women and men in one-round PR elections, division of the lists into smaller sub-lists allows only the top few names on the list to be elected. As women rarely appear at the head of these lists, the reform increased the likelihood that more men would gain election. In addition, two new laws were approved in July 2003 revising the method of election to the Senate, which increased the threshold for the application of PR from districts with three or more senators to districts with four or more senators.[27] Because the requirement to alternate between women and men applies only to Senate elections governed by PR, these reforms reduced the percentage of districts governed by parity from 70 percent to 52 percent (Zimmermann 2003, 6). The effects of these reforms were mixed: women were elected as 48 percent of the members across all regional councils and 44 percent of the French delegation to the EP, but constituted only 17 percent of all senators elected in 2004 (Zimmerman 2007, 4).

On the other hand, members of parliament also considered measures to strengthen the parity provision. In April 2003, both houses passed a new law to require strict alternation between women and men on lists for regional elections, replacing the earlier system of three men and three women in any order per group of six candidates.[28] In December 2003, the Observatory for Parity, chaired by UMP deputy Marie-Jo Zimmermann, submitted a report to Prime Minister Jean-Pierre Raffarin drawing on interviews with legislators in all the parties to suggest methods of improving the implementation of parity in future elections. For list-based elections, it proposed to introduce parity for the selection of department heads, vice-presidents, and vice mayors; reestablish proportional representation in departments with three senators; lower the threshold for parity in local elections to apply to towns with more than 2500 inhabitants; and extend parity to delegates to inter-communal bodies, which are elected indirectly from the local councils. For majoritarian elections, the report advised reinforcing existing financial penalties by installing a new fraction of public aid proportional to the number of women elected by each party, as well as establishing a means of monitoring the nomination process to enable the rejection of slates that did not comply with the provisions of the law. It further called on the parties to present equal numbers of women and men as heads of lists, viewed as a whole, and to break with the habit of designating women only in those districts judged lost in advance. To accompany the law, the report recommended that parties eliminate the practice of multiple office-holding and facilitate a better reconciling of professional, personal, and political responsibilities (Zimmerman 2003).

In 2007, some of these suggestions were taken up in a new law aimed at extending the reach of the parity law and increasing the financial penalties that were already in force.[29] It consisted of three measures: the application of parity provisions to the executives of regions and towns with more than 3500 inhabitants, including the office of deputy mayor in towns and the vice-presidency of regional councils and members of permanent commission in regions, for a period of two election cycles; the creation of 'alternates' for local councilors, who must be of the opposite sex to one another; and the strengthening of the penalty assessed on parties that do not comply with the parity requirements in legislative elections, from one-half to three-quarters of the difference between the proportions of male and female candidates. Because this last measure was scheduled to enter into force on January 1, 2008, it did not apply to National Assembly elections held in 2007.

As such, in these elections similar trends emerged, with smaller parties being more likely than larger ones to respect the provisions of the law. All of the former nominated between 47 percent and 50 percent female candidates, including the FN which nominated 49 percent. Among the latter, however, the PS improved significantly with regard to its recruitment of women: whereas the UMP and UDF fielded only 27 percent and 37 percent female candidates, respectively, the PS nominated 46 percent (*France 2*, 8 June 2007). As a result, women occupied 26 percent of the seats won by the PS, but only 14 percent of the seats won by the UMP (Observatoire de la parité 2007). Overall, women were elected to 18 percent of the seats in the National Assembly (Inter-Parliamentary Union 2008a). This seven-point increase stemmed in large part from various attempts within the parties to reform their selection practices: the Greens, PCF, and the UDF pledged to field 50 percent women, albeit with varying degrees of strictness, while the PS adopted a target of placing at least 30 percent women in winnable seats (defined as a seat that had been won by the party at some point over the last four elections), and the UMP set a goal of 30 percent women with no commitment on where they would be placed (Murray 2007). These developments coincided with extensive attention to issues of gender in the French presidential elections, which occurred around the same time and pitted a Socialist woman, Ségolène Royal, against a Gaullist man, Nicolas Sarkozy. Following the election, the victor, Sarkozy, named a new cabinet in May 2007 that included record numbers of women.

The Loi sur la Parité *and Women's Political Representation in France*

Campaigns to promote women's representation in France have thus proceeded in a less coherent fashion than in Argentina, resulting in uneven quota implementation across political parties and across levels of government. Existing research on France generally acknowledges the diverse actors and motivations behind quota adoption and, almost invariably, traces attempts at reform over time to call attention to the constraints placed on present innovations by the failures of earlier policies. The narrative of events in this chapter takes these insights one step further to unravel the paradoxes of the current parity reform, which mobilized broad coalitions of support for a seemingly radical policy that has so far only had a marginal impact on the proportion of women elected to the National Assembly. The details of the new electoral law, viewed in conjunction with patterns of quota implementation, point to differing degrees of institutional configurational change both across parties and across levels of government. These variations reveal the less systematic nature of disjointed sequences of reform, which may provide an impetus to adopt more radical policies, but which also may undermine these attempts by addressing only single institutions of candidate selection, thus resulting in only minor changes in the number of women in parliament (see table 6.4).

Table 6.4. Quota Reforms and Institutional Configurations in France

Systemic Institutions	Practical Institutions	Normative Institutions
Period 1 (1944–1999):		
Two-round majoritarian electoral system	"Sex" as irrelevant criteria Placement in unwinnable districts	Equality before the law Representation as politics of ideas
Period 2 (1999–2007):		
Two-round majoritarian electoral system	"Sex" as relevant criteria Placement in unwinnable districts	Equality of results Representation as politics of presence
Period 3 (2007–present):		
Two-round majoritarian electoral system	"Sex" as relevant criteria Placement in some winnable districts	Equality of results Representation as politics of presence

Attempts to pass a quota law in France emerged in a context of ineffective party quotas and a legal decision that had deemed quotas for local elections to be in violation of fundamental principles of the French Constitution. Before the parity reforms, therefore, all three institutions of candidate selection were highly unfavorable to women: two-round majoritarian elections provided few opportunities for women to run, party practices excluded "sex" as a category of candidate selection, and legal precedents enforced interpretations of equality and representation that precluded the application of quotas at the statutory level to improve women's access to political office. As a consequence, women's representation in France remained below 7 percent in both houses of parliament in the 1980s and early 1990s. Taking inspiration from new domestic political actors, as well as from discussions within the COE, women in France then began to mobilize increasingly around the concept of "parity." The campaign recognized that normative reform was central, given that the Constitutional Council had rejected quotas for municipal elections on normative grounds.

Separating "parity" from "quotas," advocates aimed to redefine these principles while stressing their continuities with the broader goals of French republicanism. Gaining the support of diverse actors, they proposed and obtained changes to the Constitution and the electoral law that not only permitted, but also promoted, the use of positive action to increase women's representation. The campaign's central concern with normative reform, however, was not matched by similar success in changing systemic and practical institutions. Indeed, in the context of the parity reform, all the major political parties stood against any change in the two-round system for legislative elections. At the same time, legislators devised loose regulations for implementing parity in these elections, imposing no placement requirements and only weak financial penalties for parties that did not conform to the parity provision. Thus, the adoption of the parity law entailed normative reform, but no systemic reform and very little practical reform.

The adoption of the quota law met with mixed reactions, and the fears and aspirations of both supporters and opponents were confirmed across the first three elections governed by parity in 2001 and 2002, which produced stunning variations in the impact of quota reforms. A closer look at the provisions of the law is revealing, as it indicates varying degrees of institutional configurational change at the local versus the national level. For local elections, which are governed by PR, parties must conform to specific placement mandates for female candidates or else risk having their lists rejected. Parity at the local level thus combines favorable systemic institutions with practical and normative reforms that compel the selection of female candidates and establish "sex" as a central category of political representation. For national elections, in contrast, parties compete in two-round majoritarian elections. The law requires them to nominate equal numbers of women and men across all electoral districts, but does not mandate a placement provision, enabling parties to continue to nominate women in districts where they are unlikely to be elected. While the law imposes a financial penalty on parties that deviate from the 50 percent requirement, the cost of noncompliance is greater for smaller parties, which rely more heavily on state funding, than larger parties, which can better "afford" to select fewer female candidates. At the national level, therefore, the law reforms only normative institutions, leaving existing systemic and practical institutions largely intact.

A new wave of laws in the years since these elections has shifted these patterns to a certain extent. While systemic institutions remain the same across all levels of election, parity requirements have now been extended to a wider range of political offices and impose more explicit requirements with regard to who may serve as councilors and alternates in local and regional bodies. Further, they now create stronger incentives for both smaller and larger parties to comply with the provisions of the law, as they increase the financial penalty on parties that do not nominate equal numbers of male and female candidates. At the same time, individual parties recently made various commitments to select more women to winnable seats in the run-up to the 2007 legislative elections. However, these pledges ran the gamut from 50 percent policies with strict placement provisions, as in the Greens, to less ambitious goals of 30 percent women in districts where they are likely to win, as in the PS, or simply 30 percent across all districts where the party is running candidates, as in the UMP. These developments reveal shifts in practical institutions at the national and party levels which, due to their uneven nature, have led to varied effects on the numbers of women elected to political office. These patterns, in turn, indicate that quota reforms are not yet consolidated in France, as reflected in the setbacks and advances in public discussions surrounding the parity law. As these trial-and-error processes continue, however, France may eventually head down the path of more harmonizing reform, as debates center increasingly around systemic and especially practical obstacles to more effective implementation of the parity principle.

Conclusions

Efforts to institute legislative quotas have thus followed two distinct paths in Argentina and France: reform in Argentina has been harmonizing, bringing institutions of candidate selection together in mutually reinforcing ways, while reform in France has been disjointed, generating competition among institutions in ways that work against the selection of female candidates. Although these patterns replicate the findings of earlier chapters that harmonizing sequences have a greater impact on women's representation than disjointed sequences, the juxtaposition of these two cases produces a number of particular insights for countries considering constitutional and legal reform. Most importantly, the comparison of Argentina and France reveals that quota laws themselves are rarely sufficient for spurring dramatic changes in the numbers of women elected. Indeed, in both cases, the impact of quota provisions stems from attention to the minutiae of candidate placement across different types of elections. These details rarely appear in the initial quota legislation, but rather emerge through trial-and-error as the barriers to effective implementation become increasingly evident over time.

In Argentina, the relatively quick passage of the *ley de cupos* in 1991 was followed by nearly ten years of mobilization to specify how the quota provision should be interpreted for elections to the Chamber of Deputies and the Senate, with constitutional reforms, court cases, and presidential decrees attempting to clarify exactly what is meant by 30 percent "in proportions which make their election possible." In France, in contrast, a judgment deeming quotas unconstitutional in 1982 led quota advocates to spend almost fifteen years searching for new ways of justifying measures to increase women's representation. The protracted process of gaining elite support for parity, in turn, entailed important concessions that reduced the demand of "guaranteeing parity" to one of "favoring equal access" to political office. Although the reform eventually gained the approval of both houses of parliament, as well as the Constitutional Council, the new electoral law established only weak nomination and placement requirements for elections to the National Assembly. While additional reforms have been proposed to strengthen the parity law, both at the state and party levels, these efforts have mainly entailed extending its scope, rather than binding the behavior of political elites in relation to the placement of women in winnable seats for legislative elections. Comparing these two cases over time, therefore, sheds crucial light on the relationship between institutional reform and the impact of gender quotas: the relatively mild normative reform approved in Argentina has been followed by enduring attention to systemic and practical obstacles to quota implementation, while the relatively radical normative reform in France has barely affected the systemic and practical institutions shaping the selection of female candidates for parliamentary elections. These patterns thus again confirm the central role of politics in explaining variations in women's political representation, revealing that both the adoption and implementation of gender quotas is often a deeply contested process.

SEVEN

Conclusions and Directions for Future Research

Gender quotas have become an increasingly prominent solution in recent years to the under-representation of women in electoral politics. As research on these policies has grown, scholars have sought to explain how and why quotas are adopted and, more recently, why some quota policies are more effective than others in facilitating women's access to political office. The goal of this book has been to go beyond the study of single cases to develop a more comprehensive framework for analyzing the adoption and implementation of specific quota policies, both individually and with reference to experiences around the globe. This chapter reviews this framework, as well as the insights generated by the paired comparisons of efforts to institute reserved seats in Pakistan and India, party quotas in Sweden and the United Kingdom (UK), and legislative quotas in Argentina and France. It then takes these comparisons a step further to explore what a look at all six cases together reveals about the origins and effects of quota measures. The aim is to provide additional insights for analyzing quota campaigns, and designing more effective quota policies, in these and other countries around the world. This chapter concludes with a discussion of directions for future research.

Analyzing Gender Quotas: A General Framework

This book approaches quotas as a global phenomenon and, using a comparative lens, seeks to elaborate a more general framework for analyzing variations in their diffusion and effects on the numbers of women elected to national parliaments. Because the data do not support the idea of a single universal explanation for either adoption or implementation, the book argues for rethinking two traditional assumptions in social science: *causal homogeneity*, the notion that factors work the same way in all cases, and *causal competition*, the belief that variables exert independent effects on outcomes (Ragin 1987). Drawing on recent innovations in comparative methods, it calls on scholars to consider *causal heterogeneity*, the possibility that variables may not work the same way in all instances, and *causal combination*, the idea that the effects of particular factors may depend on the presence or absence of other conditions (Mahoney and Rueschemeyer 2003; Ragin 2000). Revising these guiding assumptions has crucial implications for political analysis. Accepting causal heterogeneity means recognizing the potential for *equifinality*, or the notion that there may be multiple paths to the same outcome. Causal combination, in turn, requires that analysts conceptualize, map, and evaluate configurations rather than individual causal conditions.

To model the dynamics of quota adoption, the analysis begins by outlining four common arguments: women mobilize for quotas to increase women's representation, political elites recognize strategic advantages for pursuing quotas, quotas are consistent with existing or emerging norms of equality and representation, and quotas are supported by international norms and spread through transnational sharing. To utilize these insights to design better case studies, as well as engage in more systematic comparative research, these accounts are disaggregated into their component parts. They indicate three categories of potential actors in quota campaigns: civil society actors, like women's movements and women's sections inside political parties; state actors, like national leaders, members of parliament (MPs), and courts; and international and transnational actors, like international organizations and transnational networks. At the same time, they point to seven motivations for quota reform: principled stands, electoral considerations, empty gestures, promotion of other ends, extension of representational guarantees, international pressure, and transnational learning. To demonstrate how these elements might come together in particular quota campaigns, the book discusses a number of common alliances in quota debates. While only illustrative, these patterns suggest that many quota policies are the result of various constellations of actors that support reform for multiple and often conflicting reasons. This framework thus presents a set of shared tools for analyzing the origins of quota policies, while also remaining sensitive to diversity among quota campaigns.

Turning to quota implementation, the book is critical of recent attempts to include quotas as one variable among many that might explain cross-national variations in women's representation. It argues that understanding why some measures are more effective than others requires theorizing the dynamics of candidate selection and then exploring the degree to which quota reforms reinforce or disrupt these interactions. The analysis starts with three explanations often given in the literature, namely that the impact of quotas is linked to the details of the measures themselves, depends on the institutional framework in which they are introduced, and stems from the balance of actors for and against these measures. It then draws on earlier research on women's representation to make a case for reconciling these narratives to explore how structures, practices, and norms might work together to produce the effects of quota policies.

To this end, the book develops an alternative model of candidate selection based on configurations of three categories of gendered institutions: systemic institutions, the formal features of political systems; practical institutions, the formal and informal practices that shape political behavior; and normative institutions, the formal and informal principles that guide and justify the means and ends of political life. It then proposes that the three types of quotas reform different kinds of institutions: reserved seats revise systemic institutions, party quotas rework practical institutions, and legislative quotas redefine normative institutions. At the same time, it notes that specific quota measures also achieve varying degrees of institutional reform, interact in numerous ways with existing institutional arrangements, and intersect—at the moment of reform or at a later moment in time—with the reform and nonreform of other institutions. These theoretical tools thus frame quota impact in relation to how quota policies affect existing institutional constellations in ways that facilitate or undermine changes in patterns of women's access to political office.

After elaborating these components of quota campaigns, the book engages in a more fine-grained analysis of six individual cases of quota reform. The cases were selected according to two criteria. First, multiple attempts at quota reform have taken place. Second, within each pair, one country has witnessed dramatic shifts following the adoption of quota policies, while the other has seen little change or even stagnation in the numbers of women elected. The cases selected this way offer a relatively accurate reflection of the range of countries that have witnessed quota campaigns, in that they are politically, socially, economically, and culturally diverse. Traditional qualitative methods preclude these comparisons, on the grounds that these cases cannot be matched on most characteristics. However, differences such as these can be accommodated within an analysis focused on causal configurations, precisely because attention is trained on how factors combine, rather than on the effects of any single condition. As such, the research design uses cross- and within-case comparisons to discover why some quotas are more effective than others in achieving their stated aims by examining iterated sequences of reform and their relation to changing patterns of political representation over time. To this end, the case studies draw on primary and secondary sources to explore the actors, motivations, and contexts relevant to the adoption and implementation of reserved seats in Pakistan and India, political party quotas in Sweden and the UK, and legislative quotas in Argentina and France.

In an effort to explain differences in quota effects across these pairs of countries, the book theorizes two ideal-typical trajectories of institutional reform. These models reflect differences in how, and the extent to which, reforms of one institution intersect with the reform and nonreform of other institutions. In most instances, actors do not appear, at least initially, to be aware of how structures, practices, and norms might work together to shape patterns of political representation. Yet, as research on institutions observes, relations between institutions may be mutually reinforcing (Greif and Laitin 2004) or conflicting (Orren and Skowronek 2004), whether by historical accident or intentional design. In harmonizing sequences, actions are taken that work cumulatively to adjust institutions of candidate selection to one another, such that they fit together increasingly over time. These campaigns can be anticipated to experience dramatic success in quota implementation, as they complement institutional reform with institutional configurational change. In disjointed sequences, in contrast, actors pursue strategies that lead the three categories of institutions to clash with one another, producing conflicts and tensions that undermine efforts to promote change. These types of campaigns can be expected to produce mixed results in terms of quota adoption, as well as limited success with regard to quota implementation and impact, because they separate institutional change from institutional configurational reform. In some instances, however, these sequences may become harmonizing, if campaigners come to realize the importance of broader institutional configurations. At the same time, harmonizing and disjointed sequences may coexist across political parties or levels of government, depending on the form and reach of quota debates. As such, sequences of reform may play out in a variety of ways, with diverse effects on women's political representation.

Analyzing Gender Quotas: Case Study
Evidence

The case studies presented in the book largely confirm these expectations, revealing that harmonizing sequences are indeed more effective than disjointed reforms in increasing women's representation. In Pakistan, seats have been reserved for women since the time when the country was still part of India and ruled by the British Empire. After independence, democratic and nondemocratic regimes established quota provisions in 1954, 1956, 1962, 1967, 1970, 1973, 1980, and 1984. These policies were solely responsible for women's representation in parliament until 1977, when a woman first won a general seat, and accounted for the election of the overwhelming majority of women in parliament through 1988. Systemic institutions thus sustained women's representation from the 1950s to the 1980s, at a time when practical and normative institutions largely prevented women from contesting and winning nonreserved seats, as they did not treat "sex" as a central criteria for candidate selection or recognize "women" as a category deserving equal representation. The vital role of these provisions became clear in 1990, when the expiration of the reserved seats policy led to a dramatic drop in the number of women elected to the lower house of parliament.

Twelve years later, however, reserved seats were restored and increased through systemic reform that, combined with new restrictions on political candidacy, spilled over to practical and normative reform. More specifically, the government doubled the proportion of seats reserved for women in the national and provincial assemblies and extended reservations to local and Senate elections for the very first time. Yet, these reforms were accompanied by a series of controversial constitutional amendments that restricted candidacy to those meeting particular qualifications. These had the effect of disqualifying many former and aspiring male politicians and thus forced elites to reconsider their pool of potential candidates. Most notably, the requirement that candidates be university graduates caused some male politicians to step down in favor of their better-educated sisters and wives, while the ban on candidates who had engaged in criminal activities led to the election of women related to male leaders who could no longer run themselves. These reforms shifted practical and normative institutions in ways that benefited women, resulting in the election of more women to reserved and nonreserved seats than ever before.

In India, the first policies to institute reserved seats appeared in the 1930s, as the British government moved to include women among a list of groups that were guaranteed representation in the colonial regime. The nationalist movement, however, condemned this solution as a "divide-and-rule" strategy that sought to undermine the common identity of all Indians. For this reason, after independence the newly drafted constitution abolished special seats for women in the interest of recognizing fundamental equality between women and men. Nonetheless, practices at the local level introduced a custom of co-opting women into local councils when no women were elected directly. By the 1980s, several states had formalized these policies by reserving seats for women at various levels of local government. Thus, by the advent of the reservation debates in the 1990s, a variety of systemic and practical solutions mitigated the effects of these normative institutions in local politics. In contrast, the effects of systemic, practical, and normative institutions at the national level largely worked against the selection of female candidates.

When reserved seats for women in local government were extended to all states in the early 1990s, women's groups began to demand similar reservations for state assemblies and the national parliament. Although most parties responded by including commitments to reservations for women in their party manifestos, each new attempt by a government to introduce a bill along these lines was met with strong normative opposition from MPs, primarily on the grounds that the bill in its present form would promote upper caste Hindu women if it was not revised to incorporate sub-quotas for Other Backward Castes and Muslims. Although women's groups suggested that these concerns were simply a convenient excuse for men who did not want to lose their seats in parliament, they refused to consider normative reforms that would establish sub-reservations or practical reforms that would create quotas within their own parties, shifts that would not only eliminate these objections, but also pave the way for more effective institutional configurational change. Insisting that women should not be divided, they pointed out that sub-quotas for Scheduled Castes and Scheduled Tribes already existed in the provision, thus continuing to pursue systemic reform to the exclusion of practical and normative change. As a result, systemic, practical, and normative institutions have shifted little and women's representation in parliament remains low.

In Sweden, efforts to promote women's representation have occurred primarily at the party level, with women's groups inside and outside the parties pressing for increasingly stronger measures to ensure the selection of female candidates. Until the 1980s, most parties rejected gender quotas as a measure to improve women's access to political office, preferring instead to adopt more informal goals or targets for the recruitment of women. By the time that quotas were adopted by some parties in the 1980s and 1990s, they thus served more to consolidate women's gains than to motivate them (Dahlerup and Freidenvall 2005). Consequently, systemic institutions did not change but practical institutions shifted dramatically, as women's groups ensured that parties not only nominated women, but also placed them in winnable positions on party lists. These campaigns also succeeded in reshaping normative institutions to a certain degree by improving the proportion of women each party considered necessary for "women" to be adequately "represented," from one woman per list to at least 40 percent. Women slowly radicalized these demands in some parties, but not in others, leading to varying degrees of practical and normative reform and, in turn, slightly uneven progress across the parties in terms of the proportions of women elected to parliament. They struggled in particular with reigning normative perceptions regarding "quotas," which were largely viewed as undemocratic and as implying the selection of unqualified women.

However, the decline in the number of women elected to parliament after elections in 1991 led women across the political spectrum to organize in new ways to pressure parties to place more female candidates in safe seats on party lists. Given the strong normative aversion to "quotas" in all the parties, they pressed elites to adopt the principle of *varannan damernas*, which they stressed was not so much a quota as a method for achieving gender balance by alternating between women and men. By the late 1990s, most parties applied alternation, but differed to the extent that they treated this policy as a recommendation or as a quota. These reforms refined existing practical institutions by designating "sex" as a central organizing principle for the entire candidate list. At the same time, they altered reigning normative institutions by transforming calls for proportionate representation to demands for equal representation. While some parties were more successful than others in meeting their stated goals, most elected equal numbers of women and men by 2006, with the only exceptions being various right-wing parties, which continue to resist strict gender quotas. Together, these patterns indicate varying degrees of practical and normative reform across political formations, although all parties to a certain extent have revised their criteria for candidate selection and their willingness to intervene in local selection processes.

In the UK, campaigns to promote women's representation have unfolded at a number of different levels, with varying degrees of success in the adoption and implementation of quota policies. In the late 1980s, all institutions worked against the selection of female candidates: unfavorable systemic institutions, namely a first-past-the-post electoral system organized around single-member districts, combined with practices and norms that did not recognize "sex" as a central category of political representation. After a string of electoral defeats, however, the Labour Party underwent a series of internal reforms in an effort to capture new voter constituencies, including women. To this end, it adopted a policy of all-women shortlists (AWS) in 1993 that would apply to half of all vacant seats that the party was likely to win. This strategy required that all final lists of candidates in these districts be composed entirely of women, a solution suggested by women inside the party in light of the electoral system that made other kinds of quotas impossible to apply. Once passed, the policy became controversial on both practical and normative grounds, leading some local parties to resist AWS and two male party members to challenge the policy in court. When AWS were overturned as illegal by an industrial tribunal, a number of experts claimed that the decision was based on an incorrect interpretation of the law on sex discrimination. Party leaders nonetheless agreed to discontinue the policy, leading to reversals with regard to both practical and normative institutions.

Despite this atmosphere of legal uncertainty, in the late 1990s several parties sought to promote women's representation in the new Scottish Parliament and National Assembly for Wales. While careful to remain within the letter of the law, they took note of details of the new mixed electoral system when devising quota provisions. Labour developed a twinning strategy to ensure that equal numbers of women and men would be elected to constituency seats, by pairing districts according to geography and "winnability" and selecting a woman as the candidate in one and a man as the candidate in the other. In contrast, the Scottish National Party and Plaid Cymru considered mechanisms that would maximize the election of women from party lists. Devolution thus presented an opportunity for advocates to frame quota policies as a crucial element of democratic innovation, leading several parties to adapt their practices and norms of candidate selection to features of the new electoral system. Over the course of three elections, these patterns have endured, despite small fluctuations in the numbers of women elected, leading to equal or nearly equal numbers of women and men in the devolved assemblies.

In contrast, at the UK level, the successful legal challenge to quotas caused supporters to identify the interpretation of certain articles of the Sex Discrimination Act as the main barrier to positive action in candidate selection, and by extension, to further increases in the number of women elected to the House of Commons. In 2001, the government introduced a bill that would allow, but not compel, parties to adopt measures to reduce inequalities in representation. The focus on normative reform stemmed from a desire to clarify the legal ambiguities informing discussions on positive action. However, the need to approve the bill in both houses of parliament led advocates to settle for this more permissive formulation, in effect limiting the scope for normative change. At the same time, the debate bracketed the issue of systemic and practical reform, enabling parties to later react as they saw fit to the new provision. As a consequence, the three major parties have responded in distinct ways: Labour has engaged in full practical reform by reintroducing AWS; the Liberal Democrats have pursued partial practical reform by establishing targets; and the Conservatives initially avoided but have now begun to implement limited practical reforms by requiring equal numbers of men and women on candidate shortlists. These variations indicate the ongoing presence of multiple institutional configurations across the British party system, suggesting that suggesting that patterns of candidate selection are likely to continue to diverge across parties in the next general elections.

In Argentina, proposals to establish a quota law first appeared in the late 1980s. At that time, the only institution ostensibly favorable to women was the proportional representation (PR) list electoral system. However, because existing practical and normative institutions did not treat "sex" as a central criteria or category for candidate selection, women's representation remained low in both houses of parliament. Looking for means to alter the status quo, feminist organizations and women inside the parties looked for lessons abroad, and through transnational learning, became familiar with attempts to institute quotas elsewhere in the world. Drawing on these experiences, as well as international documents establishing the normative legitimacy of quotas, they organized within and across party lines to press for the passage of a national quota law. Legislators approved the bill, and in so doing, altered systemic and normative institutions by amending an article of the electoral law to redefine the existing principle of representation. Yet, the statement that all lists must include a minimum of 30 percent women did not specify how parties should translate this provision in their selection practices, leaving practical institutions largely untouched.

The lack of a specific placement mandate for female candidates sparked an almost decade-long battle to ensure that this requirement resulted in the election of at least 30 percent women. Although an early presidential decree introduced the first practical reforms by listing the number of women that parties had to include among their total number of candidates up for reelection, many elites offered multiple interpretations of the law and thus avoided placing women in spots where they were likely to be elected. At this juncture, women's groups initiated a legal campaign to ensure compliance with the quota law. These legal battles helped to specify various systemic and normative aspects of the quota law by establishing that it applied to all parliamentary elections, and when the constitution was reformed in 1994, that the quota did not contravene constitutional principles of equality. These efforts persisted through the late 1990s, but despite changes in systemic and normative institutions, parties continued to undermine the goals of quota law in their selection practices. In response, a new presidential decree was issued that clarified the placement of female candidates in all situations and required judges to rectify lists if parties did not do so themselves. These procedures solidified the reform of party selection practices, resulting in complete institutional configurational change and thus perfect implementation of the quota law beginning with elections in 2001.

In France, finally, attempts to pass a quota law emerged in a context of ineffective party quotas and a legal decision in 1982 that had deemed quotas for local elections to be in violation of fundamental principles of the French Constitution. Consequently, all three categories of institutions worked against the selection of female candidates: two-round majoritarian elections provided few opportunities for women to run, party practices excluded "sex" as a criterion of candidate selection, and legal precedents precluded the application of quotas at the statutory level to improve women's access to political office. As a result, women's representation in France remained very low in both houses of parliament in the 1980s and early 1990s. Around this time, however, women's groups were inspired by new domestic political actors, as well as discussions within the Council of Europe, and began to mobilize increasingly around the concept of parity. They recognized that normative reform was crucial, given that the Constitutional Council had rejected quotas for municipal elections on normative grounds. Separating "parity" from "quotas," advocates aimed to redefine principles of equality and representation, while also stressing their continuities with the broader goals of French republicanism. Gaining the support of diverse actors, they proposed and obtained changes to the Constitution and the electoral law that not only permitted, but also promoted, the use of positive action to increase women's representation.

All the same, the campaign's central concern with normative reform was not matched by similar success in changing systemic and practical institutions. Indeed, in the context of the parity reform, all the major parties opposed any change in the two-round system for legislative elections. Further, legislators approved only minimal regulations for implementing parity in these elections, imposing no placement requirements and weak financial penalties for parties that did not conform to the parity provision. Thus, the adoption of a 50 percent quota law entailed normative reform, but no systemic reform and very little practical reform. For this reason, elections governed by parity have produced stunning variations in the impact of quota reforms at the local versus national levels. In local elections, governed by PR, parties must conform to specific placement mandates for female candidates or else risk having their lists rejected. Here, favorable systemic institutions combine with practical and normative reforms to compel the selection of female candidates and establish "sex" as a central category of political representation. For national elections, in contrast, parties compete in two-round majoritarian elections. The law requires equal numbers of women and men across all electoral districts, but does not mandate a placement provision, at the same that it imposes a financial penalty on parties that deviate from the 50 percent requirement, creating a higher cost for noncompliance for smaller parties over larger ones. At the national level, therefore, the law reforms normative institutions, but leaves existing systemic and practical institutions largely intact. However, a new wave of laws has led to several recent setbacks and advances in public discussions around the quota law, indicating that debates may continue regarding ways to overcome the remaining systemic and practical obstacles to more effective quota implementation.

In addition to these insights, each two-case comparison in the book offers several empirical observations for countries considering or undergoing each type of quota reform. The juxtaposition of Pakistan and India reveals, somewhat troublingly, that democratic regimes may present important obstacles to the adoption of reserved seats, while dictators may perceive quotas as a relatively easy solution for legitimizing their rule. It also points to potential conflicts between various claims for group representation, illustrating how guarantees for other groups may facilitate but also thwart provisions for women. The comparison between Sweden and the UK uncovers why similar party quotas rarely have one uniform effect on women's representation. It reveals that understanding the impact of these measures requires two levels of analysis, the party level and the party system level, that together shape how specific policies affect the overall numbers of women elected. The study also nuances the distinction between harmonizing and disjointed sequences by noting that the latter sometimes present rather than prevent opportunities to pursue broader institutional configurational change. The examination of Argentina and France, finally, reveals that quota laws themselves are rarely sufficient for spurring dramatic changes in women's representation. Rather, their effectiveness often hinges on attention to the minutiae of candidate placement across different elections, as the barriers to effective implementation become increasingly more evident over time.

Comparing Gender Quotas: Conclusions and Directions for Future Research

The main lesson of this book is that quotas are a global phenomenon, and as such, are best studied through a broader comparative framework. Consequently, the analysis contained in this book is primarily intended as a theory-building exercise, aimed at synthesizing and elaborating the growing literature on gender quota provisions. Based on this work, it is possible to offer six main conclusions regarding quota campaigns, which together reveal the analytical benefits of recognizing causal heterogeneity and causal combination.

First, corroborating the intuition that there may be multiple paths to the same outcome, *the key actors in quota debates vary widely across countries and may pursue quota reform for feminist and nonfeminist reasons.* Actors may involve a single individual, who is able to make a decision overnight to pursue quota policies, but may also include much larger swathes of the population, who may need to mobilize over a more extended period of time to secure quota reform. For example, the most influential actors in Pakistan across all efforts to institute reserved seats have been individual male leaders. Most recently, seats were set aside for women in a Chief Executive's Order issued by General (and later President) Pervez Musharraf in January 2002. Similarly, the main actors in India have been state-level actors, like party leaders and MPs, who quickly passed one-third reservations for the local level in 1992, but have repeatedly held up efforts to extend these provisions to the state assemblies and the national parliament since 1996.

In contrast, the crucial actors in quota campaigns in the four other countries examined in this book have stretched across society, state, and even international and transnational arenas. In Sweden, women inside and outside the parties began lobbying party elites as early as the 1920s and gradually gained concessions that culminated in a policy of alternation in most parties by the end of the 1990s. In the UK, women started mobilizing only in the late 1980s, and almost exclusively within the Labour Party. However, when AWS were overturned in 1996, a wide range of advocates and opponents at the level of state and society appealed to international organizations and international law to bolster their arguments for and against positive action. In a mirror fashion, proposals for a quota law in Argentina emerged in the late 1980s from transnational contacts, as women inside and outside the parties learned of quotas elsewhere in Western Europe and Latin America. Yet, the law was later passed and implemented due in important part to the support of President Carlos Menem and, later, President Fernando de la Rúa over the course of the following decade. In France, women in parliament pursued a quota for local elections that gained the outward support of nearly all MPs but was immediately declared unconstitutional by the Constitutional Council in 1982. Debates in the Council of Europe several years later, however, inspired a second campaign organized by women in civil society around parity, which won cross-partisan support in both houses of parliament and resulted in constitutional and legal reform in 1999 and 2000.

Second, and related to the first, *the actors most often overlooked in quota accounts are international organizations and transnational networks.* Indeed, upon further inspection, it becomes clear that nearly all quota reforms involve some external actors or influences, despite a tendency in the literature to focus on international and transnational trends only in more recent quota campaigns, especially in developing countries. The three early cases of quota adoption examined in this book suggest a range of less traditional international and transnational effects. Perhaps most unusually, reserved seats policies in India originated in a colonial-era policy established by the British government, which many nationalists suspected sprang less from interests to increase the representation of women and other marginalized groups, and more from concerns to extend colonial domination during the last years of British rule. These colonial influences, in turn, spread and endured as a result of secession: quotas in Pakistan were adopted upon independence from India, and quotas in Bangladesh were adopted upon independence from Pakistan. In Sweden, policies to promote women in politics also appeared early, but developed locally with some contacts with women's groups and parties in other Nordic countries. Later, the country came to serve as a powerful, if inaccurate, model for other countries considering quota reform.

Compared with these examples, the three other campaigns analyzed in the book are much more typical of international and transnational effects at work within the broader universe of cases. In efforts to undermine quota adoption, opponents in the UK repeatedly referenced international and European law to question the legality of gender quotas, even as domestic and European analysts stressed that international and European law did not eliminate possibilities to pursue positive action. In a more supportive fashion, contacts with international and transnational actors inspired national-level quota campaigns in Argentina and France. In each case, these connections offered new ways forward in the specific domestic circumstances of democratic transition and earlier failed attempts to institute quotas. Taken together, these various patterns indicate multiple mechanisms of diffusion across quota campaigns. Importantly, however, they also reveal that international and transnational actors may deflect, as well as promote, quota demands in particular national contexts.

Third, when it comes to motivations and strategies, *normative questions play a central role in quota debates*. Although a majority of these discussions revolve around competing definitions of equality and representation, the exact content of these norm-based arguments vary widely across country and party contexts. In Pakistan, for example, many women claimed that reserved seats were necessary to give women more experience in politics, so that they would later be able to contest general seats. Along related lines, some male leaders expressed the belief that reserved seats for women were essential to establishing the legitimacy of a particular regime. Opponents countered these assertions, however, by arguing that women's participation in politics violated central principles of Islam, which forbade mixing among women and men and did not allow for women to act as national leaders. In India, normative debates took an entirely different form. Supporters maintained that reservations for women were the only way to promote fair access to politics. Opponents responded in two ways: some defended the existing definition of equality before the law, which precluded positive action of any sort, while others threatened to block reserved seats for women unless they were accompanied by guaranteed representation for other groups.

In a third vein, Swedish and British parties struggled with competing partisan and national ideologies when contemplating quota reform. While notions of justice and democratic participation justified special measures for women, values of formal equality and open competition privileged individual merit over group identity and thus invalidated special treatment for any particular group. In Argentina, similar doubts emerged but were quickly thwarted by constitutional reforms that established the legality of positive action. For this reason, quotas for women soon became associated with efforts to make the country more inclusive within the context of democratic transition. Finally, in France the earlier rejection of quotas on the grounds that they contravened reigning notions of equality and representation sparked a new campaign focused specifically on devising new normative definitions that justified positive action for women by arguing for the recognition of the two sexes of the universal citizen. Normative debates thus mainly invoke competing definitions of equality and representation, but also frequently tap into more context-specific values related to religion, party ideology, democratic transition, and the broader political system.

Fourth, despite the importance of political norms, *strategic motivations often play a significant role in getting quotas on the political agenda.* Indeed, fierce normative opposition can often be mitigated by electoral concerns to attract female voters. Such arguments reflect, and in turn foster, a belief that quotas are desirable because they appeal to women and are thus an effective way to win their support. All the same, it is rarely clear whether or not politicians truly intend to alter patterns of male dominance in electoral politics. These dynamics manifest themselves in similar ways across many national contexts. In Pakistan, national leaders repeatedly declared public support for reserved seats in overt attempts to appeal to women. Democratic leaders made their most radical proposals to restore and extend reserved seats just prior to elections, although they rarely followed through on these promises, while dictators periodically raised the number of seats reserved for women as support for their regime began to wane. In India, reserved seats were initially viewed as a tool for preserving colonial domination by giving various groups a stake in maintaining the existing regime. More recently, party leaders and MPs have repeatedly pledged to extend reservations for women in state assemblies and the national parliament. Before each election, each side has claimed that the other was not serious about allocating seats for women and pledged to institute reserved seats once they came or returned to power, although no government has yet fulfilled this promise.

In similar ways, political parties in Sweden and the UK have clearly perceived the need to distinguish themselves on the question of women's representation. In Sweden, mobilization by women inside the parties led elites to fear serious electoral repercussions if they did not take steps to promote female candidates. In the UK, however, mobilization by women inside Labour, combined with research by internal party bodies and external think tanks, persuaded the party that closing a gap in support among female voters was key to overcoming a string of electoral losses. Politicians in Argentina and France sensed analogous pressures and passed quota laws nearly unanimously in both houses of parliament. Their commitments to increasing women's representation, however, were soon revealed as shallow rhetoric, as officials in all parties sought to circumvent the spirit—and even the letter—of the law during the first rounds of implementation. Enduring pressure from women in Argentina forced elites to fulfill their promises, while debate continues in France in terms of ways of improving the provisions of the law to ensure more effective implementation. These dynamics reveal that many politicians perceive quotas as a means for gaining women's votes, but that many also implicitly acknowledge, mainly through non-implementation, that promoting women requires demoting themselves or their male colleagues. These contradictory tendencies thus shed light at once on the mechanisms of party competition that facilitate quota adoption and the instincts of self-preservation that hinder quota implementation.

Fifth, turning to the importance of causal combination, *the impact of quotas depends on how they interact with elements of the political environment, whose various effects must be disentangled by tracing changes in the configurations of these conditions over time.* As already noted, relations between new and old institutions may be reinforcing or conflicting, and consequently, produce harmonizing or disjointed sequences of reform. Pakistan constitutes a clear case of the former. Each regime maintained or increased provisions for

reserved seats for women between 1935 and 1990. Upon their expiration, these measures remained on the agenda as a policy issue until
2002, when they were reintroduced for lower house elections and
extended to upper house elections for the very first time. Spilling
over into a limited degree of practical and normative change, these
provisions have increased women's representation in Pakistan to
historically high levels. In India, in contrast, reform processes were
much more disjointed. Although a policy reserving one-third of all
seats in local government for women was quickly approved, a similar
bill seeking for state assemblies and the national parliament has not
yet reached a vote, because opponents insist on including sub-quotas
for lower castes and religious minorities.

Sweden offers a second case of harmonizing reform. Under pressure from women's groups, parties initially adopted informal recommendations and targets for selecting female candidates. Over the
years, these policies evolved into more formal quotas, as a result of
continuous mobilization on the part of women's groups to ensure that
parties nominated women and placed women in electable positions
on party lists. The UK, in comparison, is an instance of more disjointed reform, in light of multiple parties with distinct quota strategies and the various levels of government that have been the subject
of quota campaigns. When AWS were overturned, this decision not
only invalidated the specific policy, but also created an obstacle to
further attempts to establish quotas. Despite this legal uncertainty,
commitments made during the devolution campaigns convinced several parties to adapt their practices and norms of candidate selection
to features of the new electoral system. At the UK level, advocates
eventually succeeded in reforming the Sex Discrimination Act, but
only some parties adjusted their recruitment practices as a result.

In Argentina, quota reform has followed a harmonizing path. Proposals for a legislative quota first emerged as a result of contacts with
women in other countries around the world. Once adopted, various
presidents and electoral court judges solidified its effects by continually refining and upholding regulations regarding the placement of
women. A presidential decree in 2000 eventually cemented these
gains by offering the final word on the placement of female candidates in absolutely all situations. France, in contrast, reflects a more
disjointed set of reforms. Frustrated with their experiences with party
quotas, female MPs pressed for quotas in local elections, which were
approved nearly unanimously by both houses of parliament but later
rejected by the Constitutional Council. This decision prevented the

application of quotas for local elections and blocked further attempts to pursue quotas. Advocates regrouped and devised a new strategy for quota reform based on the concept of parity, which drew on the existing values of universalism and republicanism to redefine equality and representation by giving two sexes to the universal citizen. Yet, subsequent reform of the electoral code set up distinct requirements and incentives for implementation for national and local elections, leading to the uneasy coexistence of new and old institutions of candidate selection.

Sixth, given the central importance of causal combination and the possibility of multiple paths to the same outcome, *there are limits to prediction and prescription when it comes to quota adoption and implementation.* This point gains particular salience in light of the fact that the case studies reveal that the reinforcing or competing dynamics among institutions may be intentional as well as unintentional. This has crucial implications for how others might design similar or distinct quota policies, as it signals the limits and possibilities for translating the formulas that "work" in some cases to other quota campaigns. In Pakistan, as already noted, institutions are mutually reinforcing, but this effect is largely unintended. Reserved seats maintained a minimum level of female representation between 1935 and 1990, but when they were reintroduced in 2002, they appeared at the same time as several other reforms placing restrictions on political candidacy which disqualified many male incumbents. Systemic reform thus spilled over into practical and normative reform, resulting in the election of more women to reserved and nonreserved seats than ever before. In India, in contrast, institutional configurations are competing, but this effect—at least from the perspective of quota advocates—is largely intentional. Members of parliament were quick to pass a bill reserving one-third of all seats in local government for women, but have delayed addressing a similar bill for state assemblies and the national parliament, due to calls for reservations for women to include sub-quotas for lower castes and religious minorities. Closer examination of these debates, however, suggests that many male MPs simply articulate concerns about the increased representation of other marginalized groups as a way to frustrate passage of the bill and thus retain their own seats in parliament, drawing on normative and practical considerations to thwart systemic reform.

In Sweden, institutional configurations are mutually reinforcing by intention. Proponents of quotas initially lobbied for recommendations and targets but gradually radicalized their demands, eventually securing commitments from most parties to alternate between women and men on candidate lists. To achieve equal representation, parties repeatedly adjusted practices and norms of candidate selection to the rules of the electoral system to bring systemic, practical, and normative institutions increasingly more in line with one another. In the UK, in comparison, institutional configurations are intentionally reinforcing at one level, but unintentionally competing at another. In Scotland and Wales, quota campaigners pressured major parties to adapt their practices and norms of candidate selection to features of the new electoral system, resulting in a dense network of systemic, practical, and normative institutions supporting equal representation. At the UK level, however, advocates faced a situation in which positive action for women had been rejected in court and widely delegitimized as a strategy for increasing women's representation. In this environment, proponents responded by focusing exclusively on normative institutions as the major barrier to change, and thus overlooking possibilities for systemic and practical reform.

In Argentina, as in Sweden, institutional configurations are reinforcing by design. Supporters drew connections to the earlier Peronist party quota during the campaign for the quota law, and upon adoption, continually brought legal challenges against parties whose lists did not comply with the law. These efforts, combined with constitutional reform establishing the legality of positive action, resulted in presidential decrees and favorable court decisions that strengthened placement mandates and compelled parties to redo lists that did not follow the letter or the spirit of the law, steps that together adjusted the rules, practices, and norms of candidate selection to ensure effective quota implementation. In France, most complicated of all, institutional configurations, depending on the particular actors and levels of reform, are unintentionally competing, intentionally competing, and intentionally reinforcing. As in the UK, proponents confronted a situation in which quotas for local elections had been declared unconstitutional and responded by pursuing normative reform as a first order of business, overlooking the importance of systemic and practical reform. When reform was finally achieved, opponents sitting in the two houses of parliament were able to undermine the impact of parity by creating distinct requirements for quota implementation across various levels of government. At the national level, the new law mandated that parties nominate equal numbers of women and men across all electoral districts, but did not specify any sort of placement provision, enabling parties to continue to place women in districts where they were unlikely to be elected. In this case, new normative institutions competed with existing systemic and practical institutions to thwart change in patterns of representation. At the local level, however, the law imposed much stricter regulations that compelled parties to conform to strict placement mandates or else risk having their lists rejected. In these instances, new normative institutions combined with existing systemic institutions and new practical institutions to promote nearly equal representation between women and men.

Taken together, these six conclusions are rooted in a substantial body of case study evidence. However, they are by no means the final word on gender quotas. In the spirit of theory-building, they are offered instead as a way to take the first steps toward developing more cumulative research on strategies to increase women's political representation, using ideas about causal heterogeneity and causal combination. Through its synthesis of research on gender quotas, the framework developed in this book aims to contribute to this project by facilitating comparisons across instances of quota reform to develop better knowledge as to the diffusion and effects of various kinds of quota policies. Ideally, future work will focus on analyzing single cases and situating them in relation to other quota campaigns, discovering and giving value to similarities and differences across quota debates, and testing hypotheses about quota adoption and implementation across a wider group of cases, among other potential research questions. These kinds of studies, in turn, are likely to generate a host of new insights for adding, modifying, or even discarding aspects of this framework. At the same time, modeling the dynamics of adoption and implementation constitutes only the first step in understanding the origins and outcomes of quota policies. The next stage will require exploring the broader impact of quotas, above and beyond their effects on the absolute numbers of women elected. This question will be central for future research, as scholars seek to understand what quotas might "mean" for democracy and for women as a group, in terms of the types of women elected, the pursuit of "women's interests" in public policy, and the empowerment of female candidates and voters. These possibilities suggest a rich field for further study, building on comparative knowledge of the actors, strategies, and contexts of quota reform.

Appendix

Candidate Gender Quota Policies Worldwide[a] as of January 1, 2008

Reserved Seats in Single or Lower Houses of Parliament

Region/Country	% of Seats	House of Parliament	Year Adopted	% Women (Year)
Africa				
Djibouti	10	single house	2002	11 (2003)
Eritrea[b]	30	single house	Unknown	22 (1994)
Kenya	3	single house	1997	7 (2002)
Rwanda	30	lower house	2003	49 (2003)
Somalia	12	single house	2004	8 (2004)
Sudan	13	single house	2005	18 (2005)
Tanzania[c]	30	single house	2005	30 (2005)
Uganda[d]	18	single house	2001	30 (2006)
Asia				
Bangladesh[e]	13	single house	2004	15 (2001)
India (*previously*)	4	lower house	1935	8 (2004)
Pakistan[f]	18	lower house	2002	21 (2002)
Philippines (*previously*)	10	lower house	1986	23 (2007)
Middle East[g]				
Afghanistan	27	lower house	2004	27 (2005)
Egypt (*previously*)	8	single house	1979	2 (2005)
Jordan	5	single house	2003	6 (2003)
Morocco	9	single house	2002	11 (2002)

Sources: Inter-Parliamentary Union (2008a); Krook (2005, 493–503), updated.

[a]Quota percentages refer to the minimum percentage of female candidates that must or ought to appear on party lists for elections to the national parliament. When quotas are framed in gender-neutral terms (i.e., "no more than 80 percent of candidates of the same sex"), the quota regulation is translated into the terms of a female quota (i.e., "20 percent women"). When provisions

are framed as proportions (i.e., "one-third"), the regulation is translated into percentage terms (i.e., "33 percent"). Only the most recent provisions are recorded in the chart; earlier policies are signaled in footnotes.

[b]An earlier reserved seats policy adopted in 1994 set aside 10 percent of seats for women in Eritrea.

[c]Earlier reserved seats adopted in Tanzania include a 6 percent policy in 1961, 15 percent policies in 1975 and 1995, a 20 percent policy in 1996, and a 20–30 percent policy in 1999.

[d]Earlier reserved seats adopted in Uganda include a 13 percent policy in 1989 and a 14 percent policy in 1995.

[e]Earlier reserved seats adopted in Bangladesh include a 5 percent policy in 1972 (for 10 years), a 10 percent policy in 1978 (for 15 years), and a 10 percent in 1990 (for 10 years). Although separate elections were not organized, the 2004 provision was allocated to parties in both 2004 and 2005 based on the proportion of the vote they won in 2001.

[f]Earlier reserved seats adopted in Pakistan include 3 percent policies in 1954 and 1956; 4 percent policies in 1962, 1970, and 1973; a 7 percent policy in 1981; and a 9 percent policy in 1984.

[g]In Bahrain, 15 percent of seats in the upper house were reserved for women in 2002. The current level of female representation in this chamber is 25 percent; however, it is only 2.5 percent in the lower house (Inter-Parliamentary Union 2008a).

Party Quotas in Single or Lower Houses of Parliament

Region/ Country	% Candidates	Party	Year Adopted	% Women (Year)
Western Europe				
Austria	50	Greens-Green Alternative	1986	32 (2006)
	40	Social Democratic Party[a]	1993	
	33	Austrian People's Party	1995	
Belgium	20	Flemish Liberal Party	1985	35 (2007)
	33	French Christian Democrats	1986	
	50	Flemish Green Party	1991	
	25	Flemish Social Democrats	1992	
	50	French Green Party	2000	
	50	French Social Democrats	2000	
Denmark (*previously*)	50	Left Socialist Party	1985	37 (2005)
	40	Socialist People's Party	1988	
	40	Social Democratic Party	1988	
France	30	Socialist Party	1996	18 (2007)
Germany	50	Alliance 90-Greens	1986	32 (2005)
	40	Social Democratic Party[b]	1998	
	50	Party of Democratic Socialism	1990	
	33	Christian Democratic Union	1996	
Greece	40	Pan-Hellenic Socialist Movement	Unknown	13 (2004)
Iceland[c]	50	Left-Green Movement	1996	32 (2007)
	40	Progressive Party	1996	
	40	United Front	2002	

(*continued*)

Party Quotas in Single or Lower Houses of Parliament (*continued*)

Region/ Country	% Candidates	Party	Year Adopted	% Women (Year)
	40	Social Democratic Alliance	2007	
Ireland	40	Workers Party	1991	13 (2007)
	25	Labour Party	1991	
	40	Green Party	1992	
Italy[d]	40	Democrats of the Left	1989	17 (2006)
	50	Green Federation	1991	
	30	Democracy is Freedom	2001	
	40	Communist Refoundation	Unknown	
	20	Italian People's Party	Unknown	
	33	Italian Democratic Socialists	Unknown	
Luxembourg	33	Christian Socialist Party	2002	23 (2004)
	50	Green Party	Unknown	
	50	The Left	Unknown	
Netherlands	50	Labour Party	1987	37 (2006)
Norway	40	Socialist Left Party	1975	38 (2005)
	40	Labour Party	1983	
	40	Centre Party	1988	
	40	Christian People's Party	1993	
	40	Liberal Party	Unknown	
Portugal	33	Socialist Party	2004	21 (2005)
Spain	40	Socialist Workers Party[e]	1996	36 (2004)
	40	United Left	1997	
Sweden	40	Liberal Party	1972	47 (2006)
	50	Green Party	1981	
	50	Left Party	1987	
	40	Christian Democrats	1987	
	50	Social Democrats	1993	
Switzerland	40	Social Democratic Party	Unknown	25 (2003)
United Kingdom	50	Labour Party	1993	20 (2005)

Party Quotas in Single or Lower Houses of Parliament (*continued*)

Region/ Country	% Candidates	Party	Year Adopted	% Women (Year)
Eastern Europe				
Albania	30	Social Democratic Party	2001	7 (2005)
	25	Democratic Party	2003	
Armenia	20	Union for National Self-Determination	Unknown	9 (1995)
Bosnia-Herzegovina	30	Social Democratic Party	2001	14 (2006)
Croatia	40	Social Democratic Party	2000	22 (2003)
Cyprus	30	Social Democrats	Unknown	14 (2006)
Czech Republic	25	Social Democratic Party	1996	16 (2006)
Georgia	30	Citizens Union	2003	9 (2004)
Hungary	Unknown	Social Democratic Party	1999	10 (2006)
	20	Hungarian Socialist Party	Unknown	
Lithuania	33	Social Democratic Party[f]	Unknown	25 (2004)
Macedonia	30	Social Democratic Union	Unknown	28 (2006)
Malta	20	Labour Party	Unknown	9 (2003)
Moldova	50	Christian Democratic Party	Unknown	22 (2005)
Montenegro	Unknown	Social Democratic Party	1999	9 (2006)
Poland	30	Labour Union	1997	20 (2005)
	30	Democratic Left Alliance	1999	
	30	Freedom Union	Unknown	
	50	Zieloni 2004	2003	
Romania	30	Democratic Party	Unknown	11 (2004)
	30	Social Democratic Party	2001	
Serbia	30	Social Democratic Party	2000	20 (2007)
Slovakia (*previously*)	20	Party of the Democratic Left	Unknown	19 (2006)
Slovenia	25	Liberal Democracy Party[g]	1998	12 (2004)

(*continued*)

Party Quotas in Single or Lower Houses of Parliament (*continued*)

Region/ Country	% Candidates	Party	Year Adopted	% Women (Year)
	40	Social Democrats[h]	1997	
Ukraine	33	Social Democratic Party	Unknown	9 (2006)
Africa				
Botswana	30	Botswana National Front	1994	11 (2004)
	30	Botswana National Congress	1999	
Burkina Faso	25	Alliance for Democracy	2002	15 (2007)
	25	Congress for Democracy	2002	
Cameroon	25	Cameroon People's Free Movement	1996	14 (2007)
	25	Social Democratic Front	1996	
Cape Verde	Unknown	Movement for Democracy	Unknown	15 (2006)
Equatorial Guinea	Unknown	Social Democratic Convergence	Unknown	18 (2004)
Ethiopia	30	People's Revolutionary Democratic Front	Unknown	22 (2005)
Ghana	40	National Democratic Congress	2000	11 (2004)
	30	Great Consolidated People's Party	Unknown	
Ivory Coast	30	Ivorian Public Front	2002	9 (2000)
Kenya	33	Democratic Party	Unknown	7 (2002)
Malawi	30	Malawi Congress Party	Unknown	14 (2004)
	25	United Democratic Front	Unknown	
Mali	30	Alliance for Democracy	Unknown	10 (2007)
Mozambique	30	Front for the Liberation of Mozambique	1999	35 (2004)
Namibia	50	South West Africa People's Organization	1997	27 (2004)

Party Quotas in Single or Lower Houses of Parliament (*continued*)

Region/ Country	% Candidates	Party	Year Adopted	% Women (Year)
	50	Congress of Democrats	1999	
Senegal	25	Senegal Socialist Party	1996	22 (2007)
	33	Senegalese Liberal Party	Unknown	
South Africa	30	African National Congress	1994	33 (2004)
Latin America				
Bolivia	50	Movement without Fear	1999	17 (2005)
Brazil	30	Brazilian Workers Party	1986	9 (2006)
	30	Democratic Labor Party	1999	
	30	Popular Socialist Party	2000	
Chile	40	Party for Democracy[i]	1999	15 (2005)
	40	Socialist Party[j]	1996	
	20	Christian Democratic Party	1996	
Costa Rica	40	National Liberation Party	1996	39 (2006)
	50	Christian-Social Unity Party	2002	
	50	Citizen Action Party	2002	
Dominican Republic	25	Dominican Revolutionary Party	1994	20 (2006)
Ecuador	25	Ecuador Roldosista Party	Unknown	25 (2006)
	25	Party of Democratic Left	Unknown	
	25	People's Democracy	Unknown	
El Salvador	35	National Liberation Front	Unknown	17 (2006)
Haiti	25	Socialist Party	Unknown	4 (2006)
Mexico	20	Party of Democratic Revolution	1993	23 (2006)

(*continued*)

Party Quotas in Single or Lower Houses of Parliament (*continued*)

Region/ Country	% Candidates	Party	Year Adopted	% Women (Year)
	30	Institutional Revolutionary Party	1996	
Nicaragua	30	Sandinista National Liberation	Unknown	19% (2006)
Paraguay	20	Colorado Party	Unknown	10 (2003)
	30	Revolutionary Febrerista Party	Unknown	
Uruguay	25	Socialist Party	1984	11 (2004)
	25	Christian Democrat Party	1993	
	33	New Space	1998	
Asia				
Fiji	20	Fiji Labour Party	Unknown	Unknown
India	15	Indian National Congress	Unknown	9 (2004)
South Korea	20	Democratic Party	Unknown	13 (2004)
	30	Grand National Party	Unknown	
Philippines	25	Philippines Democratic Socialist Party	Unknown	23 (2007)
Taiwan	25	Democratic Progressive Party	1996	Unknown
	25	Chinese Nationalist Party	2000	
Thailand	30	Democrat Party	Unknown	9 (2006)
Middle East				
Algeria	40	National Liberation Front[k]	2002	7 (2007)
Israel	25	Israel Labour Party	1997	14 (2006)
	40	Meretz-Yashad		
Morocco	20	National Religious Party	Unknown	11 (2002)
	20	Socialist Union for Popular Forces	Unknown	
Tunisia	25	Democratic Constitutional Rally	2004	23 (2004)
Yemen	10	General People's Congress	2006	0 (2003)

Party Quotas in Single or Lower Houses of Parliament (*continued*)

Region/ Country	% Candidates	Party	Year Adopted	% Women (Year)
North America				
Canada	50	National Democratic Party	1992	21 (2006)
Australia				
Australia	40	Australian Labor Party[l]	2002	25 (2004)

Sources: Inter-Parliamentary Union (2008a); Krook (2005, 493–503), updated.

[a]The party adopted a 25 percent quota policy in 1985.

[b]The party adopted a 25 percent quota policy in 1988 and a 33 percent quota policy in 1994.

[c]The People's Alliance and the Social Democratic Party adopted 40 percent quotas, but were subsumed as parties into the Social Democratic Alliance and, to a lesser degree, the Left-Green Movement in 1996.

[d]The Communist Party and Italian Republican Party adopted quotas, proportions unknown, in 1987, while the Christian Democrats adopted a quota, proportion unknown, in 1989. These parties no longer exist.

[e]The party adopted a 25 percent quota policy in 1988.

[f]The party adopted a 20 percent quota policy in 1996.

[g]The party is one of the few to reduce the quota proportion over time: initially the provision was 30 percent in 1990.

[h]The party adopted a 33 percent quota policy in 1992.

[i]The party adopted a 20 percent quota policy in 1988.

[j]The party adopted a 20 percent quota policy, date unknown, and then a 30 percent quota policy in 1996.

[k]The party requires that two of the first five names on the candidate list in each province must be women (forty-eight provinces total).

[l]The party adopted a 35 percent quota policy in 1994.

Legislative Quotas in Single or Lower Houses of Parliament

Region/ Country	% Candidates	House	Year Adopted	% Women (Year)
Latin America				
Argentina	30	lower house	1991	40 (2007)
Bolivia	30	lower house	1997	17 (2005)
Brazil	25	single house	1997	9 (2005)
Colombia (*previously*)	30	lower house	1999	8 (2006)
Costa Rica	40	single house	1996	39 (2006)
Dominican Republic[a]	33	lower house	2000	20 (2006)
Ecuador[b]	30	lower house	2000	25 (2006)
Guyana	33	single house	Unknown	29 (2006)
Honduras[c]	30	single house	2004	23 (2005)
Mexico	30	lower house[d]	2002	23 (2006)
Panama	30	lower house	1996	17 (1997)
Paraguay	20	lower house	1996	10 (2003)
Peru[e]	30	single house	2000	29 (2006)
Venezuela	30	single house	1998	19 (2005)
Eastern Europe				
Armenia[f]	15	single house[g]	2007	9 (2007)
Bosnia-Herzegovina	30	single house	2001	14 (2006)
Kosovo[h]	30	single house	2000	Unknown
Kyrgyzstan	30	single house	2007	26 (2007)
Macedonia	30	single house	2002	28 (2006)
Serbia	30	single house	2004	20 (2007)
Slovenia	35	lower house	2006	12 (2004)
Uzbekistan	30	single house	2004	18 (2004)
Asia				
China[i]	22	single house	2007	20 (2003)
Indonesia	30	lower house	2003	11 (2004)
North Korea	20	single house	1998	20 (2003)
South Korea	50	single house[j]	2004	13 (2004)
Nepal[k]	5	lower house	1990	17 (2007)
Philippines[l]		Must include women	1995	23 (2007)
Africa				
Burundi	30	single house	2005	31 (2005)
Liberia	30	single house	2005	13 (2005)
Mauritania	30–50	single house[m]	2006	18 (2006)

Legislative Quotas in Single or Lower Houses of Parliament (*continued*)

Region/ Country	% Candidates	House	Year Adopted	% Women (Year)
Niger	10	single house	2004	12 (2001)
Western Europe				
Belgium[n]	50	lower house	2002	35 (2007)
France	50	lower house	1999/2000	18 (2007)
Portugal	33	single house	2006	21 (2005)
Spain	40	lower house	2007	36 (2008)
Middle East				
Iraq	25	lower house	2004	26 (2005)
Palestinian Territory[o]	20	single house	2005	Unknown

Sources: Inter-Parliamentary Union (2008a); Krook (2005, 493–503), updated.

[a]An earlier law passed in 1997 required parties to include 25 percent women.

[b]An earlier law passed in 1997 required parties to include 20 percent women.

[c]An earlier law was included as part of a new equality law passed in 2000.

[d]An earlier law passed in 1996 "recommended" that parties include 30 percent women.

[e]An earlier law passed in 1997 required parties to include 25 percent women.

[f]An earlier law passed in 1999 required parties to include at least 5 percent women, but only in the proportional representation (PR) list-component of the mixed electoral system.

[g]This regulation applies only to PR elections in the mixed electoral system.

[h]The quota was passed when Kosovo was part of the former Yugoslavia.

[i]A regulation passed in 1955 stated that an "appropriate" and increasing proportion of women should be elected; this commitment was emphasized again in 1992 to read that the proportion of female deputies should not be lower in current than in earlier congresses.

[j]This regulation applies only to PR elections in the mixed electoral system. In addition, the law recommends that parties include 30 percent women among their candidates in single member districts.

[k]The interim constitution approved in 2007 required parties to include 33 percent women, half fielded on closed party lists and half in open elections. The resulting assembly will be charged with the task of writing a new constitution, which may or may not include gender quotas.

[l]The Constitution of 1986 provided that half of all seats elected by PR lists must be filled by labor, peasant, urban poor, indigenous cultural communities, women, and youth.

[m]The regulation varies according to the magnitude of each district: in constituencies with two members, all party lists must include one candidate of each sex; when there are three members, lists must include at least one woman; when there are more than three members, each group of four candidates must include equal numbers of women and men.

[n]A law passed in 1994 required parties to include 33 percent women.

[o]Nonindependent state.

Notes

Chapter 1

1. In the early 1990s, some countries began to establish 30 percent quotas for women in local government.
2. It is not known where the 30 percent figure in fact originates, but one possibility is that it is linked to the concept of a 'critical mass,' a theory used in some research on women's substantive representation which speculates that women need to form a large minority of all legislators before they can make a difference in public policy (cf. Childs and Krook 2006).

Chapter 2

1. This is the case in India, as well as the two states that eventually seceded from India, Pakistan and Bangladesh.

Chapter 3

1. Low district magnitudes raise the "effective quota" when the laws of arithmetic necessitate rounding up the number of seats in order to meet the quota requirement, transforming a 25 percent quota into a 50 percent quota when two seats are available, a 30 percent quota when three seats are available, and a 25 percent quota when four seats are available (Schmidt 2003).
2. In unusual cases, citizens exhaust domestic remedies and appeal to international authorities to gain compliance with quota measures. Citizens in Argentina and Peru, for example, have lodged complaints with the Inter-American Commission on Human Rights (IACHR). In Argentina, the IACHR decision to admit the case pushed President Fernando de la Rúa to support a new presidential decree specifying how quotas were to be implemented (Inter-American Commission on Human Rights 2001). In Peru, the appeal to the IACHR led

the National Elections Tribunal to correctly calculate the minimum quota for the 2002 local elections (Inter-American Commission on Human Rights 2002).

3. A limited number of campaigns do take other institutions into account before quotas are adopted, for example by considering the features of the electoral system before pursuing party or legislative quotas.

4. The case of electoral systems reveals that—given the importance of configuration of causal conditions—one institution can stay stable while its overall causal effect changes as other institutions evolve.

Chapter 4

1. Many of these countries have also sought to use reserved seats to promote women's representation in local government. Indeed, campaigns in numerous countries have focused first on reserved seats at the local level as a means to empower women, who might then be inspired to pursue a national political career. While this chapter addresses local quotas, its main focus is on national quotas to retain consistency with the other two empirical chapters.

2. The only exceptions are cases where women do not stand for reserved seats, due to intimidation from male relatives or from campaigns ostensibly aimed at undermining these provisions for religious or cultural reasons.

3. More specifically, she proposed that one seat be reserved for women in each subdivision of each provincial assembly, as well as in each district of the National Assembly (Mumtaz 1998).

4. Bangladesh adopted a system of government relatively similar to the one reigning in Pakistan. The unicameral legislature consisted of 315 seats, with 300 seats elected directly and 15 seats reserved for women, who were elected by the general members. The number of seats was doubled to thirty in 1979, but expired in 1987, was renewed in 1990, and expired again in 2001. After a prolonged debate over whether or not to restore this provision, legislators agreed in May 2004 to reserve 45 seats for women in the 345-member national assembly, approximately 13 percent (Chowdhury 2002; Quota Project 2008).

5. Two other proposals were briefly voiced but also summarily rejected. One involved establishing an electoral college of women's organizations, while the other proposed twenty seats to be elected directly by male and female voters (Pakistan Commission on the Status of Women 1989; Zafar 1996).

6. The ordinance also reserved twenty seats for religious minorities, who were to be directly elected by members of those communities, in

addition to eighteen seats per province for scholars, technocrats, and professionals (Korson and Maskiell 1985).

7. In 1986, the Commission on the Status of Women recommended in addition that at least two seats be reserved for non-Muslim women in the National Assembly, women in reserved seats be elected directly by women, a political party with fewer than 20 percent female members not be allowed to contest elections, and all local councils include at least two women (Shaheed, Zia, and Warraich 1998).

8. During the election itself, Pakistan's chief mullah, Maulwi Syed Mohammad Abdul Qadir Azad, issued a *fatwa* stating that any person voting for Bhutto would be rendered non-Muslim and thereby sentenced to an afterlife in hell (Goodwin 1994).

9. This particular translation comes from Mernissi (1991b).

10. They also argued that women simply did not possess the capacities of leadership, both because they were the "weaker sex" and not well-versed enough in the Quran (Shaikh 1981; Zakaria 1990).

11. A feminist scholar who has studied the history of this *Hadith* has determined that one of its transmitters, Abu Bakra, had a political motivation for "remembering" it twenty five years after he claimed to have heard it from the Prophet: he stood to lose a great deal if 'A'isha, one of Muhammad's wives, came to power (Mernissi 1991a; Mernissi 1991b).

12. Despite Article 32, local government had been subject to legislation and executive orders. Interestingly, military regimes had viewed local elections as a means to legitimize their rule and thus of the six elections ever held—in 1959, 1979, 1983, 1987, and 1998—four had been conducted by a military regime (Bari 2001).

13. Senate seats were elected by members of the provincial assemblies.

14. For details on specific state policies, see d'Lima (1993), Jain (1996, 9–10), and Manikyamba (1989, 34–37).

15. The right-wing BJP approved this proposal unanimously in a rarely used procedure, whereby the party president presents a measure that is immediately passed without debate. Normally, party members present proposals that are followed by a debate and then voted upon (Nath 1996).

16. The category of OBC includes a heterogeneous collection of groups that together constitute 52 percent of the Indian population. While not a political minority, they are a socially and educationally deprived group and thus qualify for job quotas in the government (Jenkins 1999).

17. Numerous surveys suggested that 75 percent of men and women in India supported reservations for women in politics, as did the majority of people across various religious backgrounds, classes, and levels of literacy (Kishwar 1996b, 12; Rai and Sharma 2000, 159).

Chapter 5

1. An excellent example of these battles is the case of Kerstin Hesselgren, one of the first women to sit in the Senate (Palme 1969, 60–61).
2. This tradition was also known as "democratic dancing." Similar attempts to translate the concept of alternation to local contexts are evident in Germany, where it is called the "zipper system," and Southern Africa, where it is known as the "zebra principle." In a related fashion, the one-third requirement in Argentina is sometimes referred to as "the braid."
3. The word in Swedish, *Stödstrumporna*, is a play on words in several senses. Although its primary meaning refers to the fact that the Support Stockings were a support network for women in politics, the term rhymes with *Rödstrumporna* (Redstockings), the radical feminist movements in Scandinavia in the 1970s, and literally means support hosiery, an allusion to the fact that many of the women involved tended to be middle-aged and older.
4. This party was founded in 1985, but with only 140 members, it was too small to be registered as a party and received only about 500 votes during parliamentary elections in 1991 (Eduards 1992).
5. The emergence of the Support Stockings, however, coincided with a general trend during the early 1990s of women organizing as women as never before in Sweden (Gustafsson, Eduards, and Rönnblom 1997).
6. Cinnika Belming, vice-chairperson of the Social Democratic Youth Association, published an editorial in *Aftonbladet* in September 1993, in which she argued that it was more important to support those women already in politics that to "force" others forward. She also noted that quotas were demeaning to women because they suggested that women were only nominated because they were women. Incidentally, the party also discussed youth representation at length during this same period of time, with Carlsson arguing that half of all SAP candidates should be under the age of forty.
7. This campaign was known as *Kryss för en kvinna* (Westerlund 2002).
8. Twelve people won seats through personal voting, seven men and five women. Without personal voting, eight men and four women would have been elected (Wängnerud 1999a, 301).
9. The party conference briefly debated adoption of all-black shortlists, but the NEC decided to consider the matter further before accepting this principle (Norris 1997a).
10. The original purpose of this clause apparently was to enable parties to maintain their women's organizations without being charged with sex discrimination (Russell 2000).
11. The Treaty of Amsterdam addressed a series of political and institutional changes to the Treaty on European Union and came into force

in May 1999. It identified equality between women and men as one of the fundamental rights within the EU and authorized both the Council and member states to apply positive action when one sex is under-represented.

12. A brief discussion was also raised regarding commitments to improving the numbers of MPs from minority backgrounds, but the issue of ethnic representation was ultimately regarded as different from the issue of women's representation (Childs 2002b).

13. Following the party's defeat in 1997, the Conservative Party leader, William Hague, sought to persuade local parties to adopt positive action, but these suggestions were firmly rejected in favor of strategies to recruit more women through talent-spotting and political training (Ward 2000c; Watt 2000).

Chapter 6

1. This branch was also known as the *Partido Femenino Peronista*, or the Peronist Women's Party. One of the main goals of the party was to incorporate women into politics, especially working class women with lower levels of education (Bianchi and Sanchis 1988).

2. The only group that refused to support quotas was women in the PC.

3. For details on the debate inside the Senate, see Gallo and Giacabone (2001, 47–71).

4. For details on the debate inside the Chamber of Deputies, see Gallo and Giacabone (2001, 73–110).

5. For the text of this speech, see Fundación Friedrich Ebert 1992, 107–113.

6. This group, the Gabinete de Consejeras Presidenciales, was created by President Menem on January 26, 1993, with the goal of incorporating women's concerns into all state policies by appointing nine female advisors to the president at the rank of Secretary of State.

7. This organ, the Consejo Nacional de la Mujer, was created in 1992 as the state's main women's policy agency at the national level.

8. For details on specific court cases waged between 1993 and 2000, see Gallo and Giacabone (2001).

9. Caso 1.568/93, Darci Sampietro s/impugnación lista de candidatos a diputados nacionales del Partido Justicialista distrito Entre Ríos.

10. For details on these cases, see Chama 2001, 88–93.

11. Interestingly, no challenges were necessary to the lists for constitutional convention deputies, because parties complied fully with the quota (Durrieu 1999).

12. Caso 1.919/95, Consejo Nacional de la Mujer s/impugnan listas, Cámara Nacional Electoral Tucumán.

13. Caso 1.836/95, Cámara Nacional Electoral.

14. Case 1.851/95, Cámara Nacional Electoral; Case 1.854/94, Cámara Nacional Electoral. For further discussion of these cases, see Chama (2001).

15. Caso 1.565/93, Merciadri de Morini, María Teresa s/presentación, Cámara Nacional Electoral.

16. Décision no. 82-146 DC du 18 novembre 1982.

17. The title of this book reconfigures two central slogans of the French Revolution: *aux armes citoyens* (to arms, citizens), the refrain of the French national anthem, and *liberté, égalité, fratenité* (liberty, equality, fraternity), the motto of French republicanism.

18. The media referred to these women as "juppettes," a play on Juppé's name and the French word for "skirt."

19. The body of literature arguing in favor of parity, as well as surveying these contributions, is enormous. Central contributions include Agacinski (2001); Gaspard (1994); Gaspard (1998); Gaspard, Servan-Schreiber, and Le Gall (1992); Giraud and Jenson (2001); Halimi (1997); Scott (1998); Sineau (2002); and Viennot (1994).

20. This characterization of the United States is based on French misperceptions of the extent of affirmative action there. The United States is in fact actually quite unusual in that it is one of the few countries in the world where quotas for women in elected positions have not been proposed, despite having existed for internal party positions since the 1920s (Krook, Lovenduski, and Squires 2006).

21. Despite the history of party quotas, this was the first public announcement by the PS in favor of the parity provision (Mazur 2001).

22. Décision no 96-387 DC du 21 janvier 1997.

23. Décision no 2000-429 DC du 30 mai 2000. For commentary, see Lenoir (2001).

24. Parity does not apply in these towns because they are governed by a different type of election system, which allows voters to strike candidates' names, change the order of candidates, and add new names to the list. Drafters of the parity law felt that imposing parity on these elections would have required legislative changes to this voting method, which Jospin had already promised he would not do.

25. Approximately one-third of the 321 seats in the Senate are elected every three years.

26. In September 2002 the RPR and Liberal Democracy decided to enter into a union, creating a new right-wing political party.

27. Loi no. 2003-696 du 30 juillet 2003; Loi no. 2003-697 du 30 juillet 2003.

28. Loi no. 2003-327 du 11 avril 2003.

29. Loi no. 2007-128 du 31 janvier 2007.

References

Abou-Zeid, Gihan. 2006. The Arab Region: Women's Access to the Deci-sion-Making Process Across the Arab Nation. In *Women, Quotas, and Politics*, ed. Drude Dahlerup, 168–93. New York: Routledge.

Adams, Melinda, and Alice Kang. 2007. Regional Advocacy Networks and the Protocol on the Rights of Women in Africa. *Politics & Gender* 3 (4): 45174.

Afzal, Nabeela. 1999. *Women and Parliament in Pakistan, 1947–1977*. Lahore: Pakistan Study Centre.

Agacinski, Sylviane. 2001. *Parity of the Sexes*. Trans. Lisa Walsh. New York: Columbia University Press.

Agnew, Vijay. 1979. *Elite Women in Indian Politics*. New Delhi: Vikas Publishing House.

Ahlbaum, Jenny. 1994. *Hur SSKF har påverkat SAP i frågan om könskvotering till valet 1994*. C-uppsats, University of Stockholm.

Ahmed, Aijazz. 2002. Pakistani women: The politics of subjugation. *Asia Times Online*, October 4.

Ali, Shaheen Sardar. 2000. Law, Islam and the Women's Movement in Pakistan. In *International Perspectives on Gender and Democratisation*, ed. Shirin M. Rai, 41–63. New York: St. Martin's.

al-Mujahid, Sharif. 1965. "Pakistan's First Presidential Elections." *Asian Survey* 5 (6): 280–294.

Amar, Micheline, ed. 1999. *Le Piège de la parité: Arguments pour un débat*. Paris: Hachette Littératures.

Aminzade, Ronald. 1992. Historical Sociology and Time. *Sociological Methods & Research* 20 (4): 456–80.

Andersson, Karin. 1983. Vad hände sedan?" In *Framåt Systrar! 50 år Centerns Kvinnoförbund*, 91–94. Stockholm: LTs förlag.

Antić, Milica G, and Maruša Gortnar. 2004. Gender Quotas in Slovenia: A Short Analysis of Failures and Hopes. *European Political Science* 3 (3): 73–80.

Appleton, Andrew, and Amy G. Mazur. 1993. Transformation or Modernization: the Rhetoric and Reality of Gender and Party Politics in France. In *Gender and Party Politics*, ed. Joni Lovenduski and Pippa Norris, 86–112. Thousand Oaks: Sage.

Araújo, Clara. 2003. Quotas for Women in the Brazilian Legislative System. Paper presented at the International IDEA Workshop, Lima, Peru.

Araújo, Clara, and Ana Isabel García Quesada. 2006. Latin America: The Experience and the Impact of Quotas in Latin America. In *Women, Quotas, and Politics*, ed. Drude Dahlerup, 83–111. New York: Routledge.

Badinter, Elisabeth. 1996. Non aux quotas de femmes. *Le Monde*, June 12.

Baines, Beverley, and Ruth Rubio-Marin, eds. 2005. *The Gender of Constitutional Jurisprudence*. New York: Cambridge University Press.

Balasubrahmanyan, Vimal. 1998. *Who's Saying What On The Women's Reservation Bill*. Hyderabad: Asmita Resource Centre for Women.

Baldez, Lisa. 2004. Elected Bodies: The Gender Quota Law for Legislative Candidates in Mexico. *Legislative Studies Quarterly* 24 (2): 231–58.

Ballington, Julie, and Drude Dahlerup. 2006. Gender Quotas in Post-Conflict States: East Timor, Afghanistan, and Iraq. In *Women, Quotas, and Politics*, ed. Drude Dahlerup, 249–58. New York: Routledge.

Baqai, M. Sabihuddin. 1976. *Changes in the Status and Roles of Women in Pakistan: An Empirical Study in Karachi Metropolitan Area*. Karachi: University of Karachi.

Bari, Farzana. 2001. *Local Government Elections: December 2000-(Phase-1)*. Islamabad: Pattan Development Organization.

Baruah, Amit. 1997. Pakistani women demand quota in legislatures. *The Hindu*, May 6.

Bauer, Antje. 2002. *Afghan Women and the Democratic Reconstruction of Afghanistan: Findings and Interviews from a Journalist's Field Trip*. Trans. Dominic Johnson. Berlin: Berghof Research Center for Constructive Conflict Management.

Bauer, Gretchen, and Hannah Britton. 2006. *Women in African Parliaments*. Boulder: Lynne Rienner.

Beckwith, Karen. 2003. The Gendering Ways of States: Women's Representation and State Configuration in France, Great Britain, and the United States. In *Women's Movements Facing the Reconfigured State*, eds. Lee Ann Banaszak, Karen Beckwith, and Dieter Rucht, 169202. New York: Cambridge University Press.

Bergqvist, Christina. 1994. *Mäns makt och kvinnors intressen*. Ph.D. Diss., University of Uppsala.

Bianchi, Susana, and Norma Sanchis. 1988. *El Partido Peronista Femenino. Primera parte (1949/1955)*. Buenos Aires: Centro Editor de América Latina.

Bih-er, Chou, Cal Clark, and Janet Clark. 1990. *Women in Taiwan Politics: Overcoming Barriers to Women's Participation in a Modernizing Society*. Boulder: Lynne Rienner Publishers.

Bird, Karen. 2003. Who are the Women? Where are the Women? And What Difference Can They Make? Effects of Gender Parity in French Municipal Elections. *French Politics* 1 (1): 5–38.

Bokhari, Farhan. 2001. For Pakistan's women, election quotas are a start. *Christian Science Monitor*, May 31.

Bonder, Gloria, and Marcela Nari. 1995. The 30 Percent Quota Law: A Turning Point for Women's Political Participation in Argentina. In *A Rising Public Voice: Women in Politics Worldwide,* ed. Alida Brill, 183–93. New York: The Feminist Press at The City University of New York Press.

Bradbury, Jonathan, David Denver, James Mitchell, and Lynn Bennie. 2000. Devolution and Party Change: Candidate Selection for the 1999 Scottish Parliament and Welsh Assembly Elections. *Journal of Legislative Studies* 6 (3): 51–72.

Brady, Henry E., and David Collier, eds. 2004. *Rethinking Social Inquiry: Diverse Tools, Shared Standards.* Lanham: Rowman and Littlefield.

Brink, Josefin. 2002. Socialdemokraterna: gärna rättvisa men inget bråk." Bang 1: 11–15.

Brooks, Rachel, Angela Eagle, and Clare Short. 1990. *Quotas Now: Women in the Labour Party.* London: Fabian Society.

Brown, Alice. 1996. Women and Politics in Scotland. Reprinted in *Women and Contemporary Scottish Politics: An Anthology*, eds. Esther Breitenbach and Fiona Mackay. 2001. Edinburgh: Polygon, 197–212.

Brown, Alice, Tahyna Barnett Donaghy, Fiona Mackay, and Elizabeth Meehan. 2002. Women and Constitutional Change in Scotland and Northern Ireland. In *Women, Politics, and Change*, ed. Karen Ross, 71–84. New York: Oxford University Press.

Bruhn, Kathleen. 2003. Whores and Lesbians: Political Activism, Party Strategies, and Gender Quotas in Mexico. *Electoral Studies* 22 (1): 101–19.

Burness, Catriona. 2000. Young Swedish members of parliament: Changing the world? *NORA* 8, (2): 93–106.

Busby, Nicole, and Calum MacLeod. 2002. Maintaining a Balance: The Retention of Women MP's in Scotland. In *Women, Politics, and Change*, ed. Karen Ross, 30–42. New York: Oxford University Press.

Bystydzienski, Jill M. 1995. *Women in Electoral Politics: Lessons from Norway.* Westport: Praeger.

Camacho Granados, Rosalía, Silvia Lara Povedano, and Ester Serrano Madrigal. 1997. *Las cuotas mínimas de participación de las mujeres: Un mecanismo de acción afirmativa.* San José: Centro Nacional para el Desarrollo de la Mujer y la Familia.

Campbell, John L., and Ove K. Pedersen, eds. 2001. *The Rise of Neoliberalism and Institutional Analysis.* Princeton: Princeton University Press.

Campbell, Rosie, Sarah Childs, and Joni Lovenduski. 2006. Women's Equality Guarantees and the Conservative Party. *The Political Quarterly* 77 (1): 18–27.

Carlshamre, Nils. 1969. Kvinnorna och den konservativa rörelsen. In *Kvinnors röst och rätt*, eds. Ruth Hamrin-Thorell, Ulla Lindström, and Gunvor Stenberg, 183–92. Stockholm: AB Allmänna Förlaget.

Carrio, Elisa María. 2002. Los retos de la participación de las mujeres en la Parlamento. Una nueva mirada al caso argentino. In *Mujeres en el Parlamento. Más allá de los números*, eds. Myriam Méndez-Montalvo and Julie Ballington, 135–146. Stockholm: International IDEA.

Castle, Stephen. 2005. Feminist Party Threatens to Unseat Swedish Premier. *Independent*, April 8.

Caul, Miki. 1999. Women's Representation in Parliament: The Role of Political Parties. *Party Politics* 5 (1): 79–98.

———. 2001. Political Parties and the Adoption of Candidate Gender Quotas: A Cross-National Analysis. *The Journal of Politics* 63 (4): 1214–29.

Chama, Mónica. 2001. *Las mujeres y el poder*. Buenos Aires: Ciudad Argentina.

Chaney, Paul. 2003. Increased Rights and Representation: Women and the Post-devolution Equality Agenda in Wales. In *Women Making Constitutions: New Politics and Comparative Perspectives*, eds. Alexandra Dobrowolsky and Vivien Hart, 173–84. New York: Palgrave.

Childs, Sarah. 2002a. Concepts of Representation and The Passage of The Sex Discrimination (Election Candidates) Bill. *Journal of Legislative Studies* 8 (3): 90–108.

———. 2002b. The Sex Discrimination (Election Candidates) Act 2002 and its implications. *Representation* 39 (2): 83–93.

———. 2004. *New Labour Women MPs: Women Representing Women*. London: Routledge.

Childs, Sarah, and Mona Lena Krook. 2006. Should Feminists Give Up on Critical Mass? A Contingent Yes. *Politics & Gender* 2 (4): 522–30.

Childs, Sarah, Joni Lovenduski, and Rosie Campbell. 2005. *Women at the Top: Changing Numbers, Changing Politics?* London: Hansard Society.

Chowdhury, Najma. 2002. The Implementation of Quotas: Bangladesh Experience—Dependence and Marginality in Politics. Paper presented at the International IDEA Workshop, Jakarta, Indonesia.

Ciezadlo, Annia. 2003. Iraqi women raise voices—for quotas. *Christian Science Monitor*, December 17.

Clokie, H. McD. 1936. The New Constitution for India. *American Political Science Review* 30 (6): 1152–65.

Collie, Lizbeth, Jo Hoare, and Jacqueline Roddick. 1991. Women in the Green Party. In *A Woman's Claim of Right in Scotland: Women, Representation, and Politics*, ed. Women's Claim of Right Group, 66–72. Edinburgh: Polygon.

Collier, Ruth Berins, and David Collier. 1991. *Shaping the Political Arena: Critical Junctures, the Labor Movement, and Regime Dynamics in Latin America*. Princeton: Princeton University Press.

Connell, Dan. 1998. Strategies for Change: Women & Politics in Eritrea & South Africa. *Review of African Political Economy* 76: 189–206.

Coote, Anna, and Polly Pattullo. 1990. *Power and Prejudice: Women and Politics*. London: Weidenfeld and Nicolson.

Corrin, Chris. 2001. Post-Conflict Reconstruction and Gender Analysis in Kosova. *International Feminist Journal of Politics* 3 (1): 78–98.

Costa Benavides, Jimena. 2003. Women's Political Participation in Bolivia: Progress and Obstacles. Paper presented at the International IDEA Workshop, Lima, Peru.

Craske, Nikki. 1999. *Women and Politics in Latin America*. New Brunswick: Rutgers University Press.

Dahlerup, Drude. 1988. *Vi har ventet længe nok—håndbog i kvinderepræsentation*. Copenhagen: Nordisk Ministerråd.

———. 2001. *'Men kvinderne vil jo ikke selv': Diskursen omkring betydningen af køn ved danske kommunevalg*. Aalborg: GEP.

———. 2006a. Introduction. In *Women, Quotas and Politics*, ed. Drude Dahlerup, 3–31. New York: Routledge.

———, ed. 2006b. *Women, Quotas, and Politics*. New York: Routledge.

———. 2007. Electoral Gender Quotas: Between Equality of Opportunity and Equality of Result. *Representation* 43 (2): 73–92.

Dahlerup, Drude, and Anja Taarup Nordlund. 2004. Gender Quotas: A Key to Equality? A Case Study of Iraq and Afghanistan. *European Political Science* 3 (3): 91–98.

Dahlerup, Drude, and Lenita Freidenvall. 2005. Quotas as a Fast Track to Equal Representation for Women: Why Scandinavia Is No Longer the Model. *International Feminist Journal of Politics* 7 (1): 26–48.

Dalal, Mukesh. 2000. Women's Reservation: Another Approach. *Manushi* 120: 28–31.

Davidson-Schmich, Louise K. 2006. Implementation of Political Party Gender Quotas: Evidence from the German Lander 1990–2000. *Party Politics* 12 (2): 211–32.

Delgadillo, Tania. 2000. Ley de Cuotas burlada por partidos políticos. http://www.fempress.cl/222/revista/222_cuotas.html (accessed September 25, 2002).

Diop, Aissata de. 2002. Les quotas en Afrique francophone: Des débuts modestes. In *Les Femmes au parlement: Au-delà du nombre*, eds.

Julie Ballington and Marie-José Protais, 133–142. Stockholm: International IDEA.

d'Lima, Hazel. 1993. Participation of Women in Local Self Government. In *Women's Participation in Politics*, ed. Susheela Kaushik, 21–30. New Delhi: Vikas Publishing House.

dos Santos, Estela. 1983. *Las mujeres peronistas*. Buenos Aires: Centro Editor de América Latina.

Drangel, Louise. 1984. Folkpartiet och jämställdhetsfrågan. In *Liberal ideologioch politik, 1934–1984*. Falköping: AB Folk & Samhälle, 342–425.

Dugger, Celia M. 1999. A Woman's Place: Special Report. *New York Times*, May 3.

Durrieu, Marcela. 1999. *Se dice de nosotras*. Buenos Aires: Catálogos Editora.

Eagle, Maria, and Joni Lovenduski. 1998. *High Time or High Tide for Labour women?* London: Fabian Society.

Eduards, Maud. 1977. *Kvinnor och politik. Fakta och förklaringar*. Stockholm: LiberFörlag.

———. 1981. Sweden. In *The Politics of the Second Electorate: Women and Public Participation*, eds. Joni Lovenduski and Jill Hills, 208–27. Boston: Routledge & Kegan Paul.

———. 1992. Against the Rules of the Game: On the Importance of Women's Collective Actions. In *Rethinking Change: Current Swedish Feminist Research*, eds. Maud L. Eduards et al, 83–104. Uppsala: Swedish Science Press.

———. 2002. *Förbjuden handling. Om kvinnors organisering och feministisk teori*. Malmö: Liber.

Eduards, Maud Landby, and Gertrud Åström. 1993. *Många kände sig manade, men få blevo kallade—en granskning av arbetet för ökad kvinnorepresentation*. Stockholm: Socialdepartementet.

Edwards, Julia, and Laura McAllister. 2002. One Step Forward, Two Steps Back? Women in the Two Main Political Parties in Wales. In *Women, Politics, and Change*, ed. Karen Ross, 154–66. New York: Oxford University Press.

Ekström, Solweig. 1983. Politikens villkor—villkor för demokratin." In *Framåt Systrar! 50 år Centerns Kvinnoförbund*. Stockholm: LTs förlag, 95–99.

Ellerby, Kara. 2008. Inclusion Diffusion: The Dynamics of Quota Diffusion. Paper presented at the Midwest Political Science Association National Conference, Chicago.

Ethington, Philip, and Eileen McDonagh. 1995. The Eclectic Center of the New Institutionalism: Axes of Analysis in Comparative Perspective. *Social Science History* 19 (4): 467–77.

Everett, Jana Matson. 1979. *Women and Social Change in India*. New Delhi: Heritage.

Fagerström, Eva. 1974. *Fler kvinnor i politiken—en studie av det social-demokratiska partiets och kvinnoförbundets åtgärder för att nå detta mål mellan valen 1970 och 1973.* Stockholm: C-uppsats, Stockholm University.

Fawcett Society. 2001a. *Experiences of Labour Party Women in Parliamentary Selections.* London: Fawcett Society.

———. 2001b. *Experiences of Liberal Democrat Women in Parliamentary Selections.* London: Fawcett Society.

Feijoó, María del Carmen. 1994. From Family Ties to Political Action: Women's Experiences in Argentina. In *Women and Politics Worldwide*, eds. Barbara J. Nelson and Najma Chowdhury, 60–72. New Haven: Yale University Press.

———. 1998. Democratic Participation and Women in Argentina. In *Women and Democracy: Latin America and Central and Eastern Europe*, eds. Jane S. Jacquette and Sharon L. Wolchik, 29–46. Baltimore: Johns Hopkins University Press.

Fraisse, Genviève. 1989. *Muse de la Raison. Démocratie et exclusion des femmes en France.* Paris: Gallimard.

Franceschet, Susan. 2001. Women in Politics in Post-Transitional Democracies. *International Feminist Journal of Politics* 3 (2): 207–36.

Franceschet, Susan. 2005. *Women and Politics in Chile.* Boulder: Lynne Rienner.

Frebran, Rose-Marie. 1990. Kvinnan i den kristdemokratiska rörelsen. In *Kvinnorollen. KdS-K belyser kvinnans situation i Sverige idag.* Stockholm: Samhällsgemenskaps Förlags, 62–69.

Freidenvall, Lenita. 2005. A Discursive Struggle—The Swedish National Federation of Social Democratic Women and Gender Quotas. *NORA: Nordic Journal of Women's Studies* 13 (3): 175–86.

———. 2006. *Vägen till Varannan Damernas: Om Kvinnorepresentation, Kvotering och Kandidaturval i Svensk Politik 1970–2002.* Ph.D. Diss., Stockholm University.

Freidenvall, Lenita, Drude Dahlerup, and Hege Skjeie. 2006. The Nordic Countries: An Incremental Model. In *Women, Quotas and Politics*, ed. Drude Dahlerup, 55–82. New York: Routledge.

Fundación Friedrich Ebert. 1991a. *Cuota mínima de participación de ambos sexos. El debate en el Partido Socialdemócrata alemán.* Asunción: Fundación Friedrich Ebert.

———. 1991b. *Cuota mínima de participación de mujeres. Discusión y resoluciones del Partido Socialista obrero Español.* Asunción: Fundación Friedrich Ebert.

———. 1992. *Cuota mínima de participación de mujeres: El debate en Argentina.* Buenos Aires: Fundación Friedrich Ebert.

Galatas, Steven E. 2004. Electing the First Parliament: Party Competition and Voter Participation in Scotland. *Party Politics* 10 (2): 213–33.

Gallo, Edit Rosalía, and Carlos Alberto Giacobone, eds. 2001. *Cupo feminino en la política argentina. Ley nacional, leyes provinciales, debates parlamentarios, normativa internacional, jurisprudencia.* Buenos Aires: Editorial Universitaria de Buenos Aires.

Gandhi, Maneka. 1996. And the One Who Differs...Maneka Gandhi on the Women's Reservation Bill. *Manushi* 96: 17–19.

García Quesada, Ana Isabel. 2003. Putting the Mandate into Practice: Legal Reform in Costa Rica. Paper presented at the International IDEA Workshop, Lima, Peru.

Gaspard, Françoise. 1994. De la parité: genèse d'un concept, naissance d'un mouvement. *Nouvelles questions féministes* 15 (4): 29–44.

———. 1998. Parity: Why Not? *differences: A Journal of Feminist Cultural Studies* 9 (2): 93–104.

———. 2001. The French Parity Movement. In *Has Liberalism Failed Women?* eds. Jytte Klausen and Charles S. Maier, 55–66. New York: Palgrave.

Gaspard, Françoise, Claude Servan-Schreiber, and Anne Le Gall. 1992. *Au pouvoir, citoyennes!: liberté, égalité, parité.* Paris: Éditions du Seuil.

Genberg, Ia. 2002. Vänsterpartiet: maktanalysen i centrum. *Bang* 1: 28–31.

Giraud, Isabelle, and Jane Jenson. 2001. Constitutionalizing Equal Access: High Hopes, Dashed Hopes? In *Has Liberalism Failed Women? Assuring Equal Representation in Europe and the United States,* eds. Jytte Klausen and Charles S. Maier, 69–88. New York: Palgrave.

Gjötterberg, Tora-Brita. 1975. Fler kvinnor i politiken. In *Kvinnan i politiken,* ed. Barbro Hedvall, 153–70. Södertälje: Fredrika-Bremer-Förbundet.

Goetz, Anne Marie, and Shireen Hassim, eds. 2003. *No Shortcuts to Power: African Women in Politics and Policy Making.* New York: Zed Books.

Gómez, Patricia Laura. 1998. Representación política y Género: Notas para el análisis de la ley 24.012. *Temas de Mujeres: Perspectivas de Género.* Tucumán: Facultad de Filosofía y Letras, Universidad Nacional de Tucumán.

Goodwin, Jan. 1994. *Price of Honor: Muslim Women Lift the Veil of Silence on the Islamic World.* New York: Little, Brown and Company.

Green, Manda. 2003. La Parité—To Be or Not to Be? Paper presented at the European Consortium for Political Research, Joint Sessions of Workshops, Edinburgh.

Greif, Avner, and David Laitin. 2004. A Theory of Endogenous Institutional Change. *American Political Science Review* 98 (4): 633–52.

Guadagnini, Marila. 2005. Gendering the Debate on Political Representation in Italy: A Difficult Challenge. In *State Feminism and Political Representation,* ed. Joni Lovenduski, 130–52. New York: Cambridge University Press.

Guigou, Élisabeth. 1998. Projet de loi constitutionelle relatif à l'égalité entre les femmes et les hommes. Speech presented to the French National Assembly. http://www.justice.gouv.fr/discours/d151298. htm. (accessed April 1, 2000).

Guldvik, Ingrid. 2003. Gender quota regimes and ideas of social justice—The quota regime of the Norwegian Local Government Act. Paper presented at the General Conference of the European Consortium for Political Research, Marburg, Germany.

Gulrez, Fazila, and Sohail Warraich. 1998. Women in Politics: Update 1993–1997. In *Women in Politics: Participation and Representation in Pakistan*, eds. Farida Shaheed, Asma Zia, and Sohail Warraich, 68–87. Lahore: Shirkat Gah.

Gustafsson, Gunnel, Maud Eduards, and Malin Rönnblom. 1997. *Towards a New Democratic Order? Women's Organizing in Sweden in the 1990s*. Stockholm: Publica.

Halimi, Gisèle.1997. *La nouvelle cause des femmes*. Paris: Éditions du Seuil.

Hall, Peter A., and Rosemary C. R. Taylor. 1996. Political Science and the Three New Institutionalisms. *Political Studies* 44 (5): 936–57.

Haroon, Anis. 1995. The Women's Movement in Pakistan. In *Unveiling the Issues: Pakistani Women's Perspectives on Social, Political, and Ideological Issues*, eds. Nighat Said Khan and Afiya Shehrbano Zia, 167–77. Lahore: ASR Publications.

Hassim, Shireen. 2002. 'A Conspiracy of Women': The Women's Movement in South Africa's Transition to Democracy. *Social Research* 69 (3): 693–732.

Haug, Frigga. 1995. The Quota Demand and Feminist Politics. *New Left Review* 209: 136–45.

Haydu, Jeffrey. 1998. Making Use of the Past: Time Periods as Cases to Compare and as Sequences of Problem Solving. *American Journal of Sociology* 104 (2): 339–71.

Hirdman, Yvonne. 1990. Genussystemet. In *Demokrati och makt i Sverige*. Stockholm: Statens offentliga utredningar, 73–116.

Holli, Anne Maria, Eeva Luhtakallio, and Eeva Raevaara. 2006. Quota Trouble: Talking About Gender Quotas in Finnish Local Politics. *International Feminist Journal of Politics* 8 (2): 169–93.

Holmberg, Sören, and Tommy Möller, eds. 1999. *Premiär för personval*. Stockholm: Statens offentliga utredningar.

Howard-Merriam, Kathleen. 1990. Guaranteed Seats for Political Representation of Women: The Egyptian Example. *Women and Politics* 10 (1): 17–42.

Htun, Mala. 2002. Puzzles of Women's Rights in Brazil. *Social Research* 69 (3): 733–51.

Htun, Mala N., and Mark P. Jones. 2002. Engendering the Right to Participate in Decision-Making: Electoral Quotas and Women's Leadership in Latin America. In *Gender and the Politics of Rights and Democracy in Latin America*, eds. Nikki Craske and Maxine Molyneux, 32–56. New York: Palgrave.

Huang, Chang-Ling. 2002. Democracy and the Politics of Difference: Gender Quota in Taiwan. Paper presented at the Annual Meeting of the American Political Science Association, Boston.

Hughes, Melanie. 2007. Understanding the Positive Effects of Armed Conflict on Women's Parliamentary Representation. Paper presented at the Annual Meeting of the American Sociological Association, New York.

Human Rights Watch. 2002. Pakistan. http://www.hrw.org/wr2k2/asia9.html (accessed August 2, 2004).

———. 2003. Pakistan. http://www.hrw.org/wr2k3/asia8.html (accessed August 2, 2004).

———. 2004. Stop Violence against Women in Pakistan: Violence Against Women Leaders. http://www.hrw.org/campaigns/pakistan/defenders.htm (accessed August 2, 2004).

Huret, Marie. 2002. "L'inégalité des chances." *L'Express*, June 20. http://www.lexpress.fr/info/france/dossier/legislative2002/dossier.asp?ida=340393 (accessed July 15, 2002).

Ikramullah, Begum Shaista. 1976. Women & Politics. In *Quaid-I-Azam and Muslim Women*. Islamabad: National Book Foundation, 34–43.

Inglehart, Ronald, and Pippa Norris. 2003. *Rising Tide: Gender Equality and Cultural Change Around the World*. New York: Cambridge University Press.

Inhetveen, Katharina. 1999. Can Gender Equality Be Institutionalized? The Role of Launching Values in Institutional Innovation. *International Sociology* 14 (4): 403–22.

Inter-American Commission on Human Rights. 1999. Report No. 102/99, Case 11.307, María Merciadri de Morini, Argentina, September 27.

———. 2001. Report No. 103/01, Case 11.307, María Merciadri de Morini, Argentina.

———. 2002. Report No. 51/02, Case 12.404, Janet Espinoza Feria et al, Peru.

Inter-Parliamentary Union. 1995. *Women in Parliaments, 1945–1995*. World Statistical Survey. Geneva: Inter-Parliamentary Union.

———. 1998. Women in National Parliaments: Situation as of 10 August 1998. http://www.ipu.org/wmn-e/classif.htm (accessed September 15, 1999).

———. 2002. Women in Politics: Promising Developments in Eastern Europe and the Arab Countries. Press Release no. 130, March 1.

———. 2004. Women in National Parliaments: Situation as of 31 August 2004. http://www.ipu.org/wmn-e/classif.htm (accessed September 15, 2004).

————. 2008a. Women in National Parliaments: Situation as of 31 March 2008. http://www.ipu.org/wmn-e/classif.htm (accessed May 12, 2008).

————. 2008b. Women in National Parliaments: Situation as of 31 March 2008. http://www.ipu.org/wmn-e/world.htm (accessed May 12, 2008).

Jain, Devaki. 1996. Panchayat Raj: Women Changing Governance. http://www.undp.org/gender/resources/mono5 .html (accessed July 1, 2004).

Jenkins, Laura Dudley. 1999. Competing Inequalities: The Struggle Over Reserved Seats for Women in India. *International Review of Social History* 44: 53–75.

Jenson, Jane. 1996. Representations of Difference: The Varieties of French Feminism. In *Mapping the Women's Movement: Feminist Politics and Social Transformation in the North*, ed. Monica Threlfall, 73–114. New York: Verso.

Jenson, Jane, and Mariette Sineau. 1994. The Same or Different? An Unending Dilemma for French Women. In *Women and Politics Worldwide*, eds. Barbara J. Nelson and Najma Chowdhury, 243–60. New Haven: Yale University Press.

Jones, Mark P. 1996. Increasing Women's Representation Via Gender Quotas: The Argentine Ley de Cupos. *Women and Politics* 16 (4): 75–98.

————. 1998. Gender Quotas, Electoral Laws, and the Election of Women: Lessons from the Argentine Provinces. *Comparative Political Studies* 31 (1): 3–21.

————. 2004. Quota Legislation and the Election of Women: Learning from the Costa Rican Experience. *Journal of Politics* 66 (4): 1203–23.

Kaiser, Pia. 2001. *Strategic Predictors of Women's Parliamentary Participation: A Comparative Study of Twenty-Three Democracies.* Ph.D. Diss., University of California, Los Angeles.

Karlsson, Gunnel. 1996. *Från broderskap till systerskap: Det social-demokratiska kvinnförbundets kamp för inflytande och makt i SAP.* Lund: Arkiv förlag.

Kassé, Aminata Faye. 2003. Women in Politics in Senegal. Paper presented at the International IDEA Workshop The Implementation of Quotas: African Experiences, Pretoria, South Africa.

Katyal, Anita. 2000. Parties try to score points on women's quota bill. *Times of India*, August 30.

Katznelson, Ira. 1997. Structure and Configuration in Comparative Politics. In *Comparative Politics: Rationality, Culture, and Structure*, eds. Mark Irving Lichbach and Alan S. Zuckerman, 81–112. New York: Cambridge University Press.

Keating, Christine. 2002. The Women's Reservation Bill in India: Disrupting the Postcolonial Sexual Contract. Paper presented at the Annual Meeting of the American Political Science Association, Boston.

Keck, Margaret E., and Kathryn Sikkink. 1998. *Activists Beyond Borders: Advocacy Networks in International Politics*. Ithaca: Cornell University Press.

Khan, Nighat Said. 1985. *Women in Pakistan: A New Era?* London: CHANGE.

King, Gary, Robert O. Keohane, and Sidney Verba. 1994. *Designing Social Inquiry: Scientific Inference in Qualitative Research*. Princeton: Princeton University Press.

Kingdon, John W. 1984. *Agendas, Alternatives, and Public Policies*. Boston: Little, Brown and Company.

Kishwar, Madhu. 1989. Violence and the 1989 Election: Implications for Women. *Manushi* 54–55:2–9.

——. 1996a. Out of the Zenana Dabba: Strategies for Enhancing Women's Political Representation. *Manushi* 96:21–30.

——. 1996b. Women's Marginal Role in Politics. *Manushi* 97:9–21.

——. 1998a. The Logic of Quotas: Women's Movement Splits on the Reservation Bill. *Manushi* 107:31–39.

——. 1998b. Women's reservation bill is a setback to feminists. *India Abroad*, July 31.

Kittilson, Miki Caul. 2006. *Challenging Parties, Changing Parliaments: Women and Elected Office in Contemporary Western Europe*. Columbus: Ohio State University Press.

Kolinsky, Eva. 1991. Political Participation and Parliamentary Careers: Women's Quotas in West Germany. *West European Politics* 14 (1): 56–72.

Korson, J. Henry, and Michelle Maskiell. 1985. Islamization and Social Policy in Pakistan: The Constitutional Crisis and the Status of Women. *Asian Survey* 25 (6): 589–612.

Krasner, Stephen D. 1984. Approaches to the State: Alternative Conceptions and Historical Dynamics. *Comparative Politics* 16 (2): 223–46.

Kristdemokratiska Kvinnoförbundet. 2002. *Kristdemokratiska Kvinnoförbundet 20 år. Från 1982–2002, Korta glimtar och citat*. Stockholm: Kristdemokratiska Kvinnoförbundet.

Krook, Mona Lena. 2004. Gender Quotas as a Global Phenomenon: Actors and Strategies in Quota Adoption. *European Political Science* 3 (3): 59–65.

——. 2005. *Politicizing Representation: Campaigns for Candidate Gender Quotas Worldwide*. Ph.D. Diss., Columbia University.

——. 2006a. Gender Quotas, Norms, and Politics. *Politics & Gender* 2 (1): 110–18.

——. 2006b. Reforming Representation: The Diffusion of Candidate Gender Quotas Worldwide. *Politics & Gender* 2 (3): 303–27.

——. 2007. Candidate Gender Quotas: A Framework for Analysis. *European Journal of Political Research* 46 (3): 367–94.

Krook, Mona Lena, and Diana O'Brien. 2007. The Politics of Group Representation: Quotas for Women and Minorities Worldwide. Paper presented at the Annual Meeting of the Midwest Political Science Association, Chicago.

Krook, Mona Lena, and Lenita Freidenvall. 2007. Discourses as Institutions: Gender and Candidate Selection Reform in France and Sweden. Paper presented at the General Conference of the European Consortium for Political Research, Pisa, Italy.

Krook, Mona Lena, Joni Lovenduski, and Judith Squires. 2006. Western Europe, North America, Australia and New Zealand: Gender Quotas in the Context of Citizenship Models. In *Women, Quotas, and Politics*, ed. Drude Dahlerup, 194–221. New York: Routledge.

Kudva, Neema. 2003. Engineering Elections: The Experiences of Women in Panchayati Raj in Karnataka, India. *International Journal of Politics, Culture and Society* 16 (3): 445–63.

Kunovich, Sheri, and Pamela Paxton. 2005. Pathways to Power: The Role of Political Parties in Women's National Representation. *American Journal of Sociology* 111 (2): 505–52.

Lakshmi, Josyula, Kiran Jyoti, and Priti Sharma. 2000. *Daughters of 74th Amendment: A Study of Women Elected to Municipal Bodies in Karnal and New Delhi.* New Delhi: Multiple Action Research Group.

Lama-Rewal, Stéphanie Tawa. 2001. *Women in the Calcutta Municipal Corporation: A Study in the Context of the Debate on the Women's Reservation Bill.* New Delhi: French Research Institutes in India.

Lawless, Jennifer L. and Richard L. Fox. 2005. *It Takes a Candidate: Why Women Don't Run for Office.* New York: Cambridge University Press.

Le Doeuff, Michèle. 1995. Problèmes d'investiture (De la parité, etc.). *Nouvelles questions féministes* 16 (2): 5–80.

Leijenaar, Monique. 1997. *How to create a gender balance in political decision-making: A guide to implementing policies for increasing the participation of women in political decision-making.* Luxembourg: Office for Official Publications of the European Communities.

Lenoir, Noëlle. 2001. The representation of women in politics: from quotas to parity in elections. *International and Comparative Law Quarterly* 50 (2): 217–47.

Lipietz, Alain. 1994. Parité au masculin. *Nouvelles questions féministes* 15 (4): 45–64.

Lokar, Sonia. 2003. *Women Can Do It II: Integration of Gender Equality Issues in Parliamentary Parties' Work in South East Europe—2002 Project Report.* Novi Sad: yuTOPag.

Lorentzi, Ulrika. 2002. Moderaterna: hårdare straff och vardagsfeminism. *Bang* 1:18–21.

Lovecy, Jill. 2000. 'Citoyennes à Part Entière'? The Constitutionalization of Gendered Citizenship in France and the Parity Reforms of 1999–2000. *Government and Opposition* 35 (4): 439–462.

Lovenduski, Joni. 1997. Gender Politics: A Breakthrough for Women? *Parliamentary Affairs* 50 (4): 708–19.

———. 1999. Sexing Political Behaviour in Britain. In *New Agendas for Women*, ed. Sylvia Walby, 190–209. New York: St. Martin's.

———. 2002. Representation without the Incumbency Barrier: The Example of Scotland. In *Women, Public Life and Democracy: Changing Commonwealth Parliamentary Perspectives*, eds. Joni Lovenduski and Rosie Campbell with Jacqui Sampson-Jacent, 18–25. Sterling: Pluto Press.

———, ed. 2005. *State Feminism and Political Representation*. New York: Cambridge University Press.

Lovenduski, Joni, and Pippa Norris, eds. 1993. *Gender and Party Politics*. Thousand Oaks: Sage.

Lovenduski, Joni, and Vicky Randall. 1993. *Contemporary Feminist Politics: Women and Power in Britain*. New York: Oxford University Press.

Lubertino Beltrán, María José. 1992. Historia de la 'Ley de Cuotas.' In *Cuotas mínima de participación de mujeres: El debate en Argentina*. Buenos Aires: Fundación Friedrich Ebert, 9–43.

Lubertino, María José. 2000. *Female Citizenship, Legal Instruments* and *Constitutional Reforms: The Argentinian Experience*. Buenos Aires: ISPM.

Lundblad, Harriet. 1962. *De kvinnliga riksdagsledamöterna åren 1922–1949. Bakgrund och arbete i riksdagen*. M. Phil. Thesis, University of Stockholm.

MacDonell, Hamish. 2003. Labour's women for winnable Holyrood seats. *Scotsman*, 28 January. http://election.scotsman.com/topics.cfm?tid=782&id=108672003 (accessed November 19, 2003).

Mahan, Rajan. 1999. *Women in the Indian National Congress (1921–1931)*. New Delhi: Rawat Publications.

Mahoney, James. 2000. Path Dependence in Historical Sociology. *Theory and Society* 29 (4): 507–48.

Mahoney, James, and Gary Goertz. 2006. A Tale of Two Cultures: Contrasting Quantitative and Qualitative Research. *Political Analysis* 14 (3): 227–49.

Mahoney, James and Dietrich Rueschemeyer, eds. 2003. *Comparative Historical Analysis in the Social Sciences*. New York: Cambridge University Press.

Maillé, Chantal, and Lena Wängnerud. 1999. Looking for New Opportunities in Politics: Women's Organizations and Political Parties in Canada and Sweden. In *Women's Organizing and Public Policy in Canada and Sweden.* Ithaca: McGill-Queen's University Press, 184–209.

Mandal, Amal. 2003. *Women in Panchayti Raj Institutions.* New Delhi: Kanishka Publishers.

Manikyamba, P. 1989. *Women in Panchayati Raj Structures.* New Delhi: Gian Publishing House.

March, James G., and Johan P. Olsen. 1989. *Rediscovering Institutions: The Organizational Basis of Politics.* New York: The Free Press.

Marx, Jutta. 1994. Mujeres, participación política y poder. In *Capacitación política para mujeres: género y cambio social en la Argentina actual,* eds. Diana H. Maffía and Clara Kuschnir, 123–34. Buenos Aires: Feminaria Editora.

Marx, Jutta, and Ana Sampaolesi. 1993. Elecciones internas bajo el cupo: La primera aplicación de la Ley de Cuotas en la Capital Federal. *Feminaria* 6 (11): 15–17.

Marx, Jutta, Jutta Borner, and Mariana Caminotti. 2007. *Las Legisladoras: Cupos de Género y Política en Argentina y Brasil.* Buenos Aires: Siglo XXI Editora Iberoamericana.

Matland, Richard E. 1995. How the Election System Structure Has Helped Women Close the Representation Gap. In *Women in Nordic Politics: Closing the Gap,* eds. Lauri Karvonen and Per Selle, 281–309. Brookfield: Dartmouth.

———. 2006. Electoral Quotas: Frequency and Effectiveness. In *Women, Quotas, and Politics,* ed. Drude Dahlerup. New York: Routledge.

Matland, Richard E., and Donley T. Studlar. 1996. The Contagion of Women Candidates in Single-Member District and Proportional Representation Electoral Systems: Canada and Norway. *The Journal of Politics* 58 (3): 707–33.

Matland, Richard E., and Kathleen A. Montgomery, eds. 2003. *Women's Access to Political Power in Post-Communist Europe.* New York: Oxford University Press.

Mazur, Amy G. 2001. Drawing Lessons from the French Parity Movement. *Contemporary French Civilization* 25 (2): 201–20.

McCarthy, Rory. 2001. Pakistan's women get seats at the bottom table. *Guardian Unlimited,* May 18.

McDonald, Ronnie, with Morag Alexander and Lesley Sutherland. 2001. Networking for Equality and a Scottish Parliament: the Women's Coordination Group and Organisational Alliances. In *Women and Contemporary Scottish Politics: An Anthology,* eds. Esther Breitenbach and Fiona Mackay, 321–40. Edinburgh: Polygon.

McDougall, Linda. 1998. *Westminster Women.* London: Vintage.

McKay, Joanna. 2005. Women in German Politics: Still Jobs for the Boys? *German Politics* 13 (1): 56–80.

Mehta, G. S. 2002. *Participation of Women in the Panchayati Raj System.* New Delhi: Kanishka Publishers.

Meier, Petra. 2000. The Evidence of Being Present: Guarantees of Representation and the Belgian Example. *Acta Politica: International Journal of Political Science* 35 (1): 64–85.

———. 2003. Gender Quotas or Electoral Reform: Why More Women Got Elected During the 2003 Belgian Elections. Paper presented at the Annual Meeting of Dutch and Flemish Political Scientists, Dordrecht, Netherlands.

———. 2004. The Mutual Contagion Effect of Legal and Party Quotas: A Belgian Perspective. *Party Politics* 10 (5): 583–600.

———. 2005. The Belgian Paradox: Inclusion and Exclusion of Gender Issues. In *State Feminism and Political Representation*, ed. Joni Lovenduski et al, 41–61. New York: Cambridge University Press.

Mernissi, Fatima. 1991a. *Can We Women Head a Muslim State?* Lahore: Sang-e-Meel Publications.

———. 1991b. *The Veil and the Male Elite: A Feminist Interpretation of Women's Rights in Islam.* Reading: Addison-Wesley.

Millard, Eric, and Laure Ortiz. 1998. Parité et représentations politiques. In *La Parité: Enjeux et mise en oeuvre*, ed. Jacqueline Martin. Toulouse: Presses Universitaires du Mirail, 189–203.

Mills, John Stuart. 1974. *A System of Logic: Ratiocinative and Inductive.* 8th ed. New York: Harper and Brothers.

Minyersky, Nelly. 2001. Derechos civiles y políticos de la mujer. Medidas de acción positiva. *Plenario.* Edición Electrónica. Buenos Aires: Asociación de Abogados de Buenos Aires.

Molinelli, N. Guillermo. 1994. Argentina: The (no) Ceteris Paribus. In *Electoral systems in comparative perspective: their impact on women and minorities*, ed. Wilma Rule and Joseph F. Zimmerman. Westport: Praeger, 197–202.

Moore, Barrington. 1966. *Social Origins of Dictatorship and Democracy: Lord and Peasant in the Making of the Modern World.* Boston: Beacon Press.

Mossuz-Lavau, Janine. 1998. *Femmes/hommes pour la parité.* Paris: Presses de Sciences Po.

Mumtaz, Khawar. 1998. Political Participation: Women in National Legislatures in Pakistan. In *Shaping Women's Lives—Laws, Practices, and Strategies in Pakistan*, 319–70. Karachi: Shirkat Gah Women's Resource Centre.

Mumtaz, Khawar, and Farida Shaheed. 1987. *Women of Pakistan: Two Steps Forward, One Step Back?* London: Zed Books.

Murray, Rainbow. 2004. Why Didn't Parity Work? A Closer Examination of the 2002 Election Results. *French Politics* 2 (4): 347–62.

————. 2007. Will 2007 Be the Year for Women in French Politics? Paper presented at the Political Studies Association Annual Conference, Bath, UK.

————. 2008. The Power of Sex and Incumbency: A Longitudinal Study of Electoral Performance in France. *Party Politics* 14 (5): 539–54.

Nanivadekar, Medha. 2003a. Feasible Option of Dual-Member Constituencies: Do We Have the Political Will? *Indian Legislator*, August 4.

————. 2003b. Reservation for Women in Local Bodies: Lessons from Maharastra. Unpublished manuscript.

————. 2006. Are Quotas a Good Idea? The Indian Experience with Reserved Seats for Women. *Politics & Gender* 2 (1): 119–128.

Narayan, Jayaprakash, Dhirubhai Sheth, Yogendra Yadav, and Madhu Kishwar. 2000. Enhancing Women's Representation in Legislatures: An Alternative to the Government Bill for Women's Reservation. *Manushi* 116:5–12.

Nath, Meenakshi. 1996. Cutting Across Party Lines: Women Members of Parliament Explain their Stand on Reservation Quotas. *Manushi* 96:7–16.

National Assembly for Wales. 2007. Assembly Member Profiles. http://www.assemblywales.org/memhome/mem-profile.htm (accessed October 25, 2007).

National Commission on the Status of Women. 2002. NCSW wants 33pc women membership in political parties. http://www.ncsw.gov.pk/news/news-11.htm (accessed August 15, 2004).

Nechemias, Carol. 1994. Democratization and Women's Access to Legislative Seats: The Soviet Case, 1989–1991. *Women & Politics* 14 (3): 1–18.

Norris, Pippa. 1987. *Politics and Sexual Equality: The Comparative Position of Women in Western Democracies*. Boulder: Lynne Rienner.

————. 1997a. Equality Strategies and Political Representation. In *Sex Equality Policy in Western Europe*, ed. Frances Gardiner, 46–59. New York: Routledge.

————. 1997b. Introduction: Theories of Recruitment. In *Passages to Power: Legislative Recruitment in Advanced Democracies*, ed. Pippa Norris, 1–14. New York: Cambridge University Press.

————. 2004. *Electoral Engineering: Voting Rules and Political Behavior*. New York: Cambridge University Press.

————. 2006. Fast Track Strategies for Achieving Women's Representation in Iraq and Afghanistan: Choices and Consequences. Paper presented at the Annual Meeting of the American Political Science Association, Philadelphia.

Norris, Pippa, and Joni Lovenduski. 1995. *Political Recruitment: Gender, Race, and Class in the British Parliament*. New York: Cambridge University Press.

North, Douglass C. 1990. *Institutions, Institutional Change and Economic Performance*. New York: Cambridge University Press.

Opello, Katherine A.R. 2006. *Gender Quotas, Parity Reform and Political Parties in France*. New York: Lexington Books.

Orren, Karen and Stephen Skowronek. 2004. *The Search for American Political Development*. New York: Cambridge University Press.

Östberg, Kjell. 2001. Demokratiskt genombrott med förhinder: Kvinnorna och det demokratiska genombrottet under mellankrigstiden. In *Rösträtten 80 år. Forskarantologi*, ed. Christer Jönsson, 101–13. Stockholm: Justitiedepartementet.

Ozouf, Mona. 1995. *Les mots des femmes: Essai sur la singularité française*. Paris: Fayard.

Pakistan Commission on the Status of Women. 1989. *Report of the Pakistan Commission on the Status of Women*. Islamabad: Pakistan Commission on the Status of Women.

Palme, Sven Ulric. 1969. Vid valurnan och i riksdagen under femtio år. In *Kvinnors röst och rätt*, eds. Ruth Hamrin-Thorell, Ulla Lindström, and Gunvor Stenberg, 41–110. Stockholm: AB Allmänna Förlaget.

Perrigo, Sarah. 1996. Women and Change in the Labour Party 1979–1995. *Parliamentary Affairs* 49 (1): 116–129.

———. 1999. Women, Gender and New Labour. In *The Impact of New Labour*, ed. Gerald R. Taylore, 162–76. New York: St. Martin's.

Phillips, Anne. 1995. *The Politics of Presence: The Political Representation of Gender, Ethnicity, and Race*. New York: Oxford University Press.

Pierson, Paul. 2000. Increasing Returns, Path Dependence, and the Study of Politics. *American Political Science Review* 94 (2): 251–67.

———. 2004. *Politics in Time: History, Institutions, and Social Analysis*. Princeton: Princeton University Press.

Pires, Milena. 2002. East Timor and the Debate on Quotas. Paper presented at the International IDEA Workshop, Jakarta, Indonesia.

Pisier, Evelyne. 1995. Universalité contre parité. *Le Monde*, February 8.

Praud, Jocelyne. 2001. French Women and the Liberal Model of Political Citizenship: From Exclusion to Inclusion? *Contemporary French Civilization* 25 (2): 250–70.

Quota Project. 2008. Global Database of Quotas for Women. http://www.quotaproject.org (accessed May 12, 2008).

Ragin, Charles C. 1987. *The Comparative Method: Moving Beyond Qualitative and Quantitative Strategies*. Berkeley: University of California Press.

Ragin, Charles C. 2000. *Fuzzy-Set Social Science*. Chicago: University of Chicago Press.

Rahat, Gideon, and Reuven Y. Hazan. 2001. Candidate Selection Methods: An Analytical Framework. *Party Politics* 7 (3): 297–322.

Rai, Shirin. 1997. Gender and Representation: Women MPs in the Indian Parliament, 1991-96. In *Getting Institutions Right for Women in Development*, ed. Anne Marie Goetz, 104–20. New York: Zed Books.

———. 1999. Democratic Institutions, Political Representation and Women's Empowerment: The Quota Debate in India. *Democratization* 6 (3): 84–99.

———. 2002. Class, Caste and Gender—Women in Parliament in India. In *Women in Parliament: Beyond Numbers*, ed. Azza Karam. 2d ed. Stockholm: International IDEA.

Rai, Shirin M., and Kumud Sharma. 2000. Democratising the Indian Parliament: the 'Reservation for Women' Debate. In *International Perspectives on Gender and Democratisation*, ed. Shirin M. Rai, 149–65. New York: St. Martin's.

Raman, Vasanthi. 2002. The Implementation of Quotas for Women: The Indian Experience. Paper presented at the International IDEA Workshop, Jakarta, Indonesia.

Ramesh, Asha, and Bharti Ali. 2001. *33–1/3 % reservation towards political empowerment*. Bangalore: Books for Change.

Ramsay, Raylene L. 2003. *French Women in Politics: Writing Power, Paternal Legitimization, and Maternal Legacies*. New York: Berghahn Books.

Randall, Vicky. 1982. *Women and Politics*. London: Macmillan.

Rasmussen, Jorgen S. 1983. Women's Role in Contemporary British Politics: Impediments to Parliamentary Candidature. *Parliamentary Affairs* 36 (3): 300–315.

Rasul, Begam Aizaz. 2001. *From Purdah to Parliament*. New Delhi: Ajanta.

Remy, Jacqueline. 2002. Parité bien ordonnée…*L'Express*, June 20. http://www.lexpress.fr/info/france/dossier/parite/dossier.asp (accessed December 11, 2002).

Report of the Commission of Inquiry for Women. 1997. Islamabad: Stationery, Farms, and Publications Depot.

Reyes, Socorro L. 2002. Quotas in Pakistan: A Case Study. Paper presented at the International IDEA Workshop, Jakarta, Indonesia.

Reynoso, Nené. 1992. Ley del cupo: una prioridad del movimiento de mujeres. *Feminario* 5 (8): 10–12.

Rizvi, Muddassir. 2002. Women win record seats, but not activists' hearts. *Interpress Service*, October 15.

Rodríguez, Marcela. 1994. Sobre la constitucionalidad de la cuota mínima de participación de mujeres en los partidos políticos. In *Capacitación política para mujeres: género y cambio social en la Argentina actual*, eds. Diana H. Maffía and Clara Kuschnir, 76–104. Buenos Aires: Feminaria Editora.

Rönnblom, Malin. 1997. Halva makten? En feministisk granskning av politik. In *Makt & kön. Tretton bidrag till feministisk kunskap*, ed. Gudrun Nordborg, 151–69. Stockholm: Brutus Östlings Bokförlag Symposion.

Rukavina, Mary Ann et al., ed. 2002. *Building National Gender Equality Mechanisms in South East Europe: Women's Use of the State*. Zaghreb: Stability Pact—Gender Task Force, Regional Centre for Gender Equality.

Rundkvist, Fredrik. 2002. Kvinnorna tjänar på personvalet. *Aftonbladet*, September 19.

Russell, Meg. 2000. *Women's Representation in UK Politics: What can be done with the Law?* London: The Constitution Unit.

———. 2003. Women in Elected Office in the UK, 1992–2002: Struggles, Achievements and Possible Sea Change. In *Women Making Constitutions: New Politics and Comparative Perspectives*, eds. Alexandra Dobrowolsky and Vivien Hart, 68–83. New York: Palgrave.

———. 2005. *Building New Labour: The Politics of Party Organisation*. London: Palgrave.

Russell, Meg, Fiona Mackay, and Laura McAllister. 2002. Women's Representation in the Scottish Parliament and National Assembly for Wales: Party Dynamics for Achieving Critical Mass. *Journal of Legislative Studies* 8 (2): 49–76.

Sainsbury, Diane. 1993. The Politics of Increased Women's Representation: the Swedish Case. In *Gender and Party Politics*, eds. Joni Lovenduski and Pippa Norris, 263–90. Thousand Oaks: Sage.

———. 2004. Women's Political Representation in Sweden: Discursive Politics and Institutional Presence. *Scandinavian Political Studies* 27 (1): 65–87.

Saint-Germain, Michelle, and Martha Morgan. 1991. Equality: Costa Rican Women Demand 'The Real Thing.' *Women and Politics* 11 (3): 23–75.

Sangregorio, Inga-Lisa. 1994. Hellre kaos än enighet om fel saker! Kvinnolistan kan rubba oheliga allianser. *Kvinnobulletinen* 24 (1): 4–5.

Santos, Estela dos. 1983. *Las mujeres peronistas*. Buenos Aires: Centro Editor de América Latina.

Sarwar, Beena. 1997. Pakistan: Feuding Politicians Keep Women Out of Parliament. *Interpress Service*, June 13.

Sayeed, Khalid B. 1963–1964. Pakistan's Constitutional Autocracy. *Pacific Affairs* 36 (4): 365–77.

———. 1966. 1965—An Epoch-Making Year in Pakistan—General Elections and War with India. *Asian Survey* 6 (2): 76–85.

Schmidt, Gregory D. 2003. Unanticipated Successes: Lessons from Peru's Experiences with Gender Quotas in Majoritarian Closed List and Open List PR Systems. Paper presented at the International IDEA Workshop, Lima, Peru.

Schmidt, Gregory D., and Kyle L. Saunders. 2004. Effective Quotas, Relative Party Magnitude, and the Success of Female Candidates: Peruvian Municipal Elections in Comparative Perspective. *Comparative Political Studies* 37 (6): 704–34.

Schwindt-Bayer, Leslie. 2007. Making Quotas Work: A Statistical Test of the Effectiveness of Gender Quota Laws. Paper presented at the Annual Meeting of the American Political Science Association, Chicago.

Scott, Joan Wallach. 1998. 'La Querelle des Femmes' in the Late Twentieth Century. *differences: A Journal of Feminist Cultural Studies* 9 (2): 70–92.

Scottish Parliament. 2007a. Female MSPs: Session 3. *Scottish Parliament Fact Sheet*, August 31.

———. 2007b. List of Male MSPs: Session 3. *Scottish Parliament Fact Sheet*, August 31.

Sgier, Lea. 2003. Political Representation and Gender Quotas. Paper presented at the European Consortium for Political Research, Joint Sessions of Workshops, Edinburgh.

———. 2004. Discourses of Gender Quotas. *European Political Science* 3 (3): 67–72.

Shahab, Rafi Ullah. 1993. *Muslim Women in Political Power.* Lahore: Maqbool Academy.

Shaheed, Farida. 1991. The Cultural Articulation of Patriarchy. In *Finding our Way: Readings on Women in Pakistan,* ed. Fareeha Zafar, 135–58. Lahore: ASR Publications.

Shaheed, Farida, and Yasmin Zaidi. 2005. *Pakistan Ten Years into the Beijing Platform for Action: A Civil Society Perspective.* http://www.undp.org.pk/gender/B10-national-action-plan.pdf (accessed September 20, 2007).

Shaheed, Farida, Asma Zia, and Sohail Warraich. 1998. *Women in Politics: Participation and Representation in Pakistan, with update 1993–1997.* Lahore: Shirkat Gah.

Shaikh, N. M. 1981. *Women in Muslim Society.* Karachi: International Islamic Publishers.

Shehzad, Mohammad. 2003. Pakistani Women Lawmakers Battle Bias. Pakistan-Facts.com (accessed August 6, 2003).

Short, Clare. 1996. Women and the Labour Party. In *Women in Politics*, eds. Joni Lovenduski and Pippa Norris, 19–27. New York: Oxford University Press.

Siddiqui, Aziz. 1997. Women's presence in assemblies. *DAWN*, May 31.

Simonsson, Lennart. 2005. Swedish Feminist Party to decide on election run. *Deutsche Press-Agentur*, September 9.

Sineau, Mariette. 2001. *Profession: femme politique. Sexe et pouvoir sous la Cinquième République.* Paris: Presses de Sciences Po.

Sineau, Mariette. 2002. Institutionnalisation de la parité: l'expérience française. In *Les femmes au parlement: Au-delà du nombre*, ed. International IDEA. Stockholm: International IDEA.

Singh, Jyotsna. 1999a. India introduces women's bill. *BBC News*, November 11.

———. 1999b. Vajpayee tries to defuse quota row. *BBC News*, December 21.

Sinha, Niroj. 2000. Equality in Political Decision-Making [Some Implications of the Panchayati Raj System (Grass root Institutions) Amendment Act 1992 For Women in India]. In *Women in Indian Politics (Empowerment of Women through Political Participation)*, ed. Niroj Sinha 253–68. New Delhi: Gyan Publishing House.

Skjeie, Hege. 1992. *Den politiske betydningen av kjønn: En studie av norsk topp-politikk*. Oslo: Institute for Social Research.

Socialdemokraterna. 1993. *Är socialdemokraterna ett kvinnoparti?* Stockholm: Socialdemokraterna.

———. 1994. *Kvinnor kan—och vill! Socialdemokraternas politik för ökad jämställdhet*. Stockholm: Socialdemokraterna.

Squires, Judith. 1996. Quotas for Women: Fair Representation? In *Women in Politics*, eds. Joni Lovenduski and Pippa Norris, 73–90. New York: Oxford University Press.

———. 2004. Gender Quotas in Britain: A Fast Track to Equality? Stockholm University Working Paper 2004: 1.

Srivastava, Rashmi. 2000. Empowerment of Women through Political Participation: With Special Reference to Madhya Pradesh. In *Women in Indian Politics (Empowerment of Women through Political Participation)*, ed. Niroj Sinha, 195–217. New Delhi: Gyan Publishing House.

Steering Committee for Equality between Women and Men. 1992. *The democratic principle of representation—Forty years of Council of Europe activity*. Strasbourg: Council of Europe Press.

Steininger, Barbara. 2000. Representation of Women in the Austrian Political System 1945–1998: From a Token Female Politician Towards an Equal Ratio? *Women and Politics* 21 (2): 81–106.

Stevenson, Linda. 2000. *Gender Politics and Policy Process in Mexico, 1968–2000: Symbolic Gains for Women in an Emerging Democracy*. Ph.D. Diss., University of Pittsburgh.

Strickland, Pat, Oonagh Gay, Julia Lourie, and Richard Cracknell. 2001. *The Sex Discrimination (Election Candidates) Bill*. House of Commons Library Research Paper 01/75.

Studlar, Donley T., and Ian McAllister. 1998. Candidate Gender and Voting in the 1997 British General Election: Did Labour Quotas Matter? *Journal of Legislative Studies* 4 (3): 72–91.

Suchinmayee, Rachna. 2000. Reservation as a Strategy for Political Empowerment—The Ongoing Debate. In *Women in Indian Politics*

(Empowerment of Women through Political Participation), ed. Niroj Sinha, 235–52. New Delhi: Gyan Publishing House.

Svensson, Michael. 2006. Sex kryssade in sig i riksdagen. *Tv4.se*, September 21.

Sveriges Riksdag. 2003. Kvinnor i riksdagen 1921–2002. http://www.riksdagen.se/arbetar/siffror/siffror.kvinnori.htm (accessed September 20, 2007).

———. 2006. *Kvinnor i riksdagen*. Stockholm: Sveriges Riksdag.

Swarup, Hem Lata, Niroj Sinha, Chitra Ghosh, and Pam Rajput. 1994. Women's Political Engagement in India: Some Critical Issues. In *Women and Politics Worldwide*, ed. Barbara J. Nelson and Najma Chowdhury, 361–79. New Haven: Yale University Press.

Talbot, Ian. 2003. Pakistan in 2002: Democracy, Terrorism, and Brinkmanship. *Asian Survey* 43 (1): 198–207.

Thelen, Kathleen. 2003. How Institutions Evolve: Insights from Comparative Historical Analysis. In *Comparative Historical Analysis in the Social Sciences*, eds. James Mahoney and Dietrich Rueschemeyer, 208–40. New York: Cambridge University Press.

Thelen, Kathleen, and Sven Steinmo. 1992. Historical Institutionalism in Comparative Politics. In *Structuring Politics: Historical Institutionalism in Comparative Analysis*, eds. Sven Steinmo, Kathleen Thelen, and Frank Longstreth, 1–32. New York: Cambridge University Press.

Tilly, Charles. 1995. *Popular Contention in Great Britain, 1758–1834*. Cambridge: Harvard University Press.

Tilly, Charles. 2001. Mechanisms in Political Processes. *Annual Review of Political Science* 4:21–41.

Tinker, Irene. 2004. Quotas for Women in Elected Legislatures: Do They Really Empower Women? *Women's Studies International Forum* 27 (5–6): 531–546.

Tinker, Irene, and Mil Walker. 1956. The First General Elections in India and Indonesia. *Far Eastern Survey* 25 (7): 97–110.

Torbacke, Jarl. 1969. Kvinnolistan 1927–1928—ett kvinnopolitiskt fiasko. *Historisk tidskrift* 32 (2): 145–84.

Towns, Ann E. 2004. *Norms and Inequality in International Society: Global Politics of Women and the State*. Ph.D. Diss., University of Minnesota.

Trat, Josette. 1995. La loi sur la parité: une solution en trompe-l'oeil. *Nouvelles questions féministes* 16 (2): 129–139.

Tremblay, Manon. 2006. Democracy, Representation, and Women: A Comparative Analysis. Paper presented at the International Political Science Association World Congress, Fukuoka, Japan.

Tripp, Aili Mari. 2000. *Women and Politics in Uganda*. Madison: University of Wisconsin Press.

———. 2004. Transnational Feminism and Political Representation in Africa. Paper presented at the American Political Science Association Annual Meeting, Chicago.

Tripp, Aili Mari, and Alice Kang. 2008. The Global Impact of Quotas: On the Fast Track to Increased Female Legislative Representation. *Comparative Political Studies* 41 (3): 338–61.

Tripp, Aili, Dior Konaté, and Colleen Lowe-Morna. 2006. Sub-Saharan Africa: On the Fast Track to Women's Political Representation. In *Women, Quotas, and Politics*, ed. Drude Dahlerup, 112–137. New York: Routledge.

True, Jacqui, and Michael Mintrom. 2001. Transnational Networks and Policy Diffusion: The Case of Gender Mainstreaming. *International Studies Quarterly* 45 (1): 27–57.

Udovic, Ana. 2002. Folkpartiet: var och en väljer själv. *Bang* 1:60–63.

United Nations. 1995. *Platform for Action and the Beijing Declaration.* New York: United Nations.

Valiente, Celia. 2005. The Women's Movement, Gender Equality Agencies and Central-State Debates on Political Representation in Spain. In *State Feminism and Political Representation*, ed. Joni Lovenduski, 174–94. New York: Cambridge University Press.

Vallance, Elizabeth. 1984. Women Candidates in the 1983 General Election. *Parliamentary Affairs* 37 (3): 301–09.

Varannan Damernas: Slutbetänkande från Utredningen om Kvinnorepresentation. 1987. Stockholm: Statens offentliga utredningar.

Varikas, Eleni. 1995. Une réprésentation en tant que femme? Réflexions critiques sur la demande de la parité des sexes. *Nouvelles questions féministes* 16 (2): 81–127.

Viennot, Éliane. 1994. Parité: les féministes entre défis politiques et révolution culturelle. *Nouvelles questions féministes* 15 (4): 65–89.

Wängnerud, Lena. 1999a. Kön och personröstning. In *Premiär för personval*, eds. Sören Holmberg and Tommy Möller, 301–25. Stockholm: Statens offentliga utredningar.

———. 1999b. *Kvinnorepresentation. Makt och möjligheter i Sveriges riksdag.* Lund: Studentlitteratur.

———. 2001. Kvinnors röst: En kamp mellan partier. In *Rösträtten 80 år. Forskarantologi*, ed. Christer Jönsson. Stockholm: Justitiedepartementet, 129–146.

Ward, Lucy. 2000a. Blair's plan for more women MPs. *Guardian*, February 3.

———. 2000b. 'Change rules' to allow more women MPs. *Guardian*, March 8.

———. 2000c. Tories search for more women MPs. *Guardian*, March 31.

———. 2001a. Clarke rejects quotas for more women MPs. *Guardian*, August 9.

————. 2001b. Outcry as party rejects quotas for women candidates. *Guardian*, September 27.

Watt, Nicholas. 2000. Grassroots snub Hague plea for more women MPs. *Guardian*, February 8.

Waylen, Georgina. 1994. Women and Democratization: Conceptualizing Gender Relations in Transition Politics. *World Politics* 46 (3): 327–54.

Weir, Margaret 1992. Ideas and the Politics of Bounded Innovation. In *Structuring Politics: Historical Institutionalism in Comparative Analysis*, eds. Sven Steinmo, Kathleen Thelen, and Frank Longstreth, 188–216. New York: Cambridge University Press.

Weiss, Anita M. 1990. Benazir Bhutto and the Future of Women in Pakistan. *Asian Survey* 30 (5): 433–45.

————. 1994. The Consequences of State Policies for Women in Pakistan. In The *Politics of Social Transformation in Afghanistan, Iran, and Pakistan*, eds. Myron Weiner and Ali Banuazizi, 412–44. Syracuse: Syracuse University Press.

Westerlund, Ulrika. 2002. Centerpartiet: ett kryssande mellan strategier. *Bang* 1:49–52.

Wiberg, Ingrid Segerstedt. 1969. Kvinnorna och folkpartiet. In *Kvinnors röst och rätt*, eds. Ruth Hamrin-Thorell, Ulla Lindström, and Gunvor Stenberg, 169–78. Stockholm: AB Allmänna Förlaget.

Wilder, Andrew R. 1995. Changing Patterns of Punjab Politics in Pakistan: National Assembly Election Results, 1988 and 1993. *Asian Survey* 35 (4): 377–93.

Wintour, Patrick. 2000. Make more women MP's or lose votes, Blair told. *Guardian*, January 9.

Wisler, Dominique. 1999. Parité politique: la diffusion d'un principe. *Swiss Political Science Review* 5 (1): 110–14.

Wistrand, Birgitta. 1975. Vi trycker på för fler kvinnor i politiken. In *Kvinnan i politiken*, ed. Barbro Hedvall, 17–26. Södertälje: Fredrika-Bremer-Förbundet.

Wörlund, Ingemar. 1995. Populism kontra genus—eller varför röstar inte kvinnor på Ny Demokrati? *Mid-Sweden University Rapport* 1995: 22.

Yadav, Ritu. 1997. More than just a token. *News India*, May 16.

Yáñez, Ana María. 2003. Quotas and Democracy in Peru. Paper presented at the International IDEA Workshop, Lima, Peru.

Yoon, Mi Yung. 2001. Democratization and Women's Legislative Representation in Sub Saharan Africa. *Democratization* 8 (2): 169–90.

————. 2004. Explaining Women's Legislative Representation in Sub-Saharan Africa. *Legislative Studies Quarterly* 29 (3): 447–66.

Zafar, Fareeha. 1991. Introduction. In *Finding Our Way: Readings on Women in Pakistan*, ed. Fareeha Zafar, i–xxi. Lahore: ASR Publications.

Zafar, Fareeha. 1996. Gender and Politics in Pakistan. In *Representations of Gender, Democracy and Identity Politics in Relation to South Asia*, ed. Renuka Sharma, 39–69. Delhi: Sri Satguru Publications.

Zakaria, Rafiq. 1990. *Women and Politics in Islam: The Trial of Benazir Bhutto*. New York: New Horizons Press.

Zetterberg, Pär. 2008. The Downside of Gender Quotas? Institutional Constraints on Women in Mexican State Legislatures. *Parliamentary Affairs* 61 (3): 442–460.

Zia, Shehla. 1991. "The Legal Status of Women in Pakistan." In *Finding our Way: Readings on Women in Pakistan*, ed. Fareeha Zafar, 26–42. Lahore: ASR Publications.

Zimmermann, Marie-Jo. 2003. *Elections à venir: faire vivre la parité*. Paris: Observatoire de la parité entre les femmes et les hommes.

———. 2007. *Les clés de la parité*. Paris: Observatoire de la parité.

Index

actors, 21, 218–19. *See also* civil society actors; elites; international/transnational actors; state actors; *specific countries*

additional member (AMS) electoral system, 142, 144

Afghanistan, 227*t*

Africa, 227*t*, 228, 232*t*, 233*t*, 236*t*, 237*t*, 242n2

age,
   representation and, 124–25, 127, 128, 242n6

'A'isha, 241n11

AIWC. *See* All-India Women's Conference

Albania, 231*t*

Algeria, 234*t*, 235

All India Muslim Women's Sub-Committee (1938), 60

All-India Women's Conference (AIWC), 86–87

All Pakistan Women's Association (APWA), 60, 61

all-women shortlists (AWS), 45, 136. *See also* UK's all-women shortlists

Alva, Margaret, 90

AMS. *See* additional member (AMS) electoral system

ANP. *See* Awami National Party

anti-democracy,
   quota adoption as, 24

Anwar, Khalid, 73

Anwar, Roquayya, 63, 240n3

APWA. *See* All Pakistan Women's Association

Argentina, 179*t*, 218, 219, 223, 225–26, 236*t*. *See also specific Argentine laws, organizations, political parties*
   "the braid" in, 242n2
   Cabinet of Female Presidential Advisors for, 171, 243n6
   democracy in, 166
   IACHR and, 239n2
   legislative quotas in, 16, 161–205
   legislative representation in, 165*t*
   reforms in, 48
   Senate of, 165*t*

Argentina's *ley de cupos*
   adoption of, 168–70
   antecedents to, 163–66
   CEDAW for, 173–74
   Constitutional Assembly for, 173–74, 243n11
   elections v., 165–66
   IACHR for, 176–78
   implementation of, 170–78
   juridical interpretations of, 172–74
   lawsuits for, 171–73, 174–75, 176–78
   military regimes and, 163–65
   National Electoral Chamber for, 175
   origins of, 166–68
   political representation and, 178–81
   proposals for, 168–70
   support for, 166–68, 171–72, 174–75, 243n2

9 780199 740277